D1216833

EDWARDIAN RADICALISM
1900 – 1914

Contributors

RODNEY BARKER
CATHERINE ANN CLINE
MARGARET COLE
ROY DOUGLAS
JOHN GRIGG
GERALD H. S. JORDAN
STEPHEN E. KOSS
ALAN J. LEE
F. M. LEVENTHAL
A. J. A. MORRIS
EDWARD C. MOULTON
A. K. RUSSELL
MARVIN SWARTZ
CLIVE TREBILCOCK
HOWARD WEINROTH

EDWARDIAN RADICALISM 1900–1914

Some aspects of British Radicalism

EDITED BY
A. J. A. Morris

ROUTLEDGE & KEGAN PAUL
London and Boston

First published in 1974
by Routledge & Kegan Paul Ltd
Broadway House, 68-74 Carter Lane,
London EC4V 5EL and
9 Park Street,
Boston, Mass. 02108 USA
Set in 10pt Horley Old Style
and printed in Great Britain by
Willmer Brothers Limited, Birkenhead

ISBN 0 7100 7866 8
Library of Congress Catalog Card No. 74–79360

Of right and wrong they taught
Truths as refin'd as ever Athens heard;
And (strange to tell) they practis'd what they preach'd.

for

J.A.G.G.

and

W.J.

CONTENTS

NOTES ON CONTRIBUTORS

RODNEY BARKER, MA, PhD, lecturer in government, London School of Economics. Author of *Education and Politics 1900-1951*, editor of, and contributor to, *Studies in Opposition.*

CATHERINE ANN CLINE, AB, MA, PhD, associate professor of history, Catholic University of America. Author of a number of books and articles on Radical politics, including *Recruits to Labour.*

DAME MARGARET COLE, president of the Fabian Society. Dame Margaret's many published works include *Growing up into Revolution, Beatrice Webb, The Webbs and their Work* (ed.).

ROY DOUGLAS, PhD, lecturer in history, University of Surrey. Author of *History of the Liberal Party, 1895-1970.*

JOHN GRIGG, MA, political journalist, former editor *National English Review.* Author of *Two Anglican Essays* and *The Young Lloyd George.*

GERALD H. S. JORDAN, MA, PhD, lecturer in history ,York University, Ontario. Author of *Popular Literature and Imperial Sentiment: 1870-90.*

STEPHEN E. KOSS, BA, PhD, professor of history, Columbia University. Author of many articles on the Liberal party, his books include biographies of Morley, Haldane and Brunner. His most recent book is *Fleet Street Radical,* a life of A. G. Gardiner.

ALAN J. LEE, MA, PhD, lecturer in history at the University of Hull. Author of *Liberalism, Democracy and the Press, 1855-1914,* and contributor to Bellamy and Saville (eds), *Dictionary of Labour Biography.*

F. M. LEVENTHAL, AB, PhD, associate professor of history, Boston University. Author of *Respectable Radical: George Howell and Victorian Working Class Politics,* editor of *Trade Unionism New and Old.*

A*

A. J. A. MORRIS, LLB, MA, sometime Robert Lee Bailey visiting professor, University of North Carolina, Director of Politics, Philosophy and History, Ulster College. Author of *Parliamentary Democracy in the Nineteenth Century*, *Radicalism against War, 1906-14*.

EDWARD C. MOULTON, MA, PhD, associate professor of history, University of Manitoba. Author of *Lord Northbrook's Indian Administration, 1872-76* and many essays on Indian and imperial history.

A. K. RUSSELL, MA, DPhil, administrator and historian. Author of *Liberal Landslide*.

MARVIN SWARTZ, MA, PhD, assistant professor of history, University of Massachusetts, Amherst. Author of *The Union of Democratic Control in British Politics during the First World War*.

CLIVE TREBILCOCK, MA, fellow of Pembroke College, Cambridge. An authority on the armaments industry, he has published articles on the subject, and is currently completing a book.

HOWARD WEINROTH, MA, PhD, lecturer in history, McGill University. Author of numerous articles on Radical attitudes to foreign policy and armaments in the pre-1914 period.

INTRODUCTION

A. J. A. MORRIS

'If it was so, it might be; and if it were so, it would be: but as it isn't, it ain't.' That, Tweedledee affirmed, was logic. He could as well have been describing the inherent paradox of British Radicalism. The role of Radicalism in British political life had been recognized, its extremist dimension and revolutionary dynamic abandoned, long before Edward succeeded Victoria, before stolid Sir Henry Campbell-Bannerman, 'the first Radical Prime Minister', took office in December 1905, indeed, before the Fabians hymned the virtues of the inevitability of gradualness, a lyric sweetly tuned to the English genius for moderation in all things, especially change.

The way was made straight for British Radicalism when Jeremy Bentham disclaimed any connection between his views on that subject and those of revolutionaries like Tom Spence. Bentham wrote a tract with, for him, an unusually terse title: *Radicalism Not Dangerous*. Thus, place if not fortune was secured for Radicalism. Foreigners might wish to change everything from God to the calendar, but Englishmen seemed disposed to preserve as much as possible. Once Bentham and then Mill assumed that they could organize a representative system so that the interests of governors and governed could be reconciled harmoniously, then English Radicalism was well on its way to being assimilated into Liberalism. To become practical and, perhaps more importantly, respectable, Radicalism consciously chose to put aside its revolutionary and Utopian characteristics. Of course, some found this exercise easier than others. But who better to celebrate this successful transmogrification than John Morley? To a meeting of the Eighty Club in 1889, he avowed:[1]

The name of Radical is good enough for me . . . do not let us

> quarrel about nicknames . . . . If we are agreed upon certain definite ends for today, that is enough for me. Let us achieve the task which is assigned to us: do not let us endeavour to settle millennial problems, let us do what we have to do.

When Morley was apotheosized as Viscount Morley of Blackburn, despite the comforting plebeian ring of the latter part of the title, James Keir Hardie in the columns of his *Labour Leader* darkly pronounced it 'a fitting reward for one whose policies have been thoroughly reactionary'.[2]

Radicalism was born of paradox, sustained by paradox and, in the end, confounded by paradox. It is not illogical to talk of a Radical tradition. Radicals more naturally divined their course by consulting the actions of the past exemplars of their faith than by advancing new ideas. Fox, Bright, Cobden and, most important, W. E. Gladstone – these were their tribal gods to be summoned in turn to play prophet for actions enjoined and justification for attitudes indulged in. Nor was this all. A selective memory invested this tradition and these men with virtues and wisdom beyond those which any mortal might possibly have possessed. The debilitating effects of this ancestor-worship could be illustrated by a dozen examples, but one may be sufficient. Most Radicals during the Boer War assumed, without question, the paradigm of their reaction to Imperialism with Gladstone's Midlothian campaign. The trouble was, however, that the nation stubbornly refused to provide a 'unified moral conscience' to which they might have appealed. Nor had they a leader of sufficient political stature to enthuse even the faithful with constant reminders of the righteousness of their opposition. With Gladstone gone, the Radicals, as Rosebery gleefully pointed out, lacked their 'crutch'. He enjoined them, along with the rest of the Liberal party, to embrace the new philosophy of Imperialism. But the Radicals were the last people to be tempted down that primrose path to perdition.

Radicals of the old school were ill-equipped to deal with the politics of the twentieth century. It could not have been otherwise. They were the true children of the Victorian era, an age of paternalism, certitude and progress, of evolutionary optimism and principled dissent in politics. There was no easy escape into cynicism for them. They possessed an unshakeable optimism rooted in their simple faith in the good sense of men. It could be said that optimism was the mainspring of the Radical spirit. But this, the source of their greatest strength, was also a source of political vulnerability.

Quite simply, their hope was proof against experience. Felix Moschelles, posing the question after the Agadir crisis in 1911, 'Is it Peace or War?', argued:[3]

> War will go simply because the dispossessed will no longer sacrifice their lives for the possessed, and will not allow themselves to be perennially sweated at home and periodically dismembered abroad. Anti-militarism and anti-patriotism will triumph over these two insidious enemies of mankind, Caesarism and national egotism; and the patriotism which today we crown with laurels, will cease to be a standing menace to the peace of the world and pass away. . . . You may deplore and disbelieve; I have faith and rejoice.

It is easy to understand why such men were surprised, hurt and infuriated when the deeds of a Liberal government – the Tories, of course, could never be trusted – did not correspond with its pledges and promises.

Such optimism was ill rewarded. In the confusion and disarray caused by war with Germany, many Radicals acquiesced in the surrender of their patrimony to a parliamentary socialist party that had even forsworn its name, and whose bubble of revolutionary pretension had long been pricked by an Establishment whose pleasant toleration had been harder to combat than open contempt. C. F. G. Masterman, writing in the *Nation* in 1907, noted that there were 'no wild revolutionaries, harbingers of the uprising of the lower orders' in Labour's parliamentary ranks. He could discover only 'a mixture of old-fashioned Trade Unionists with a sprinkling of well behaved and pleasant Socialists'.[4] What was the strange alchemy of British political life that could effect such dramatic change? What transformed the visionary of the street-corner meeting, or the Marxist dialectician of the Socialist International, into just another parliamentary sheep bleating, none too convincingly, much of the Liberal-Radical litany? R. Cunninghame Graham remarked, with disgust, to Wilfrid Scawen Blunt:[5]

> When Labour members get into Parliament they are at once bitten with the absurd idea that they are no longer working men, but statesmen, and they try to behave as such. I tell them . . . that they would do more good if they came to the House in a body drunk and tumbling about the floor.

It can be argued that the demise of English Radicalism was inevitable because the psychological and material conditions that had fostered and enhanced it no longer existed after 1914. In a society increasingly susceptible to a mistaken conception of determinist philosophies, there could no longer be a place for men whose political judgment was answerable to outdated moral and religious imperatives. Causal explanations under the determinist umbrella suggested that Radicalism all along had been merely the justification of the particular prejudices of a middle class whose real intent had been to share the spoils of power: exit the idea of moral accountability in politics, and the way was thrown open for excuse, the father of pragmatism. The twentieth century was born in the shambles of Armageddon and it was wiser to look back in anger than forward in the deluded hope of a millennium of universal prosperity and brotherhood among men of all nations.

Such an explanation may be part, but only part, of the story. Notions of moral accountability, however, bring us conveniently to the vexed question of the role of the so-called 'Nonconformist conscience' in the fortunes of Edwardian Radicalism. Was it an aid or a hindrance? At its best, and yet, paradoxically, its least politically effective, it provided impulse and justification for the Radical campaigns for peace, disarmament, Anglo-German understanding, and the succour of small nations struggling for independence. These 'pacifist' Radicals (the adjective was coined and used in a pejorative manner) did not see themselves as others saw them – vague idealists proposing Utopian policies. They were convinced that the Liberal government in its conduct of international affairs had fallen into the fundamental error of denying that *moral* power was the force that really commanded predominance in the world. At its worst, and yet most politically effective, the Nonconformist conscience largely shaped the education controversy of 1902. Dr Clifford's 'Rome on the rates' was an effective battle slogan. It was, however, as accurate as the splenetic nonsense pumped out by the denominational journals that delighted in picturing their readers as latter-day Hampdens defending democracy while thwarting the Cecils' intent to revive the policies of Archbishop Laud!

The trouble was that the dissenting conscience divined moral judgments by instinct. Thus, moral indignation was readily summoned, but it thrust some problems deep into the shadows of prejudice as easily as it illuminated others with a startling clarity. As a political force, the real problem was that the dissenting conscience could not grasp the notion that moral frontiers divined by instinct can seldom be accommodated within the boundaries of party programmes.

The conscience of dissent presents an inherent paradox. It is the product of two opposing forces – emotion and reason. In the inevitable battle between these two, emotion, or call it 'instinct' or 'the still small voice', is more usually the victor. This is apparent in the assumption that a pious exhortation or an earnest avowal of faith was sufficient to answer complex political problems. In turn, this dictated that while the faithful remained convinced, those not of the elect were quite unmoved. The public voice of dissent was not confined to the pulpits of the Bethels in the provinces. C. P. Scott's *Manchester Guardian*, for example, was not so much a newspaper as an anointed vehicle by which dissent's intellectual establishment was pleased to reveal the truth. It is said that a certain Nonconformist minister once began an extemporary prayer, 'O Lord, Thou has doubtless seen it reported in the *Manchester Guardian* . . . ' We may be sure that the congregation would not have been in the least surprised by this revelation of the Deity's reading habits. The mistake is to suppose that the public voice of dissent was ever as certain or as consistent on matters of policy as it would have had its hearers believe.

Edwardian Radicalism possessed its theorists who proved to be better endowed as writers than as prophets. Indeed, there was no lack of publicists and apologists. Gardiner, Massingham, Hammond, Hirst, Hobhouse, Brailsford and Hobson, together with a host of lesser luminaries, was no mean literary galaxy. They broadcast loudly and persistently the voice of Radicalism. That it was not better heeded was the fault of these men. Theirs was the voice of disagreement, a minority voice, but this was never admitted. This was not because the authors were perverse by nature but because they cared so deeply that they succumbed to the temptation to claim they spoke for a larger, more influential body of opinion than they did. They did not envy the success of their opponents because they despised the methods employed that gave weight to the 'opinions' of a newspaper like the *Daily Mail*. Leo Maxse, the ultra-Tory editor of the *National Review*, may have been an 'egregious gobemouche'; Robert Blatchford's scaremongering 'odious and inaccurate'; and J. L. Garvin's 'the Eight, the whole Eight, and nothing but the Eight' both 'immoral and ineffably vulgar'. But if the language employed by the 'Jingo Yellow Press' was shrill and impolite, and its information rather less than the truth, it was much to the taste of most ordinary people. When war came in 1914, the *Daily Mail* published with pride its claim to have been a better prophet of doom than A. G. Gardiner's *Daily News*. With delight, *New Age* declared:[6]

> Who in future will pay attention to the *Daily News* . . ., the *Manchester Guardian* and other journals of the same stamp? These idealists . . . who refuse to look reality in the face and prefer to be deceived and to deceive their followers.

One might suppose from the smug attitudes adopted by the 'patriotic' press that war was something to welcome rather than avoid. But in August 1914 most Englishmen subscribed to that belief even as, when they rushed to the colours, they supposed they were enlisting to fight 'For God, King and Country'.

The difficulties were discernible even in January 1906 when 'peace, retrenchment and reform', the old Radical battle-cry, seemed about to be realized. The landslide victory when 'the Babylon of Toryism with all its false gods was shattered', when the righteous seemed about to inherit power borne to Westminster upon a Radical flood tide, was to prove the prologue not to triumph but to disaster, defeat and extinction. In some ways, Radical success in the 1906 election was the supreme paradox. It proved to be, not so much a Radical victory as a conservative reaction – a product of *l'ennui de la fin du siècle*. After years of impotent dissension, internecine strife and failure, political realities went unheeded in the general euphoria induced by crushing victory at the polls. The Radicals were not alone in their delusion. Rejected by the Manchester electorate, Arthur Balfour, Tory leader and worst of political pundits, wrote:[7]

> If I read the signs aright . . . C-B is a mere cork, dancing on a torrent which he cannot control, and what is going on here is the faint echo of the same movement which has produced massacres in St. Petersburg, riots in Vienna and Socialist processions in Berlin.

Balfour could not have been more wrong, about either Radicalism or Campbell-Bannerman.

Radical attitudes towards Sir Henry Campbell-Bannerman provide an interesting example of unrealistic political judgment. W. T. Stead wrote, for once without exaggeration, 'Sir Henry commands the confidence of the Radicals'. The Radicals thought of Campbell-Bannerman as one of themselves. 'We look confidently to the Prime Minister' was one of the constant refrains in the

Radical press. According to *Concord*, it was due entirely to Campbell-Bannerman that the Radicals were rid of[8]

> Rosebery . . . and his Liberal League; that Chamberlain was worn out, Balfour discredited, and once again there was a clear issue between reform and reaction, peace and provocation, with a solid majority on the right side in command of the Commons and Whitehall.

Should they ever hesitate for a moment in their trust of any Liberal minister or measure, 'the old chief's word was law to the extremists of his party'.[9] Radicals believed that Sir Henry would firmly control the Liberal Imperialists in the Cabinet – Asquith, Grey and Haldane. Of the Relugas triumvirate, they least trusted Haldane. But even he, they supposed, would be 'compelled to abjure his heresies and support the democratic policies of his chief'.[10] In fact, Campbell-Bannerman was to prove Haldane's best aid, both in Cabinet and Commons, when establishing army reforms that many of the Radicals decried as profligate and unnecessary. As to Campbell-Bannerman keeping a watch over Grey, this proved impossible. The Foreign Secretary virtually excluded the Prime Minister, as he did the rest of his Cabinet colleagues and the Commons, from the mysteries of diplomacy. In any event, though Campbell-Bannerman retained a certain emotional idealism that inspired his principles – 'methods of barbarism', 'the League of Peace', 'Vive la Douma' – as Prime Minister, experience and practicality tempered his decision-making. 'Criticism in opposition', he told Viscount Esher in confidence, 'is one thing; accomplished fact is another'.[11] Sir Henry was merely echoing a familiar lament that W. E. Forster had sounded many years earlier. 'Before the Queen made me a Cabinet Minister I was much more of a Radical. After that I did what I could and not what I would.'

The Radicals expected much of the Liberal leadership – and the impossible of Campbell-Bannerman. His prime task, after all, was to give some homogeneity of purpose to the unwieldy coalition majority of 'Limps', orthodox Gladstonians, even a few Whigs, as well as Radicals that together jostled uncomfortably under the umbrella of Liberalism. Radicals exaggerated Campbell-Bannerman's contribution and influence in politics. Even a contemporary Radical critic was prepared to admit that they tended 'to take a too personal view of political life'.[12] When Sir Henry died, the Radicals, in a desperate attempt to claim the leadership of the Liberal party and thus determine its policies, for a moment even contemplated

Asquith as a Prime Minister cast in their mould. The *Nation*, least inclined of all Radical journals to keep up its spirits by whistling in the dark, strangely presumed that 'of late (spring 1908) Asquith has been showing an increasing inclination to the Left'. This, by their calculation, was just as well, for 'only by and with the Left [would] Asquith be able to govern. Five-sixths of the Liberal Parliamentary Party are Left wing'. The influence of Liberal Imperialism had been 'only a passing phase', and now 'the normal tendencies [had] regained their accustomed strength'.[13] The *Labour Leader* poured scorn on this suggestion. When Asquith's Cabinet list was announced, its damning verdict was 'different yet the same'.[14] Wilfred Blunt had said as much about Campbell-Bannerman's administration when it was announced in December 1905. 'People talk about violent democratic changes. I do not believe in them. The new Cabinet is a Whig Cabinet.'[15]

Wherever the Radicals turned to find a potential leader at Cabinet level, they were foiled. John Burns, Lord Loreburn and John Morley were incapacitated by their vanity. Bryce was soon banished. Churchill, after a promising beginning, was lost to the Radical cause when he discovered that his *métier* was dreadnoughts rather than 'do-gooding', and embraced his destiny at the Admiralty. Undoubtedly, David Lloyd George proved the greatest disappointment to the Radicals for he had promised so much, first as President of the Board of Trade and later as Chancellor of the Exchequer. But, by 1911, his Radical impetus seemed to wither in the sun of his growing parliamentary prospects. The pursuit of the holy grail of his own political fortunes left Lloyd George little time for other and hopeless crusades. It seemed to backbench Radicals that office corrupted. Even the young were not immune. Charlie Masterman's appointment to a junior government post was, sternly counselled the *Labour Leader*, a matter not for joy but for sorrow. Office was an effective muzzle, and though Masterman was an 'avowed Socialist' (!), he was 'not likely to vote against the Government any longer'.[16]

Why this desperate search for a leader – any leader? To some extent the Radicals were conscious of their particular dilemma. The 'rich pattern of dissent' in England owed something to tradition, but more to eclecticism. Radicals were rather in the position of the errant adolescent who cannot satisfactorily resolve the conflict between dependence and the desire for independence. They, like the unhappy adolescent, could appear truculent, and for the same reason. It was intended to conceal a crisis of identity. Radicals were for ever pursuing their particular 'crusade' of the moment with never a thought for the equally earnest efforts of colleagues in another direction. They were as often in opposition to one another as to the government they supported. Morley put his finger exactly on this weakness when he confidently predicted that Radical opposition to the Anglo-Russian Convention would collapse. They were, he wrote, 'of all sorts of political temperament' and capable of agreeing on few things in concert. Their energies were 'dissipated upon a number of different projects'. To a determined, single-minded minister, they would never present a serious difficulty.[17]

Socialists, with an unwarranted degree of smugness and moral self-satisfaction, upbraided the Radical penchant for making pious resolutions. Objecting to 'theoretic moonshine' as a substitute for direct action, a correspondent wrote to *New Age:* 'Passing resolutions is the paradisaical occupation par excellence of the English Radical.'[18] The judgment was true, but it obscured more than it revealed. The Radicals desperately wanted to be loyal to the Liberal government. Because of this, they preferred to formulate resolutions and motions rather than press their opposition to a public avowal of disloyalty in a parliamentary division. For example, those who for years sought to diminish the burden of armaments had not only to struggle with their consciences and notions of loyalty, but to overcome the subterranean efforts of ministers persuading them to desist by raising the spectre of the Tories voting with them and bringing down the Liberal government. A misguided Liberal administration advocating the building of four dreadnoughts was bad enough, but the prospect of what a Tory government would spend on naval armaments was too dreadful to contemplate. After the 1910 elections the small Liberal parliamentary majority, bolstered by uncertain political bargains with Irish and Labour members, put added pressure on Radical loyalties. Problems related to the conduct of foreign affairs were particularly difficult. When Sir Edward Grey put his finger to his lips in the Commons, refused to give information, or provided misleading information, the Radicals, though they might grumble, would always give in. The Foreign Secretary, they said, was 'secretive', obsessed with an unreal fear of Germany, unduly influenced by his Foreign Office advisers. But Grey had only to threaten resignation for the Radicals to flock to his support. They all wanted to believe Grey; some of them actually did. For most, there was no practicable parliamentary alternative other than 'to grin and bear it'. The *Nation* spelled this out in June 1912. When Radicals went 'reluctantly' into the government lobby to vote 'on the partition of Persia, or the handling of

Anglo-German relations, or the increase of armaments', they were in fact 'voting for Free Trade and Home Rule and Social Reform'.[19]

So the Radicals could do nothing save splutter and rage and threaten. They subscribed to a parliamentary system that seemed designed to make them impotent as critics of government when the Liberals were in office. As, once more, Winston Churchill had his way with another massive increase in the naval estimates, *Concord* could 'understand well the difficulties of our friends in the House of Commons'. But such understanding could not altogether temper the frustration and puzzlement.[20]

> Yet we cannot but think that they might have done something more to bring home to the country and the Cabinet, the monstrous character of the Admiralty programme. . . . . Parliamentary control is becoming weaker instead of stronger. . . and old constitutional safeguards are coolly defied in order to serve an inordinately ambitious policy.

Were the Radicals, as some of even their friendlier critics now suggested, merely playing games?[21]

> The game is as innocuous as bridge for love, at which all that can be lost is honour or temper – things that do not matter. It is not war and it is not discussion. It is Parliamentary Debate. The reports should be published, not by Hansard, but by de la Rue.

It was no accident that the British invented and popularized team games, or that the Edwardian period is known as the 'Golden Age of Sport'. The British political system, especially its concept of an institutionalized and 'loyal' opposition, already enshrined the great sporting adage – 'the game and not the winning matters'. If procedural rather than substantive issues provide the inspiration of parliamentary democracy, is it too cynical to suppose that this, in part at least, could explain why the Radicals were prepared to believe that trimming the powers of the House of Lords was a 'dominant' political issue? That the rules of the parliamentary 'game' were sacred and immutable was much more part of the Liberal-Radical tradition than of that of the Conservative-Unionists. This is not so strange as at first it might seem. The political progenitors of Radicalism were, after all, mainly responsible for inventing the rules. The Tories, unencumbered by sentimental attachment, were more sympathetically disposed to the idea of, on occasion, if not cheating at least 'bending' the rules. Revolution by resolution was the Radical-Liberal disposition: only the Tories went in for 'dying in the ditch' or arming revolutionaries in Ireland in the name of defending the constitution.

In 1884, Gladstone, addressing a group of aspiring young politicians, had declared:[22]

> The word procedure has in it something homely and it is difficult for anyone except those who pass their lives within the walls of Parliament to understand how vital and urgent a truth it is that there is no more urgent demand, there is no aim or purpose more absolutely essential to the future victories and the future efficiency of the House of Commons, than that it should effect . . . some great reform in the matter of its procedure.

But, in 1886, when some of his Radical backbenchers had the temerity to express their dissatisfaction because they considered procedure had so strengthened the Cabinet's hands that they could no longer effect any policy changes, Gladstone upbraided them as 'impracticable' men. Theirs was an unwonted interference in matters which were not their concern.[23] No less a person than Gladstone had defined the Radicals' part in parliamentary affairs. At the time when they might hope to exercise their greatest influence upon policy decisions, it was decreed that they should be least effective.

Is it, therefore, altogether unfair to postulate that Edwardian Radicalism was so often a frustrated and ineffectual political force, not only because of inherent debilitating paradoxes of spirit and purpose but also because Radicals relied on a system that was designed to make them impotent? Is it stretching analogy too far to equate debate at Westminster with Wilf Rhodes fiddling out batsmen at Bradford, or to compare Lloyd George's thundering perorations with the Rev. Alban Davies's 'Terrible Eight' burying English rugby football for a decade in the mud of Cardiff Arms Park? Isn't it tempting to see in those portraits of Campbell-Bannerman's Cabinet a group photograph of rather ancient Corinthian Casuals? The abiding popular image of the Edwardian era remains, not one of sweat shops and strikes, of poverty and discontent, a violent domestic prelude to international anarchy, but of halcyon days, of parties in great houses, of leisure and pleasure, when those 'below stairs' knew their place in the scheme of things, and were content. God was in his English heaven, and all was right with the world. The Gentlemen matched their skill with the Players, and

Eton played Harrow at a Lords that was perpetually bathed in golden sunlight.

> And it's not for the sake of a ribboned coat,
> Or the selfish hope of a season's fame.
> But his Captain's hand on his shoulder smote —
> 'Play up! play up! and play the game!'

The Radicals always played the game. Perhaps that is why, in the end, they lost it.

NOTES

1 Quoted in A. M. McBriar, *Fabian Socialism and English Politics*, Cambridge, 1962, p. 241.
2 *Labour Leader*, 17 April 1908.
3 *Concord*, December 1911, pp. 112-13.
4 *Nation*, 24 August 1907.
5 W. S. Blunt, *My Diaries*, London, 1919-20, vol. 2, p. 205.
6 *New Age*, 13 August 1914.
7 Quoted in Blanche E. Dugdale, *Arthur James Balfour*, London, 1939, vol. 1, p. 329.
8 *Concord*, April 1908, p. 37.
9 W. S. Churchill, *The World Crisis*, London, 1923, vol. 1, pp. 34-5.
10 *Concord*, January 1906, p. 4.
11 M. V. Brett (ed.), *Journals & Letters of Reginald, Viscount Esher*, London 1934-8, vol. 2, p. 128.
12 *Albany Review*, May 1908, pp. 237-8.
13 *Nation*, 11 and 18 April 1908.
14 *Labour Leader*, 17 April 1908.
15 Blunt, *op cit.*, vol. 2, p. 129.
16 *Labour Leader*, 17 April 1908.
17 John Morley, *Recollections*, London, 1917, vol. 2, pp. 172, 175.
18 *New Age*, 23 May 1907.
19 *Nation*, 9 June 1912.
20 *Concord*, April 1914, p. 3.
21 *New Age*, 2 March 1911.
22 Quoted in Morley, *Life of Gladstone*, London, 1908 ed., vol. 2, p. 272.
23 For debate, see *Hansard*, iii: 33: 1386 ff.

I

LLOYD GEORGE AND THE BOER WAR

JOHN GRIGG

Until recently most people who had any view on the matter at all would have said that David Lloyd George opposed the Boer War because he was, at the time, a pacifist and a Little Englander, and because as a Welsh Nonconformist he felt spiritually akin to the Boers. Even now, many still believe that those were the reasons for his opposition.

In fact Lloyd George was never a pacifist, never a Little Englander and never an *indiscriminate* pro-Boer. He regarded Kruger as an old Tory whose regime would have been supplanted by a more liberal one but for the crass ineptitude of British imperial policy. Lloyd George's quarrel was with a particular imperial policy, Joseph Chamberlain's, not with Imperialism as such – any more than he objected to war as such. He was against the Boer War because it seemed to him unjust and impolitic, and he was against it not least because he saw it as gravely damaging to the long-term interests of the Empire. His denunciations of the war were, of course, emotional as well as rational, but his emotions were not those of a Gladstonian Liberal, nor those of an international socialist, nor those of a Celtic separatist. His basic premises were very similar to Chamberlain's. The profound difference between them concerned means, not ends.

From his earliest years Lloyd George had a macrocosmic view of politics. It is utterly wrong to think of him as, initially, a little potbound Welsh agitator who gradually became aware of the bigger world as he mixed with men of more spacious vision at Westminster. He stood up for Wales and, when he was first an MP, tended to concentrate upon Welsh issues – or issues in which Wales had a special interest – not because he was incapable of glimpsing wider horizons, but because he knew that he must work his way forward one step at a time, making full use of his assets. One of these was, of course, the Welsh national movement, of which he became the most effective spokesman. But his idea of Welsh nationality was not incompatible with the idea of Empire: on the contrary, he saw the two as complementary. In a speech at Caernarvon, little more than a year after his election to Parliament, he said:[1]

> As Welsh Liberals we are Imperialists because we are nationalists, and we are also Liberals for the same reason. We know . . . that by the sum of the success, prosperity and happiness attained by little Wales, the greater Empire of which she is a part will be the more glorious.

His Imperialism was, however, in the tradition of Lord Durham, and he reacted sharply against the standardizing, centralizing tendency of Joseph Chamberlain's Imperialism, which seemed to him a manifestation of English racial arrogance. Just as he advocated 'Home Rule all round' for the United Kingdom, so he advocated it for the Empire, and it was significant that in the late summer of 1899, when the Transvaal crisis was coming to a head, he was on a visit to Canada. It was from Vancouver that he sent a message to his brother, on 18 September.[2]

> The news from the Transvaal threatens to alter my arrangements. War means the summoning of Parliament, and the former seems now inevitable. The prospect oppresses me with a deep sense of horror. If I have the courage I shall protest with all the vehemence at my command against the outrage which is perpetrated in the name of freedom.

War was declared on 11 October, and Lloyd George was soon making his first protest in the House of Commons.[3] His indignation sprang from a conviction that the war had been deliberately provoked, and that the government's alleged motives for going to war with the Dutch republics were hypocritical and bogus. He could not take seriously the claim that Britain was fighting to win democratic rights for the Uitlanders, while no attempt was made to remove flagrantly oligarchic features of the British Constitution. In any case, he despised the Uitlanders who, among other things, aroused his rather strong anti-Semitic feelings. It was obvious to him, as indeed it is to posterity, that Chamberlain and the High Commissioner in South Africa, Sir Alfred Milner, were determined to assert British paramountcy, whatever the cost. But, since the legal grounds for doing so were virtually non-existent, moral rather than legal reasons had to be adduced. This put the government at a disadvantage when facing a critic of Lloyd George's relentless force and acuity.

Though no pacifist, he was genuinely disgusted by the spectacle of an unnecessary war. In his view, war was so beastly and wasteful that it could be justified only when truly vital interests were at stake, and was certainly not justified for the purpose of establishing a British hegemony in Southern Africa. He felt that Boer loyalty might be won by conciliation, but would never be won by coercion. Moreover, having read Motley as a boy in North Wales, he was convinced that the Dutch farmers on the African veld would show the same spirit that their ancestors had shown in resisting the imperial power of Spain. They would, he believed, be very hard to beat, and the cost of beating them would be disproportionately high – diverting funds that were urgently needed for social reform at home. Speaking at Carmarthen at the end of November 1899, he told his audience that every lyddite shell exploding in South Africa would be carrying away an old age pension.[4] And writing a few days later to his friend Alfred Thomas, chairman of the Welsh group of MPs, he said: 'This is a horrible business. It will cost us 10,000 men and £50,000,000 before it is over – and all for a stupid mistake or two'.[5] His estimate would have seemed wildly pessimistic to most people at the time, yet it fell far short of the eventual figures. The war cost Britain £250 million and the lives of 22,000 soldiers.

The war's first phase consisted of a series of spectacular disasters for the British Army, culminating in 'Black Week', mid-December 1899. In fact, the Boers' tactical successes masked a fundamental failure of strategy, in that they had made the mistake of invading Natal rather than Cape Colony, and had wasted much of their very limited strength in operations against the beleaguered garrisons of Mafeking, Kimberley and Ladysmith. The war's second phase began when the British government, shaken out of its complacency, dispatched the veteran Lord Roberts to South Africa as commander-in-chief, with Lord Kitchener as his chief of staff. This formidable partnership soon turned the tide of conventional warfare, and by June 1900 the capitals of both Boer republics had fallen, Mafeking and the other garrisons had been relieved, and the British were as victorious as they could ever, in the circumstances, hope to be.

While the Boers had been doing well Lloyd George was secretly delighted. Their feats of arms appealed to his imagination, which was always stirred by the David-and-Goliath motif, and they also helped to vindicate his views of the war. To that extent he was undoubtedly pro-Boer. But he was careful not to attack the British Army, and throughout the war he insisted – whatever the fortunes of battle – that his criticisms were political, not military. All the same, his anti-war line became very unpopular, even in Wales, more especially when Roberts was advancing in triumph. At his home town of Criccieth Lloyd George was burnt in effigy, and, in April 1900, after a meeting in his constituency at Bangor, he was struck with a bludgeon. Yet in the 'Khaki' election, which was fought in September-October, he held his seat with an increased majority. In this he was not unique – most other opponents of the war were returned – and it is quite wrong to interpret the election result as an overwhelming mandate for the war, with Caernarvon an isolated peace stronghold in a swirling torrent of Jingoism. If the government had gone to the country, as Lloyd George expected, immediately after Mafeking night and the fall of the Boer capitals, pro-war sentiment might have been overwhelming. But by early autumn the nation's mood was less excited, and in the popular vote the Liberals did surprisingly well, though the Conservatives came back with a big majority in the new House of Commons.

It is fair to assume that the Liberals lost because they were divided on the war, rather than because some of them were opposed to it. The party had been disunited ever since Gladstone resigned, with the personal antagonism of Rosebery and Harcourt roughly reflecting a conflict of ideas and policies. Their incompatibility was, in fact, more temperamental than ideological, but it was also in some measure true that Harcourt represented the Gladstonian tradition in foreign affairs, whereas Rosebery's foreign policy was scarcely distinguishable from Salisbury's. By 1899, Harcourt and Rosebery had both resigned their positions of leadership within the party, but others carried on the struggle, to which, of course, the Boer War gave a new urgency and relevance. Campbell-Bannerman, Harcourt's successor as Liberal leader in the Commons, was essentially Gladstonian, and from the first he took the view that the war was unnecessary. But several of his most important colleagues – notably Asquith, Grey, Haldane and Fowler – regarded the war as inevitable and just. The latter became known as Liberal Imperialists, which was and is a misleading term, because it suggests that all those Liberals who opposed the war were also opposed to the British Empire on principle. Of many, however, including Campbell-Bannerman and Lloyd George, this was not at all true.

On 25 July 1900 the party split three ways in a Commons vote on the war, with Lloyd George and thirty Liberal MPs voting against the government action, Campbell-Bannerman and thirty-four abstaining, while the Liberal Imperialists voted with the government. Campbell-Bannerman was by nature more cautious than Lloyd George, but in any case he had to do his best to keep the party together. At that stage he did not wish to be too closely identified with the anti-war faction, though he never changed his view that the war was wrong.

Just before Parliament was dissolved for the 'Khaki' election, there was a tense scene in the House of Commons when Lloyd George raised the issue of Chamberlain's family link with the armaments industry. As early as 1895 – during the general election of that year – Lloyd George had touched on the theme of Kynoch's, the armaments manufacturers.[6]

> Mr Chamberlain is anxious to know whether the Government has given sufficient orders to a firm called Kynoch & Co. of Birmingham. What is the history of that company? The chairman is Mr Chamberlain's brother. There are four Chamberlains who have large holdings in the firm.

In August 1900 Lloyd George had the advantage that a select committee had reported a week earlier on the placing of War Office contracts, suggesting that Kynoch's had been unduly favoured. In his short speech before Parliament rose, he said that the House was entitled to demand ruthless action, and that a government ostensibly so anxious to purify the administration of the Transvaal should set an example at home. Chamberlain replied, rather lamely, that he had not read the committee's report, but that he had nothing to do with his brother's private concerns, any more than his brother – the chairman of Kynoch's – had anything to do with his public concerns.[7]

After the election, in the debate on the Address, Lloyd George returned to the charge with an amendment to the effect that ministers of the crown ought to have 'no interest, direct or indirect' in any firm 'competing for contracts with the Crown', unless such precautions were taken as would 'prevent any suspicion of influence or favouritism'. Introducing the amendment in a long and devastating speech, he did not accuse Chamberlain, or his son, Austen, until recently Civil Lord of the Admiralty, of deliberate corruption, but he did argue that they had acted improperly and had failed to conform to the standard laid down by Chamberlain himself when in

Opposition – the standard that men in high places ought to be above suspicion, like Caesar's wife.[8] It might be argued, in retrospect, that Lloyd George was not the ideal man to champion the cause of Ministerial purity. But he did so most tellingly, and his amendment was supported by some of the Liberal Imperialists, including Asquith and Haldane. It was, of course, defeated by the government's automatic majority, but the honours of the debate went to Lloyd George.

At the end of 1900 the war entered its third phase, which proved agonizingly long, and, to Britain, even more discreditable than the first phase. The Boers ceased to fight in regular military units, but operated in guerrilla groups, known as commandos, whose members executed daring raids and then returned to their farms. To counter this unconventional mode of warfare Roberts started the policy of farm-burning, which Kitchener, Roberts's successor as commander-in-chief, developed into a systematic war of attrition. By covering the veld with lines of blockhouses and barbed wire, and by herding Boer families into concentration camps, he gradually deprived the commandos of their bases of support. It is only fair to say that he would have preferred to make peace on honourable terms before the most odious consequences of the new strategy took effect. In late February 1901 he met the Boer general, Botha, at Middelburg in the Transvaal and came near to reaching agreement with him. But the British government would not allow Kitchener to promise an amnesty for Boer rebels in the British South African colonies, and on that relatively minor point the peace negotiations broke down.

As a result, the war lasted another fifteen months, during which disease struck the camps and 20,000 people died in them. At one time the average mortality was 117 per thousand, and in one camp the mortality among children was nearly 500 per thousand. This scandal greatly increased the odium in which Britain was already held abroad on account of the war, and created deep uneasiness at home even among the government's supporters. Chamberlain had the responsibility for the camps transferred from the War Office to his own department, and he gradually improved their administration. By the end of the war the death rate in the camps was down to twenty per thousand. But by then the harm was irretrievably done.

Middelburg and the camps naturally changed the emphasis of Lloyd George's attacks on the government. They remained, however, attacks on policy rather than on the military conduct of the war. In its early stages he had concentrated upon the bullying and mishandling of the Boers which had brought the war about. Later, he denounced the policy of annexation. By 1901, however, he was saying that it was no longer profitable to discuss the origins of the war, and was tacitly assuming that the Boer republics would have to accept British paramountcy. Yet he was soon lambasting the government for failing to make peace, and as the tragic news of the mortality in the camps came through his indignation was compounded.

Meanwhile he had scored a remarkable coup when, at the end of 1900, he had arranged for the pro-war *Daily News* to be taken over by an anti-war syndicate, in which the key figure was the Birmingham Quaker and chocolate manufacturer, George Cadbury.[9] In response to an appeal from Lloyd George, which took the, for him, unusual form of a letter, Cadbury put up an initial sum of £20,000, and assumed a responsibility for the paper which was to cost him much more in the future. The general significance of this coup was that it secured one of the London Liberal penny dailies for the anti-war cause. Previously, the *Daily Chronicle*, since shortly after the outbreak of war, and the *Daily News* had been on the other side. But in Lloyd George's career, its significance is that it shows how influential he had become among *English* Radical Nonconformists. His reputation had been made, very largely, as the most eloquent champion of Welsh Nonconformists and tenant farmers, though after 1895, when the Liberal party was virtually leaderless, he was beginning to be accepted as an unofficial leader on national as well as provincial issues. It was the Boer War, however, which enabled him to appear once and for all in his true colours. In March 1901, one of his Welsh colleagues was writing: 'George is now . . . a below the gangway English radical – nothing more – and is doing that work admirably'.[10]

The horror of the camps brought Lloyd George and Campbell-Bannerman still closer together when, on 14 June, Campbell-Bannerman made his famous speech at the Holborn Restaurant, referring to the 'methods of barbarism' that were being used in South Africa. This speech put Campbell-Bannerman beyond the pale in the eyes of the Liberal Imperialists, but at the same time both the camps and the continued failure to win the war had severely damaged the government's credit. In the circumstances an ex-premier, who had backed the war without being in any way responsible for what had gone wrong, had a good chance of mobilizing support among Unionist malcontents as well as among his natural followers, the Liberal Imperialists. The man in question was Rosebery who emerged as a potential saviour from his self-imposed exile, but then acted and spoke with such ambivalence that the chance was missed. His speech at Chesterfield, in December 1901, was the high-water mark of his revival, but the eager anticipation with which it was awaited gave way to disillusionment when its contents were studied. The Liberal League, which was formed two months later with Rosebery as president and with Asquith, Grey and Fowler as vice-presidents, became, in effect, more anti-Campbell-Bannerman than pro-Rosebery in character. As a party within the Liberal party it cut little ice, because its objectives were so vague. Meanwhile, the bulk of the Liberal rank-and-file remained loyal to Campbell-Bannerman.

Lloyd George remained loyal to him, too. Though he rather admired Rosebery, whose outlook on some issues he shared, he was aware of Rosebery's difficult temperament, and above all was deterred by his equivocal attitude towards the most crucial immediate problem of ending the war. Rosebery's intervention was encouraging as a symptom of the doubts and anxieties afflicting people formerly wholeheartedly committed to the war, and as such it was welcomed and exploited by Lloyd George. But he never showed any sign of transferring his allegiance from Campbell-Bannerman to Rosebery. Right through the war there was an underlying solidarity between him and his leader in the Commons, which was never seriously shaken. They did not become intimate friends, but they grew to respect each other, and Campbell-Bannerman was content that Lloyd George should often take a more aggressive line than he would have found expedient himself. Even when Lloyd George attacked him in one debate, saying that he 'had been treated by his captors (the Liberal Imperialists) as the Boers treated their prisoners . . . stripped of all his principles and left on the veld to find his way back the best way he could',[11] privately Campbell-Bannerman was not at all displeased, because it was convenient for him to be accused by Lloyd George of being the *Liberal Imperialists'* captive. Since his 'methods of barbarism' speech, the charge which he normally had to face was that he had been captured by Lloyd George. While there is no evidence that the attack referred to was deliberately contrived – the result of collusion between the attacker and his supposed victim – it is a matter of record that Campbell-Bannerman saw 'nothing to regret in the whole thing',[12] since it served to enlarge and consolidate the centre of the party.

To supporters of the war, Lloyd George was always the arch-villain, and the period of the war was disagreeable, even dangerous, for him and his family. His elder son, Richard, was so bullied by his Tory travelling-companions on his daily journey to Dulwich that he had to be moved to a school in North Wales. The Lloyd George daughters did not suffer so badly, but were made to feel outsiders because their father would not allow them to sport patriotic favours. His own meetings were frequently rowdy, and at times violent. The worst, Bangor apart, were at Glasgow, Liskeard, Liverpool and, of course, Birmingham.

The Birmingham meeting of 18 December 1901 has passed into folklore, and Lloyd George's escape, disguised as a policeman, from the riot in the Town Hall is known to many who know little else about his early career. The riot was, in fact, largely fomented by the Liberal Unionist press in Birmingham whose predictions that there would be violence were obviously intended to be self-justifying. Chamberlain, for his part, did nothing to restrain them, and later, asked why Lloyd George had been allowed to escape, remarked – probably half in jest – that what was everybody's business was nobody's business. Certainly, Lloyd George's worst offence in the eyes of the Birmingham Unionists was that he had besmirched the honour of their hero, Chamberlain; the offence of being a pro-Boer was secondary.

Throughout the last phase of the war Lloyd George's speeches were subtly modulated to appeal not only to the humanitarian instincts of the British people but also to their war-weariness and even to their cupidity. A good example was his speech at Wrexham made a few days before the Birmingham meeting. He quoted an estimate that the war would last another two years, showed that its total cost would therefore be £300 million, and then asked what Wrexham's share would be. It would, he calculated, be £120,000, and the town would then have to pay a further four shillings in the pound for garrisoning South Africa after the war. He also calculated that Wrexham's share of the seven thousand children who had died in the camps was six children. So they had added £120,000 to their town debt, plus £13,000 a year which they would have to find in hard cash – 'per contra six little graves in Africa'.[13] Shakespeare's Mark Antony appealed similarly to the high and the low in his audience, when he gave the details of Caesar's will after recalling Caesar's merits and the love he had inspired.

When peace was eventually signed in June 1902, Lloyd George regarded the terms as 'generous . . . for the Boers. Much better than those we offered them 15 months ago – after spending £50,000,000 in the meantime'.[14] The terms were indeed generous, but behind the generosity was a recognition of stark necessity. The war had to be ended: so the Boers were allowed to keep their rifles, and the use of their language in schools and courts of law, in return for an acknowledgment of British sovereignty – which was to prove very different from British power. Lloyd George had regarded the war as unwinnable, and he later maintained that Britain's apparent victory was illusory. When, thirteen years later, he was talking about it to Frances Stevenson, and she suggested that he was, after all, glad that Britain had won, he replied with emphasis:[15]

> *We didn't win.* The Boers – the Dutch – are the rulers in South Africa. We had to give them back their land to rule – for us! And more – for whereas they had ruled the Orange Free State and the Transvaal, they were given in addition Cape Colony and Natal to rule. Had we not done this, we should now [1915] have been driven from South Africa . . . . Botha and others would have gone back to their farms, and waited for the moment – this moment – when all our energies are wanted elsewhere, to drive us from South Africa. We didn't win the Boer War!

In other words, Lloyd George did not, in his heart, believe that the Boers had been reconciled to Britain by Tory or Liberal magnanimity. He thought that, while saving Britain's face, they had struck a bargain very favourable to themselves, and that Britain was in no position to drive a harder bargain.

Looking back, we can see that his judgment of the practical realities was as sound as his nerve was steady, during his first major test as an undeniably national politician. There was nothing opportunistic about the line he took, which exposed him to political and personal risks of no ordinary kind. Nor was his opposition to the Boer War inconsistent, as many have assumed, with his later support for British entry into the European war in 1914. He favoured war in 1914 on a principle which, among others, had moved him to oppose war in 1899 – that he disliked the spectacle of small nations being trampled underfoot by large empires. Moreover, he was satisfied in 1914 that Britain's own vital security was threatened, whereas in 1899 it had been evident to him that there was no such threat.

Morally, Lloyd George's attitude towards the conflict in South Africa was in one sense no better or more enlightened than

Chamberlain's. Beatrice Webb reflected, long after the event, that hardly anyone involved in the controversy 'ever mentioned the claim of the native population . . . even to be considered in the matter, let alone be admitted to the government, or even to be given a vote, in the vast territories in which they had been living for generations',[16] and in which they constituted the overwhelming majority. The Fabian Society, it should be said, was no less divided on the war than the Liberal party. The Webbs themselves were much influenced by their friendship with Haldane, which reduced them to incoherence on the issue. Far from approving of Lloyd George's line, it was with obvious distaste that Beatrice Webb noted, in July 1901, that he was effectively leading the Liberal party in the House of Commons.

On the subject of race, Lloyd George had the common prejudices of a white northern Protestant. He felt, instinctively, that the darker races were inferior, and it hardly occurred to him that the real underdogs in South Africa were not the Boers but the Bantu and the immigrant Indians. In one speech, admittedly, when attacking the moral pretensions of the government, he did refer to the black Africans. 'There might be something magnanimous in a great Empire like ours imperilling its prestige and squandering its resources to defend the poor helpless black. Unhappily, here again is a fiction.'[17] The Kaffir workmen on the Rand, he said, were better treated than Cecil Rhodes's at Kimberley and in Matabeleland. But it was only a party point. Neither the government nor Lloyd George was really much concerned for the welfare of the Kaffirs.

Nor did either care much what became of the Indian community in South Africa, whose leader was a young lawyer, M. K. Gandhi. The Indian question had a much larger dimension, since the granting of democratic rights to the Indians in South Africa would have had inescapable implications for the political future of India itself. Lloyd George had nothing to say on the lesser issue, but he did throw out tantalizing hints on the larger. As an apostle of 'Home Rule all round' he was more or less bound to make some allusion, however imprecise, to India's future, and he did so most arrestingly in a speech on Imperialism delivered at Birkenhead in November 1901, when he said that the British Empire must be kept together on the basis of national freedom without 'racial arrogance'.[18]

> We ought to give freedom everywhere – freedom in Canada, freedom in the Antipodes, in Africa, in Ireland, in Wales,

B

> and in India. We will never govern India as it ought to be governed until we have given it freedom.

The wording was paradoxical, but at least the word 'freedom' was used in connection with India. Unfortunately, when he was prime minister, Lloyd George failed to meet India's demand for self-government within the Empire.

Lloyd George's radicalism – in the Boer War and subsequently – did not apply to race. But he was genuinely and fearlessly radical in his criticism of the war's origins, in his belief that the Empire could be united by conciliation, not by coercion, in his rejection of the policy of unconditional surrender and the tactics of attrition, in his righteous wrath when thousands were dying in the camps, and in his awareness that the vast sums spent on the war should have been devoted to social reform. He was also radical in his polemical methods which aroused – then as later – the extremes of enthusiasm and hostility in the country at large.

In the House of Commons, where the fortunes of every British politician are made or broken, his speeches on the war were invariably listened to, even by his opponents, with attention and grudging respect. He thus emerged from the war with a vastly enhanced reputation, and as the natural pace-setter for Edwardian Radicalism.

NOTES

1 Speech at Caernarvon, 29 May 1891.
2 Lloyd George to William George, 18 September 1899, quoted, W. George, *My Brother and I*, London, 1958, p. 177.
3 See *Hansard*, iv: 77: 782-4.
4 Speech at Carmarthen, 27 November 1899.
5 Lloyd George to A. Thomas, 7 December 1899, Pontypridd Papers.
6 Speech at Bangor, 4 July 1895.
7 *Hansard*, iv: 87: 1005-14.
8 Ibid., iv: 88: 397-476.
9 The most recent account of this transaction is in Stephen E. Koss, *Fleet Street Radical*, London, 1973, pp. 38-40.
10 A. C. Humphreys-Owen to Lord Rendel, 23 March 1901, Glansevern Papers.
11 *Hansard*, iv: 101: 537-43.
12 Campbell-Bannerman to Lord Ripon, 24 January 1902, quoted, J. A. Spender, *Life of Campbell-Bannerman*, London, 1924, vol. 2, p. 25.
13 Speech at Wrexham, 12 December 1901.
14 Lloyd George to Margaret George, 2 June 1902, Lloyd George Papers, National Library of Wales, Aberystwyth.

15 Entry for 25 January 1915, in A. J. P. Taylor (ed.), *Lloyd George: A Diary by Frances Stevenson*, London, 1971, p. 247.
16 Beatrice Webb, *Our Partnership* (ed. B. Drake and M. I. Cole), London, 1958, p. 192.
17 Speech to the Palmerston Club, Balliol College, Oxford, 27 January 1900.
18 Speech at Birkenhead under auspices of Ruskin Hall Debating Society, 21 November 1901.

2

BRITISH RADICALS AND INDIA IN THE EARLY TWENTIETH CENTURY

EDWARD C. MOULTON

One of the great ironies of the British India connection was that while India was widely regarded as the brightest jewel in the crown it normally received very little attention from the British public or Parliament. Through the long history of contact, however, there were prominent individual Whigs or Liberals who raised their voices in defence of India. This tradition began with Burke in the eighteenth century, was carried on by a number of liberal utilitarians in the early 1800s, and found expression in the third quarter of the century in the pro-India activities of John Bright and Henry Fawcett, the latter earning for himself the title of 'Member of Parliament for India'. Their mantle was in turn assumed by Charles Bradlaugh who, in the years immediately preceding his death in 1891, became a noted advocate of Indian constitutional reform. For the remainder of that decade the chief India spokesmen in Britain were Dadabhai Naoroji, a prominent Indian nationalist who was Liberal MP for Finsbury from 1892 to 1895, and his close associate William Wedderburn, a retired Indian Civil Service (ICS) officer and Liberal MP from 1893 to 1900. Vocal and active though Naoroji and Wedderburn were, achieving any significant impact was singularly difficult in that era of Conservative rule and rampant Imperialism. That was to change, however, in 1906 when the Liberals returned to power with a significant number of pro-India Radicals who received consistent support from the Labour party. Never had India excited more interest among British Radicals than during the next few years; never before had India more desperately needed the backing of British supporters dedicated to the idea that the *raj* should be guided by principles of justice and constitutionalism.

The main reason for the unusual interest in India was that from 1905 the country entered a new, militant phase of nationalism which many British interests feared might disrupt the Empire. The development of modern nationalism in India dated from the 1870s and was a logical outcome of the growth of English education among the new élite of urban India. Until the early twentieth century the nationalist movement, which found its main institutional expression in the Indian National Congress, was characterized by constitutionalism and general policies of moderation. Confined to the educated middle class, the Congress was no match for the British bureaucracy in the heyday of Imperialism. Most of its demands were ignored.

By 1905, twenty years after its establishment, Congress had little tangible to show for its efforts in the way of administrative or constitutional reform. Even stalwarts of the movement were discouraged and in 1903 four of them, Naoroji, Wedderburn, W. C. Bonnerjee and A. O. Hume, issued 'A Call to Arms', an urgent plea for more concerted effort in the nationalist cause. Hume, whose radical tradition had not been stifled by his career in the ICS and who had played the key role in establishing the Congress, was the most outspoken. He reminded Congress members that nations were created only by struggle and 'self-sacrifice' and referred them to the example of the Irish who 'have been fighting tooth and nail . . . for nearly a century'. Hume chided Indian leaders for naively assuming that 'any despotic Government . . . *will willingly* yield you . . . political privileges' and appealed to them to[1]

> be in earnest; disregard all threats – spurn all coercion – prove to the British nation that you are really determined to be fairly dealt with in this matter [of constitutional rights and reforms]; that you are resolved never to give them a day's peace till you *are* so dealt with; that you will spend your time, your money, your lives, if need be, in bringing this about.

Hume's appeal alarmed cautious Congress leaders in India who evidently tried to suppress its circulation. But events there were already moving in the direction Hume urged as young firebrands such as Bal Gangadhar Tilak, Bepinchandra Pal and Lala Lajpat Rai, disillusioned by lack of Congress achievement and influenced by the recent Hindu revival, rejected the politics of moderation. Ironically, the growth of militant nationalism received strong impetus from the actions of Lord Curzon, that great imperial proconsul who had fondly aimed to undermine the Congress movement. Curzon, who was viceroy from 1898 to 1905, believed in efficient government by a cast-iron bureaucracy as the key to continuing British rule in India. It was this principle, coupled with unconcealed contempt for the educated middle class which shaped Indian public opinion, that governed his administration.

Curzon never concealed his disparaging attitude towards his Asiatic subjects or his belief in the essential primacy of British exclusiveness in administration. On one occasion he publicly asserted that 'craftiness and diplomatic wile' were the hallmarks of the East whereas 'the highest ideal of truth is to a large extent a Western conception'.[2] Another time he warned Indians against seeking the salvation of their country through politics, for the English, because of their innate superiority, must continue to control high offices in India. This statement, as educated Indians noted indignantly, was contrary to the spirit of British official pledges dating to 1833. In the realm of policy, and ostensibly in the interest of efficiency or bureaucratic control, Curzon drastically reduced the number and powers of elected Indian members of the Calcutta Municipal Corporation, and increased official control over the universities. By these actions the liberalizing policies of earlier years were undermined.

The crowning act of Curzon's unpopular measures, however, and the one which quickly became the *bête noire* of British Radicals, was the partition of Bengal. Few questioned that the province, which included three distinct linguistic and cultural units – Bihar, Orissa and Bengal proper – with a total population of some 80 million, was an administrative nightmare. Instead of detaching the non-Bengali units, Curzon chose to divide Bengal proper. This was a homogeneous, linguistic and cultural entity with a highly articulate and politicized educated middle class. The partition created a new province of East Bengal and Assam with a population of approximately 31 million, of whom 25 million were Bengali, the majority of them being Muslim in religion. The old province of Bengal was left with a population of 18 million Bengalis, most of whom were Hindu. But now they were greatly outnumbered by the less advanced Biharis and Oriyas. Politically conscious Bengalis saw the partition scheme as a blatant case of 'divide and rule'. Numerous protest meetings were organized and hundreds of anti-partition memorials signed. But Curzon refused to be deterred and in October 1905, only a few months before his departure from India, partition became a reality. Meanwhile Bengal, led by nationalists of all political hues, had embarked on a boycott of British textiles and other goods and a corresponding campaign – the *swadeshi* movement – to promote Indian products and services. For the first time Bengal and much of urban India experienced a wave of mass nationalism.

As reaction to Curzonian imperialism mounted in India, Radicals in Britain became more active. In 1900 the tide of militarism and imperialism had been running so high in Britain that William Wedderburn, whose persistent criticism of so much of British rule in India and more especially his strong opposition to the Boer War got him into trouble with his own constituents, had decided not to seek re-election to Parliament. Dadabhai Naoroji's attempt at a political comeback was also unsuccessful with the result that between 1900 and 1905 India had no strong spokesman in Parliament. As a consequence the Indian parliamentary committee which Wedderburn and Naoroji had formed in 1893 remained dormant. Wedderburn did not, however, abandon work on India's behalf, even though for the next few years it was carried on largely outside Parliament. He remained chairman of the British Committee of Congress which he had been instrumental in establishing in 1889 and which consisted of a small core of British Radicals and Indian nationalists responsible for co-ordinating and directing Congress interests in Britain. The active core of the Committee during the difficult years following the turn of the century was Naoroji, Hume and Bonnerjee. It was these three, together with their untiring chairman, Wedderburn, who were also instrumental in keeping alive the journal *India*, a Congress publication which the Committee had established in 1890 to provide systematic information in Britain on subjects and issues concerning India. While financing this weekly publication remained a headache, the journal helped to keep Indian issues before British MPs and journalists.

The British Congress Committee was much strengthened in 1902 with the addition to its ranks of Sir Henry Cotton, a newly retired ICS officer cast very much in the mould of Hume and Wedderburn. Cotton was a Liberal Radical who as early as 1885 in his book *New India*, had stressed the political significance of the emerging Indian middle class and the urgency of the *raj* reacting constructively to this development by instituting a graduated programme of constitutional reform leading ultimately to the establishment of representative institutions on the white colonial model. This measure of identification with Indian aspirations probably prejudiced Cotton's subsequent advancement in the governing bureaucracy,[3] but his views on the need to establish representative institutions grew stronger as time progressed. With his retirement from the service he was 'unmuzzled' at last,[4] and plunged enthusiastically into the work of the British Congress Committee. Realizing that he would be able to exert greater influence from a seat in the Commons, one of his first efforts was to secure nomination as a prospective Liberal candidate for the next general election. This he achieved in the spring of 1903 when he was adopted by the Liberal Association of Nottingham. While Cotton gave considerable time during the next two years to building up support in his constituency, he was also a strong critic of Curzon's administration. He vigorously condemned Curzon's dispatch of a British expedition to Tibet and opposed Bengal partition from the outset.

As a tribute to Cotton's genuine service to India over the years, he was invited by Congress to become the president of its twentieth annual session in 1904, an invitation which he gladly accepted. For a time Wedderburn had been hopeful that all the great veterans in England would accompany Cotton. But Hume and Bonnerjee had to forgo the trip because of ill-health, and Naoroji was too busy campaigning for the forthcoming general election. As a result Wedderburn alone accompanied Cotton to the Congress session held that year in Bombay. In India, much to the chagrin of British officials, Cotton and Wedderburn were treated like national heroes. Thousands of Indians of all classes turned out to welcome them upon their arrival in Bombay and there was an audience of some 12,000 for Cotton's presidential address. In his speech Cotton identified himself completely with the Congress cause, stressed the crucial necessity of substantial reform in the Indian administration, and urged Congress to redouble its efforts to forge India's diverse communities into a strong and united nation. Both he and Wedderburn claimed that the Imperialist wave had already crested, and persuaded Congress to send delegates to England to campaign with the Radicals in the forthcoming general election.

Cotton and Wedderburn undoubtedly helped to infuse a new sense of enthusiasm among Congressmen. Following the session they embarked on a wider tour of the country. Wedderburn went to Madras and the south where he was given a rousing reception by Congress supporters. 'My visit', he wrote, 'stirred them all up, and at Tanjore they have started a vigorous young Association.'[5] Cotton's visit to Bengal and eastern India, the area in which he had worked for so many years, produced an even more electric effect. Everywhere he was received like a public hero, the biggest demonstration being a massive protest meeting at the Calcutta

Town Hall against the proposed partition of Bengal. In his keynote speech Cotton condemned the proposed scheme, advocating instead one which would not divide Bengal proper. He urged the Bengalis to keep up their agitation against Curzon's scheme and promised support from Radical sympathizers in Britain. In fact a recurring theme in the speeches of both Cotton and Wedderburn was the confident expectation that once the Liberals returned to power India would receive better treatment.

Back in Britain in early 1905, Wedderburn, Cotton and the British Congress Committee turned their attention to mobilizing support for India in the general election, expected later that year. In this connection the most important event, apart from Cotton's and Naoroji's campaigns for election to Parliament,[6] was the visit of Congress delegates from India. For a time Wedderburn had been hopeful of persuading Sir Pherozeshah Mehta, the dominant power in the Congress and one of its most cautious and conservative members, to head the delegation, but was obliged to settle for his younger but equally capable disciple, G. K. Gokhale. Gokhale arrived in October, having been preceded by Lajpat Rai, a more militant nationalist. Lajpat Rai's relations with the British Congress Committee were rather strained because of the close contact which he established in London with Shyamaji Krishnavarma, a noted young Indian revolutionary who, through the columns of his monthly magazine, the *Indian Sociologist*, condemned the politics of moderation and advocated revolutionary action to free India of British rule. When Lajpat Rai joined Krishnavarma on a public platform in London to demand Home Rule for India, some members of the British Committee were disturbed and it took considerable effort on Wedderburn's part to smooth things over. Wedderburn himself did not approve of Krishnavarma's politics, noting regretfully that he and H. M. Hyndman, the leader of the Social Democratic Federation and the most thoroughgoing British critic of the *raj*, were denouncing the Congress Committee as 'useless and even mischievous Moderates'.[7] But Wedderburn knew that Lajpat Rai, though a fiery young nationalist, was no violent revolutionary and was anxious to have him publicize India's grievances as widely as possible. He therefore arranged an extensive speaking tour which, during July, took Lajpat Rai to major cities in the Midlands, northern England and Scotland. Wedderburn was quite satisfied with the results, for he confided to Gokhale that 'Lajpat Rai has been doing very well here' on India's behalf.

The main thrust, however, of pre-election activity publicizing

India's grievances came in October with the arrival of Gokhale, the favoured son of the British Congress Committee. Gokhale had first visited England in 1897 and had established contact with John Morley and other influential Liberals. On this second visit, during which he stayed at the National Liberal Club of which he was made a temporary member, Gokhale built upon these earlier contacts. Thanks to Wedderburn's thorough advance planning, his seven-week stay was filled with personal interviews or public-speaking engagements. Among the former were meetings with influential Liberals including Morley, Lord Ripon, Lloyd George, Asquith and Campbell-Bannerman. In London he gave major addresses to the Political Committee of the National Liberal Club, the New Reform Club, 'an influential body of earnest, advanced Liberals and Radicals',[8] and the Fabian Society. He also spoke at Cambridge, Bradford, Manchester, Birmingham and Glasgow. Dominant themes in his speeches, which even Lajpat Rai considered 'very vigorous',[9] were the reactionary and oppressive nature of Curzon's imperial regime, and the urgent need to change the whole direction of British rule, which should be based on an alliance with the educated middle class and explicitly directed towards the establishment of colonial self-government. He repeatedly and forcefully condemned the partition of Bengal; justified, even before a critical Manchester audience, the Indian boycott of British textiles; and warned that India was 'seething with discontent' as never before in its history.[10] Gokhale emphasized that Congress expected the Liberals and Labour to redress India's grievances and to inaugurate an era of progressive reform. He made similar points in his personal meetings with Liberal leaders, no doubt being careful to stress the importance of their supporting Congress moderates in order, as Wedderburn put it, 'to obviate underground conspiracy' in India.[11]

While Lajpat Rai and Gokhale formed opposite assessments of what to expect from the Liberals,[12] their activities, along with the dedicated work of Cotton, Naoroji and the entire British Committee, influenced a substantial number of Radicals and Labour candidates to a new awareness of India and its problems. Shortly after the general election in January 1906, Wedderburn reported enthusiastically that the new House contained nearly one hundred 'old (India) sympathizers, or promising new Radical and Labour members'.[13] Among the former were Liberals like Sir Charles Dilke, J. Herbert Roberts and Charles Schwann who had long shown an interest in Indian affairs. New Radical MPs who were to play an active role on India's behalf included C. J. O'Donnell,

Frederic Mackarness and V. H. Rutherford. Naoroji unfortunately failed to get elected, but Cotton was returned for Nottingham and became the leader of the India caucus in Parliament. On most issues which they pressed to a division the Irish nationalists sided with them, but the most vigorous support came from Labour with James O'Grady, Ramsay MacDonald and more especially Keir Hardie playing the key roles.

Though not in Parliament, Wedderburn, as chairman of the Congress Committee, remained at the centre of Indian affairs in Britain. As soon as Campbell-Bannerman came into office, Wedderburn wrote 'beseeching him' not to appoint as Indian Secretary either 'Sir H. Fowler or Lord Elgin', 'hidebound' statesmen in whom Congress leaders had no confidence.[14] When the position went to John Morley, the leading intellectual of the Radical school, Wedderburn was delighted. He speculated that Morley's willingness to take the position might well have been influenced by the heart-to-heart talk on India which Gokhale had had with him only a few weeks earlier. Wedderburn was confident that Morley would 'go thoroughly into the facts' and that his historical experience would 'lead him to right conclusions'. Cotton, the British Committee generally and leading moderate nationalists in India shared this enthusiasm. Now that Curzon had resigned and India had a more responsive viceroy in the person of Lord Minto, they looked forward to the dawn of a new progressive era in Indian administration. As Cotton later wrote, 'above all it was felt in Bengal, where Partition was such a fresh and rankling sore, that inquiries would surely be made which would lead to its reversal or modification'.[15]

The first test of strength for the India caucus in the new Parliament came early in the first session. In anticipation of that event Wedderburn, Cotton, Roberts and others had taken the initiative of reconstituting the Indian Parliamentary Committee in mid-February 1906. The Committee, which according to Wedderburn numbered over 200, decided to move an amendment to the King's Speech expressing concern over 'the wide-spread dissatisfaction and unrest of India due to the recent policy of the Government', requesting the modification of the Bengal partition, and urging the ministry to give its consideration to 'the reasonable demands of the Indian people for a larger share in the administration of their affairs'.[16] The amendment was introduced by Roberts on 26 February and seconded by Cotton in a forceful but long-winded speech. Morley, whose Radicalism was fast waning, at least on issues affecting India, was not impressed. He admitted that partition 'went wholly and decisively against the wishes of most of the people concerned' but insisted that it was now 'a settled fact'. Despite this slap in the face, the Indian Parliamentary Committee – probably hoping that if Morley were not pushed too hard he might yet change his mind – temporized and did not force a division. Morley's inflexibility, so characteristic of the bureaucratic tradition of the *raj*, dismayed Indian moderates and encouraged the militants to more forceful action.

Meanwhile in the new province of East Bengal and Assam Lieutenant-Governor Fuller, Curzon's appointee, unleashed a veritable reign of terror against anti-partition agitators. When Fuller, in April 1906, used the police to violently disperse the Bengal Provincial Conference of Congress, summarily arrested Surendranath Banerjea, conference president and Bengal's most influential nationalist leader, and immediately suspended some three hundred students from government colleges, Cotton and the Radical caucus seized upon the issue as further compelling evidence of the injustice of partition. While their constant harrying questions in the Commons may have helped to induce Morley to seek Fuller's resignation, which came in the latter part of July, on the more fundamental issue of partition itself the Secretary of State refused to budge. Ironically, Cotton and O'Donnell indirectly contributed to this continuing inflexibility. In September Morley secretly learned that earlier in the year they had advised Bengal political leaders that if they mounted unceasing province-wide agitation Morley was bound to yield.[17] A singularly proud man, Morley was intensely piqued by this revelation and stubbornly, but unwisely, determined never to undo partition.

Having achieved little by its compliant behaviour in the debate on the King's Speech, in July the Indian Parliamentary Committee utilized the discussion of the Indian budget to force a trial of strength. On the whole the debate was not particularly impressive, perhaps its main significance being that it marked the beginning of major involvement by Keir Hardie in Indian affairs. While he traced his general interest in India to an association with Naoroji which went back to 1886, Curzonian Imperialism and the Congress agitation in England in 1905 stirred Keir Hardie to deeper involvement. In view of his interest and that of Labour in Indian reform, the Indian Parliamentary Committee decided that Keir Hardie should move a formal resolution proposing that the salary of the Secretary of State for India, like that of the Colonial Secretary, should be charged to the British Exchequer. Congress had been urging such a reform for several years, the hope being that such a change would induce Parliament to assert more effective control over Indian questions. In his speech, for which he was coached by Gokhale, then on his third visit to Britain to promote support for Congress reform policies, Keir Hardie not only argued for the justice of the amendment but deplored the famine and poverty which the country suffered under British rule, condemned the British middle classes for keeping India 'as a preserve for their own sons', and urged that educated Indians be given a larger share in the administration of their homeland.[18] Herbert Roberts, seconding the amendment, warned that unless Parliament exerted its influence to ensure reform in India the constitutional nationalists might be discredited, thus creating a grave 'political danger'. Only one or two other Radicals spoke in the debate but 89 members came into the division lobby to support the amendment.[19] This was no threat to the government which, with 30 Conservatives joining it, commanded a vote of 153. Yet the strength of the India vote was impressive. Significantly, it caused Morley considerable concern, indicating as it did that the Radical fringe should not be too lightly ignored.

In real terms, however, Cotton and the Radical caucus had singularly little to show for their efforts on India's behalf as the first session of the new Parliament drew to a close. They had failed to persuade the Liberal government to modify Curzon's most ill-advised policies. Even Wedderburn, the most patient of the India caucus leaders, was disappointed and much concerned about adverse reaction in India. In August he wrote to Tilak and Lajpat Rai, the leaders of the younger, militant nationalists, imploring them to 'keep the Congress on its present lines' of moderate constitutionalism a little longer in the hope that Morley's 'Liberalism' would soon assert itself.[20] Gokhale, nearing the conclusion of his third British visit during which he had had five long private interviews with Morley, made a similar appeal to impatient fellow-nationalists. These appeals, coupled with the diplomatic selection as that year's Congress president of Dadabhai Naoroji, kept the movement together. Under Naoroji's leadership, Congress for the first time boldly adopted resolutions on *swadeshi*, boycott and self-government. During the next year, however, it became apparent that moderates and militants were poles apart in the interpretations which they placed on these resolutions and more especially on the tactics for achieving *swaraj* or self-rule. Tilak, Lajpat Rai, Bepinchandra Pal and their militant followers were no longer prepared to put up with the politics of petitioning and pleading. At the Surat session of the Congress in December 1907 'the so-called Extremists', to use Cotton's words, 'put the Moderates to rout'.[21] This Cotton interpreted as an 'acute' symptom of 'popular unrest', the result of growing 'resentment' and 'despair', caused in no small part by the failure of the Liberal government to set a decisive new course in Indian administration.

The polarization within Congress was, as Cotton intimated, closely related to the wider climate of unrest which had begun to grip much of India in the wake of the Bengal partition. The unrest was centred at first in East Bengal, and though state repression eased somewhat following Fuller's resignation in mid-1906, violence did not. Communalism, stimulated in no small part by Fuller's blatantly pro-Muslim sympathies, continued to raise its ugly head. In March and April 1907, there were Hindu–Muslim riots in several districts of East Bengal. A little later, and just before the fiftieth anniversary of the 1857 'Mutiny', violence erupted in the strategic province of the Punjab. Though it was largely a reaction to press and political prosecutions and unpopular agricultural measures, the Punjab government, noted for its authoritarianism, took no chances. Utilizing an almost forgotten regulation of 1818, it arrested and deported without trial Lajpat Rai and Ajit Singh, a younger and more outspoken nationalist. Many of the Radicals knew Lajpat Rai personally and greatly respected him. They felt, to quote Cotton,[22]

> that it was a gross outrage on the first principles of their political creed to arrest, deport, and detain indefinitely in custody . . . individuals against whom there may not be sufficient ground to institute any judicial proceeding.

When Morley, accepting the position of senior officials in India, upheld this act of repression, the Radical India caucus was appalled and, led by Cotton and Mackarness, mounted a vigorous assault in the Commons. Morley, as Cotton not unfairly described it, was driven 'from corner to corner in his replies' and in November 1907, after six months' imprisonment, Lajpat Rai and Ajit Singh were unconditionally released. For this, the Radicals deserved much credit.[23]

Unfortunately, this episode was only the beginning of a long series of coercive measures which were to cast a blight over the Liberal government's handling of Indian affairs and to become a *cause célèbre* for the Radicals. Two days after Lajpat Rai had been arrested the Indian government issued a special ordinance to control public meetings. In November this was given permanence in the form of a Seditious Meetings Act. The government crackdown in turn led sections of the extremist press to ever more violent criticism of the *raj*. During the summer of 1907 a number of newspaper editors, mostly in Bengal, were prosecuted for sedition. Soon sedition gave way to terrorism. In December 1907 unsuccessful attempts were made on the life of the Lieutenant-Governor of Bengal and an English magistrate of Dacca. A few months later, at Muzaffarpur in Bengal, a bomb intended for Magistrate Kingford, who had earlier had a college student flogged for assaulting a policeman, killed two English women. These events created hysteria among the British community and in June 1908 the Indian government hastily adopted an Explosive Substances Act and a Newspapers Act, establishing rigid control over the Indian press. Another product of the general official hysteria was the arrest later that month of Tilak, the most influential of the extremist leaders, on a charge of sedition. Tried by a jury of seven Europeans and two Parsis, Tilak was harshly sentenced to six years' imprisonment in Burma. Later in the year the government amended the criminal law, allowing magistrates to formulate charges in the absence of the accused and to deprive them of the rights of bail and trial by jury. This legislation also empowered the government, without prior warning, to declare any association illegal. In December 1908 the government again resorted to Regulation III of 1818, arresting and deporting, without charge or trial, nine Bengali Hindus. The engine of repression failed to bring peace. In 1909 violence spread to London where a young Punjabi student assassinated Curzon-Wyllie, India Office aide-de-camp. In India there was an attempt on Minto's life, and an English collector was killed. The government responded with sedition prosecutions, adopted an even more rigorous Press Law in 1910, and initiated a number of major conspiracy cases. The pattern of violence, however, persisted until after Gandhi came on the scene in 1915.

As the wave of militant nationalism, government repression and violent outbreaks mounted, India became an even more focal concern for the Radicals. This was reflected in the visit to India in the autumn of 1907 of Rutherford, Keir Hardie and H. W. Nevinson. Rutherford, sponsored by the British Congress Committee as its delegate to that year's Indian National Congress session, was anxious 'to make the most of this golden opportunity' to 'render good service to India in Parliament'.[24] He visited leading cities in northern India, associated with extreme and moderate nationalists and did his best to mediate between them at the Surat Congress.

Nevinson, whose tour overlapped with Rutherford's, went to India as a special correspondent 'to discover the causes of the present discontent and to report without prejudice the opinions of leading Indians as well as officials'.[25] Between October 1907 and February 1908, Nevinson visited most parts of India and, unlike Rutherford, made a number of public speeches. In Madras he enthusiastically supported Indian nationalism, apologized for Morley's shortcomings and hoped that in dealing with India the Liberals would still be guided by the principles of freedom, democracy, and self-government as at home. In Calcutta he reportedly urged Indians 'to stand up and show their independence to the white man both socially and politically'.[26] He also toured extensively in troubled East Bengal, later attending the Surat Congress with Rutherford. Nevinson's activities fanned the agitation in India, while his reports to the British newspapers presented a highly sympathetic view of India and its problems. His book *The New Spirit in India*, published in 1908, showed considerable sympathy for the extremists, blamed the government for the unrest, and challenged Britain 'to welcome the spirit of freedom and nationality' in India.[27]

More controversial and important was Keir Hardie's visit extending from September to November. It was a combination of Reuter's 'alarming and clearly biased reports', Morley's weakness as Secretary of State and the resulting inability 'to get at the truth' which induced him to spend so much time in India during his broader Asian tour of that year.[28] His objective was 'to see and learn, without too much physical exertion, as much as possible of the actual condition of the people', to 'acquire information' which he could put to use on his return. Consequently, he deliberately avoided large public meetings, concentrating instead on smaller, intimate gatherings and personal interviews.

Despite his avoidance of public platforms, Hardie's tour of investigation, which was almost entirely in the hands of Congress leaders, proved to be an important political event. He went first to East Bengal, and everywhere he was welcomed by enthusiastic crowds, often being greeted with the singing of 'Bande Mataram', the popular national song of Bengal – an act that in itself was considered seditious by many officials. At a press interview Hardie claimed that official efforts to break the *swadeshi* movement 'savoured more of Russian than British methods', and likened reports 'of the forcible abduction and violation of Hindu women by Mohammedan rowdies . . . to Armenian atrocities'.[29] When a distorted and exaggerated version of this statement appeared in *The Times*, Morley reacted forcefully. He telegraphed Minto:[30]

> I wish to be promptly and continuously informed of the speeches or utterances of Keir Hardie. . . . Should any case happen of violent public disorder of a serious kind as a direct result of his speeches or utterances I should be prepared to sanction whatever measures, no matter how strong, may seem advisable.

Minto, who relished strong-arm methods against political agitators, was delighted by Morley's attitude. He wanted to 'pack [Keir Hardie] off and send him straight home' if the government could 'find any legal ground for doing so'.[31] Deportation of a British MP would be a serious business and Minto and his council concluded that they did not yet have a strong enough case for such action. Instead Minto informed the provincial governors of Morley's views, instructed them to keep a close police watch on Keir Hardie's activities and to apprehend him if circumstances justified. Minto informed Morley that Keir Hardie's[32]

> general attitude as an unfriendly critic of the Government and his utterances as reported in the press have undoubtedly tended to stimulate unrest, to promote sedition in the press, to give fresh life to the boycott and to encourage agitators to hope that their most extreme claims will receive support from an organized party in Parliament.

Meanwhile, Keir Hardie, closely followed by the secret police, travelled from Bengal to Benares, Delhi and the Punjab and then to Bombay, Poona, Madras and the south. Like the other Radical visitors of that year, he associated with political extremists as well as moderates. In Poona, at a meeting organized by Tilak, Keir Hardie vehemently condemned the police espionage to which he was being subjected. Despite continuing official anxiety, his tour concluded without major incident.

Back in Britain in 1908, Keir Hardie and Rutherford, together with Cotton and Mackarness, led the Radical fight against government repression in India. In the press they received considerable support from Nevinson and W. T. Stead. While Keir Hardie's

India visit was severely condemned by most leading British newspapers, his own account was published in the *Labour Leader*. These articles in turn formed the basis for a book, *India: Impressions and Suggestions*, published in 1909. At the same time the British Congress Committee's publication, *India*, continued to give comprehensive coverage of Indian developments, though heavily biased towards the moderates after the Congress split of 1907.

For the Radical India caucus, the two main issues during 1908 and 1909 were coercion and reform. They did not condone violence, and agreed that order must be preserved. But they emphatically rejected the need or justification for most of the coercive measures, and considered that these measures, rather than basic popular disaffection, created sedition and terrorism.

In the debate on the Address in January 1908 Rutherford warned that Liberal repression, following so hard upon Curzon's 'reign of terror', had completely destroyed Indian confidence in 'the justice of British rule'.[33] Later that year, in the Indian budget debate, Cotton, by this stage almost totally disillusioned with Morley, lashed out at the government. He attacked the harsh punishment of political agitators, describing the prosecution of Tilak as 'suicidal', a course designed to 'create discontent and unrest' in western India.[34] The 'very bad' tone of some Indian newspapers was a reaction to Anglo-Indian press descriptions of Indians as 'polecats and cowards'. Instead of coercion and transportation Cotton argued for a thorough change in the spirit of British administration, a change from 'absolute autocracy' to 'government . . . through, by, and in conformity with, the wishes of the people'.

The renewed deportations under Regulation III of 1818 and the legislation amending the criminal law produced a concerted Radical assault during 1909. In February 1909, Mackarness moved an amendment to the Address criticizing the 'imprisonment and deportation' of Indian subjects who had neither been charged with nor 'convicted of any crime'.[35] He argued that the provisions of the Criminal Law Amendment Act were 'absolutely unparalleled in . . any . . . civilized country'; even more severe than coercive legislation for Ireland which Gladstone, Morley and other Liberals had strongly denounced. Mackarness passionately believed that, as subjects of the crown, Indians should be able to 'count upon personal liberty and the protection of the law'. The amendment was seconded by T. Hart-Davis, a former ICS officer and active member of the Indian Parliamentary Committee, who urged the release of all political 'offenders' not guilty of 'actual violence'.

Two of the strongest speeches in support of the amendment came from Keir Hardie and Cotton, both of whom knew several of the deportees personally. On this occasion the Radical caucus pushed the House to a division, the vote being 76 for the amendment and 195 for the Government.

Despite this defeat, the Radicals refused to drop the issue. They concentrated especially on the deportations, persistently using the Commons' question time to embarrass the government. On this issue they soon mobilized the support of practically the full nominal membership of the Indian Parliamentary Committee, getting 150 MPs to petition Asquith against the deportations.[36] When that failed to produce the desired effect, Keir Hardie, on 18 May, attempted to move the adjournment of the House to discuss the detentions and deportations. The Speaker, however, ruled that it was not a matter of urgency. No better success attended a subsequent move by Mackarness to introduce a Bill restricting arbitrary deportations.

Following these setbacks, the Radicals used the Indian budget debate of August 1909 for their most outspoken verbal assault against the deportations, albeit to an almost empty House. Cotton charged that the only 'real crime' against the Bengal deportees was that they were *swadeshi* leaders.[37] Their movement, he argued, was similar in many respects to Tariff Reform in Britain. 'What is regarded as a patriotic movement in England', Cotton asserted, 'is sedition in India.' Cotton graphically reminded the House that 'scores and scores of journalists', newspaper editors and publishers were 'languishing' in Indian jails. In short, the government was using coercion to suppress 'public opinion in India'. Keir Hardie, who followed Cotton in the debate, continued in a similar vein, but with particular emphasis on the role of the Indian police as agents of state repression. Keir Hardie and Mackarness had been critical of police excesses for some time and, as an increasingly large number of government-initiated sedition and conspiracy cases collapsed in the appeal courts, their criticisms were amply justified. In many of the cases, the judiciary, to quote Cotton, gave 'scathing condemnations of the methods employed by an untrustworthy and unscrupulous police to promote the prosecution of so-called political offenders'.[38]

Eventually these hard-hitting attacks began to tell on the government. While it did not repudiate the coercive legislation, in January 1910, just before the new Parliament met, Morley instructed Minto to release the nine Bengal deportees. Minto complied reluctantly, blaming the 'parliamentary left' for Morley's cave-in.[39] It was indeed a Radical victory.

Besides preoccupation with the Curzonian legacy and subsequent repression, the Radicals gave much attention to the important issue of Indian political and constitutional reform. Like Congress leaders, who had long been imploring the British to grant representative institutions, Radicals such as Cotton, Keir Hardie and Rutherford believed that constitutional reform was the key to the solution of India's problems, economic as well as political. Cotton was convinced that the only answer to administrative injustice and the resulting Indian 'unrest' was to replace the 'bureaucratic, autocratic and despotic form of government' with a 'more popular and representative' system.[40] In a similar vein Keir Hardie maintained that 'there can be no real pacification, no allaying of discontent, no breaking down of the barrier rising between European and Asiatic, until the people of India have some effective form of self-government'.[41] In short, Radical leaders fully supported the Congress position that self-governing institutions, modelled on those of white British colonies such as Canada, should be progressively extended to India. They therefore differed basically from Morley who candidly informed Gokhale that it was a mere 'dream' to expect that India could be placed 'on the footing of a self-governing colony' for years to come.[42] While the 'spirit' of free institutions might be introduced and more Indians appointed to high office in government, Morley consistently maintained that British political institutions could not be transplanted 'wholesale' into India.[43] Within this somewhat limited framework, however, Morley was determined to introduce reforms. On this score the Radicals, from 1906 onward, urged Morley to move with boldness and a sense of urgency.

While the Radicals differed philosophically from Morley on the applicability of British constitutional principles to India, they were also severely critical of certain features of the reform scheme ultimately devised by Morley and Minto. In his first definitive statement on India in the Commons in July 1906, Morley indicated that he favoured establishing a representative element in the legislative councils and permitting members to debate budgets and move financial amendments. These principles, which Congress and the Radicals had long advocated, were embodied in the Indian Councils Bill that eventually came before Parliament in 1909. There was, however, one new feature of the Bill which dismayed the Radical caucus – namely, the introduction of separate electorates for Muslims who were also to have weighted representation.

Wedderburn, who was more enthusiastic about the general features of the Bill than most Radical leaders, deplored the introduction of 'sectarian' representation which he believed Morley had 'most unwillingly accepted'.[44] Stronger condemnation came from Cotton, O'Donnell and Keir Hardie during the debates in the Commons. Regarding the special concessions as another expression of the official bias in favour of Muslims which had already caused such grievous damage in Bengal, they warned of the dire consequences of setting the major religious communities against one another. O'Donnell passionately urged the House to uphold 'the old principle that we should treat all religions with equality' and not 'awake' communal 'fanaticism' in India.[45] These were prophetic words, but they represented the view of only a tiny Radical minority and were brushed aside.

Apart from this issue, the Radicals expressed general satisfaction with the reforms. They welcomed the establishment of non-official majorities in the provincial legislative councils and were equally pleased by the appointment of the first Indian to the Viceroy's Executive. In part their approval was influenced by Gokhale and other Indian moderate leaders who, for strategic reasons involving their continuing conflict with the extremists, desperately wanted to put the best possible interpretation on the reforms. Certainly some Radicals considered the reforms much too modest. Rutherford, for example, criticized the government for not extending the non-official majority to the central legislative council, a reform which would have 'given some decent, honest measure of power to the Indians'.[46] Unlike Morley, who had no desire that the reforms should lead to 'the establishment of a Parliamentary system in India',[47] the Radicals hoped they would constitute a stage on the road to progressive self-government. 'India', as Rutherford stated, 'can never be truly contented until she governs herself.'[48] In a similar vein, Cotton warned that the ICS 'must abnegate' much of its traditional power and 'agree in the necessity of governing the country upon more democratic lines'.[49] Finally, the Radicals passionately argued that the political effect of the reforms in India would be shallow unless they were accompanied by a general political amnesty and the reunifying of Bengal. Unfortunately, however, Morley gave no attention to 'the pig-headed section of the Ultra-Radicals',[50] and this golden opportunity for genuine conciliation was lost. The result was that even Gokhale soon acknowledged that 'except for the Mahomedans' practically all enthusiasm for the reforms in India had been 'killed'.[51]

With the enactment of the Indian reforms in 1909 and the rise of major constitutional issues at home, Radical attention on India began to wane. In fact, 1909 marked the culmination of the resurgent phase of Radical involvement which had begun in 1906. It also marked the high point of Liberal–Radical commitment to India. Indian issues were never popular with British voters, and in the elections of 1910 Radical leadership was decimated by the defeat of Cotton, Rutherford, O'Donnell and others. Another Radical stalwart, Mackarness, resigned to assume a judicial position. The relegation of these key leaders to the sidelines was much regretted in India where public opinion looked increasingly to Labour as the only reliable source of British support. This shift occurred not because Labour members in the 1906 Parliament had been significantly more forceful advocates of India's interests than the Liberal Radicals. Rather it resulted from the realization that whereas the Liberal Radicals represented only a small leftist fringe of their party, Labour as a whole was committed to India. This position was consolidated by a three-month visit to India by Ramsay MacDonald in late 1909. Two years later he was invited to be Congress president, an honour which he regrettably had to give up at the last moment because of his wife's severe illness. Yet, notwithstanding Labour support, the India caucus did not regain its former strength during the pre-war years. For example, when Wedgwood and Keir Hardie forced a division in the Commons in July 1910 on the continuing repression in India, they marshalled only 48 votes. That marked the last significant Commons debate on India until Dominion status became an issue in 1917.

While the Liberals between 1906 and 1910 lost their final opportunity of setting a bold new course in Indian administration, their failure was no fault of the Radicals. In the best traditions of the British left, the Radicals had fought valiantly against arbitrary government and repression in India and had persistently advocated the application of the principles of justice, freedom and representative government to India. Though they achieved few of their objectives, the Radicals helped to some extent to mitigate state repression. Moreover, in 1911 the partition of Bengal, that seriously mistaken policy against which the Radicals had pleaded for so long, was at last annulled. For that the Radicals clearly deserved credit, though the decision came too late to have much positive effect. Without persistent Radical prodding the constitutional reforms of 1909 would probably have had fewer liberalizing features. Perhaps the greatest Radical achievement, however, was the encouragement which they gave to Indian nationalists at a time when voices of protest were being ruthlessly stifled in India. The result was that for a time London was in the forefront of Indian nationalist agitation. More important still in the long run, the Radicals helped to perpetuate the faith of the great majority of Indian nationalists in the principles of justice and constitutionalism.

NOTES

1 A. O. Hume to all supporters of the Congress Movement in India, printed in *A Call to Arms* (1903), India Office Library, Tract. 973.
2 Henry W. Nevinson, *The New Spirit in India*, London 1908, pp. 5-8.
3 His highest position was that of Chief Commissioner of Assam, 1896-1902. Cotton and many of his Indian sympathizers thought he should have got a higher position.
4 Henry Cotton, *India and Home Memories*, London, 1911, p. 279.
5 Wedderburn to Gokhale, 14 January 1905, Gokhale Papers (GP), File 579/17.
6 Naoroji ran as an unofficial Liberal candidate in North Lambeth. For details, see R. P. Masani, *Dadabhai Naoroji*, London, 1939, pp. 480-92.
7 Wedderburn to Gokhale, 3 August 1905, GP, File 579/25.
8 Gokhale to Nateshrao, 27 October 1905, ibid., File 203/60.
9 V. C. Joshi (ed.), *Lajpat Rai: Autobiographical Writings*, Delhi, 1965, p. 108.
10 For further information see D. G. Karve and D. V. Ambekar (eds), *Speeches and Writings of . . . Gokhale*, Bombay, 1966, vol. 2, pp. 321-49.
11 Wedderburn to Gokhale, 17 October 1905, GP, File 579/27.
12 Unlike Gokhale, Lajpat Rai concluded that 'the Liberal executive is as indifferent to . . . Indian affairs as the Conservative' and only Labour, the Socialists and the Irish favoured Home Rule for India. See V. C. Joshi (ed.), *Lala Lajpat Rai, Writings and Speeches*, Delhi, 1966, vol. 1, pp. 87-9.
13 Wedderburn to Gokhale, 16 February 1906, GP, File 579/38.
14 Wedderburn to Gokhale, 8 and 14 December 1905, GP, File 579/32 and 33.
15 Cotton, op. cit., p. 314.
16 *Hansard*, iv: 152: 830-44.
17 Stanley A. Wolpert, *Morley and India, 1906-1910*, Berkeley 1967, pp. 102-4.
18 *Hansard*, iv: 161: 594-7.
19 The party breakdown was as follows: Irish Nationalist, 39; Labour, 18; Liberal, 32.
20 Enclosure, Wedderburn to Gokhale, 23 August 1906, GP, File 579/57.
21 Cotton, op. cit., p. 324.
22 Ibid., p. 319.
23 See Wolpert, op. cit., p. 111, for Morley's concern over parliamentary opposition to the deportations.
24 Rutherford to Gokhale, 23 October 1907, GP, File 473/5. The British Committee paid £100 towards the cost of his visit.
25 Report, Criminal Intelligence, 19 October 1907, Home Dept Proceedings (G. of I.), Political B (October 1907), No. 85.
26 Report, Criminal Intelligence, 21 December 1907, Home Dept Proceedings (G. of I.) Political B (January 1908), No. 26.

27 H. W. Nevinson, op. cit., p. 337.
28 Keir Hardie to Gokhale, 9 July 1907, GP, File 224/2.
29 J. Keir Hardie, *India*, London, 1909, pp. 24-5 and 112-14.
30 Telegram, 3 October 1907, Home Dept Proceedings, Political A (February 1908), No. 50.
31 Memo, Minto, 5 October 1907, Home Dept Proceedings, Political A (February 1908), No. 50.
32 Telegram, 6 October 1907, Home Dept Proceedings, Political A (February 1908) No. 50.
33 *Hansard*, iv: 183: 376-89.
34 Ibid., 193: 208-12.
35 Ibid., v: l: 807-17.
36 John Morley, *Recollections*, London, 1917, vol. 2, p. 308.
37 *Hansard*, v: 8: 2069-74.
38 Cotton, op. cit., p. 327.
39 Stephen E. Koss, *John Morley at the India Office, 1905-1910*, New Haven, 1969, p. 170.
40 *Hansard*, iv: 183: 391-4.
41 Keir Hardie, op cit., p. 117.
42 Morley, op. cit., p. 181.
43 *Hansard*, iv: 161: 587-8.
44 Wedderburn to Gokhale, 12 February and 15 May 1909, GP, File 579/112 and 114.
45 *Hansard*, v: 3: 551.
46 Ibid., 599.
47 Ibid., iv: 198: 1985.
48 Ibid., v: 3: 600.
49 Ibid., 565.
50 Quoted in Koss, op. cit., p. 206.
51 Gokhale to Wedderburn, 3 December 1909, GP, File 203/159.

Note: The author wishes to thank the Shastri Indo-Canadian Institute for a fellowship that made research for this essay possible.

3
THE RADICAL PRESS

ALAN J. LEE

In 1899 there were only three London Liberal morning papers. The *Daily News* since 1896 had been the spokesman of Liberal Imperialism, and in November the *Daily Chronicle* also became Imperialist, when its Radical editor H. W. Massingham was replaced by W. J. Fisher. With Harold Spender and Vaughan Nash, Massingham found employment at the major provincial anti-war paper, the *Manchester Guardian.* Nash also became private secretary to Campbell-Bannerman. This left only the halfpenny *Morning Leader* to hold the Radical line. The picture was only a little brighter in the evening press and in the provinces. As Robert Spence Watson lamented to Lord Ripon 'the papers are so bad, so many of whom [*sic*] I respect have gone wrong and grown unfair'.[1]

Much of the blame for this malaise of a once flourishing Radical–Liberal press was attributed by Radicals to the 'new journalism'. W. T. Stead and T. P. O'Connor had introduced a livelier, even a sensational note to daily journalism in the 1880s, and had allied this to Radicalism, but the term 'new journalism' was now applied also to the popular press of Harmsworth and Pearson, whose journalism seemed highly dangerous to those nurtured in an older tradition. As Massingham put it in 1906, 'it is this want of seriousness in the popular press which is its most discouraging feature'.[2] Edward Dicey was told by a 'new journalist' in 1905 that

> the newspaper reading public of today wants to be amused, not instructed. They do not wish to use their minds more than they can help. They like to have their mental food in minces and snippets, not in chops and joints. They prefer short headed paragraphs to able leading articles.

'The worst of it all is that the statement is true', commented Dicey.[3] For some, this was the inevitable result of democracy and popular education; but Radicals sought the reason rather in Jingo politics and the encroachment of commerce upon journalism. L. T. Hobhouse, one of the brightest intellectual leaders of the 'new liberalism', wrote in 1909 that 'the Press, more and more the monopoly of a few rich men, from being the organ of democracy has become rather the sounding board for whatever ideas commend themselves to the great material interests'.[4] This was the staple radical argument. It tended to ignore the fact that the Radical press had first flourished in the context of sensation, crime and sport. If the simple causal connection was mistaken, there was certainly reason to see in the spread of this form of journalism a threat to the exposition of opinion and ideas. Radical journalists were loth to adopt methods of survival which would conflict with what was, for them, the very purpose of journalism, and yet the alternatives were dependence upon the generosity of a few rich men or extinction. For the most part compromises were ineffective, and the munificence of benefactors proved to be limited. The result was, at least in quantitative terms, the steady erosion of the Radical press. The decline was not so marked in the provinces or in the weeklies, or in the Radical–Labour and Radical–Socialist papers. Nevertheless, the Radical press as a whole was inescapably that of a dwindling minority, its only consolation being that it was not an insignificant minority.

The only Radical morning paper in London at the beginning of 1901 was the *Morning Leader*,[5] founded in 1892 by Sir Frederick Wilson, J. J. Colman, Sir John Brunner and other Liberal industrialists. These men had earlier founded the evening *Star*, whose editor Ernest Parke also became the *Leader*'s editor, and remained so until the paper was merged with the *Daily News* in 1912. It successfully established itself amongst low-paid clerks and a portion of the working class, attracted, so it was said, by the cricket reporting, although under the Gladstonian influence of one of the directors, James Stuart, it managed to pursue a Radical line in social policy as well as in foreign affairs. Its greatest contribution was made to the Radical movement during the Boer War, when George Cadbury, the Quaker chocolate manufacturer, subsidized its distribution in the imperialist heartland of the Midlands.

It became clear, however, that the Radicals required something heavier than the *Leader*, and Lloyd George formed a committee, chaired by Corrie Grant, to raise funds for a new paper.[6] In the end it was deemed wiser to go for an existing paper, and there was no more obvious choice than the *Daily News*. In 1895 the proprietors of this old Liberal paper, Arnold Morley MP, the financier Henry Oppenheim, and the industrial peers Ashton and Brassey, had replaced the Radical editor P. W. Clayden with E. T. Cook of the *Westminster Gazette*, who brought the paper round behind Rosebery and Milner. This led to conflict within the paper. Sir John Robinson, the manager, considered resigning, and Lord Ashton had become a fervent pro-Boer. Within a few months following the outbreak of war, circulation had fallen by more than a third. Lloyd George discovered through Robinson's assistant, David Edwards, that the proprietors would sell for £100,000. With the help of some £20,000 each from Cadbury and a wealthy cotton-spinner, J. P. Thomasson, plus the money which the committee had raised, the purchase was made. One of the new proprietors, Rudolph Lehmann of *Punch*, rather strangely was appointed editor, and Massingham and Nash were retrieved from the *Guardian*. Already circulation had started to recover as war-weariness began to affect Liberal readers, and a much-needed tonic had been administered to an ailing Radical press.

Yet as Thomasson had foreseen, the new proprietors were hardly more united than the old over issues other than the war, and in 1902 they began to withdraw, leaving Cadbury with most of the property, and the losses. Lehmann lasted but a few months as editor, and until the appointment in 1902 of A. G. Gardiner, then editor of the *Blackburn Weekly Telegraph*, the paper was run by a committee. As well as obtaining Gardiner, Cadbury persuaded the proprietor of the Blackburn paper, T. P. Ritzema, to become manager. Under this new direction the *Daily News* quickly became the leading exponent of a Radicalism which was coming to be known as the 'new liberalism'. It favoured increased state intervention for the provision of welfare, land reform, and the accommodation of Labour. In practical terms it was also active in organizing relief for the Bethesda strikers and the London dock-workers in 1904-5; in arranging the famous Sweating Exhibition of 1906; and in supporting Labour candidates in the by-elections at Woolwich, Wakefield and Barnard Castle. In one respect, however, the paper remained true to its traditional Nonconformist constituency – in 1901 there were two Quakers and a leading Methodist amongst the proprietors. Cadbury insisted that no betting news should be carried – a policy with which the proprietor of the *Manchester Guardian* was in agreement, but which he was not so imprudent as unilaterally to implement. Ritzema insisted also upon the exclusion of liquor advertising. A few years later a similar if less stringent line was adopted by the *Tribune*. In both cases, the tactic, though well-intentioned, was misconceived, financially injurious, and arguably less effective than the sensational *Daily Mail* campaigns about dear soap and cheap bread. In February 1904 the *Daily News* had little choice but to follow its sister Liberal paper, the *Daily Chronicle*, in reducing its price to a halfpenny. This only intensified its dependence upon the advertisers whom it scorned, and its vulnerability was underlined in 1905 by the attempt of some Free Food Unionists to take it over.[7]

As the *Daily Chronicle* could hardly be said to have regained its Radical identity, even after Robert Donald had become editor in 1904, Radical readers had next to turn to two evening papers. The halfpenny *Star* had been established in 1888 by that group of Liberal industrialists mentioned in connection with the *Morning Leader*. The first editor, T. P. O'Connor, claimed that it would oppose all privilege, and consider everything 'from the Radical standpoint'.[8] After a quarrel with the proprietors, O'Connor was replaced in a year or so, first by Massingham, who proved too inclined to socialism, and then by Ernest Parke. Though the *Star*'s Radicalism was now tempered, it proved an invaluable Radical support in London. It remained, of course, an example of the snippety 'new journalism' so decried by some Radicals, but it provided information, and, as Henry Labouchere once put it, 'so long as there are grievances and scandals a newspaper will be a Radical agent'.[9]

The *Echo* was an older evening paper that had established a Radical reputation under the ownership of J. Passmore Edwards. He sold it in 1896 to a group of Liberal politicians, who had little commercial success against the competition of the *Star* and the *Evening News*. In 1901 it was once again Lloyd George who intervened, persuading F. W. Hirst to approach his friend F. W. Pethick Lawrence with a view to purchasing the paper. With the help of some friends the purchase was made, and Lawrence gathered round him an impressive and Radical editorial staff: Percy Alden as editor, H. N. Brailsford as chief leader writer, and J. R. MacDonald, under the pseudonym of 'Spectator', as a Labour columnist. The new *Echo* was particularly concerned about relations between Liberals and Labour. In October 1901 it launched an unsuccessful campaign for an alliance between them. In 1902 Lawrence became editor and further capital was raised with the help of the Liberal

MP, H. J. Wilson. A bevy of talent and a purseful of money, however were insufficient to defeat the inexorable logic of the newspaper industry. Circulation rose by 60 per cent, but a half-penny paper existed on its advertisement revenue and the final blow came when tobacco advertising was at least halved by the formation of the Imperial Tobacco Company trust. In 1905 the *Echo* was at last wound up.[10]

This meant that only the *Star* and the *Westminster Gazette* were left to defend Liberalism, let alone Radicalism, in the London evening press against the forces of the *Evening News* the *Evening Standard*, the *Globe*, the *Pall Mall Gazette*, and the *St James's Gazette*. The *Westminster* had the benefit of the brilliance of J. A. Spender as editor, F. C. Gould as cartoonist, and, for a time, H. H. Munro as satirist. Apart, however, from being a formidable free trade protagonist, it was not Radical and served rather as a bridge between the Liberal factions.[11]

The popular Sunday papers were still the nearest there was to a mass-circulation press – even the *Daily Mail* failed to pass the million mark before the outbreak of the First World War. Of these only *Reynolds News* – the property of Lloyd George's friend, J. H. Dalziel, and edited by W. M. Thompson, the founder in 1900 of

TABLE 3.1 Provincial daily press of England and Wales 1901 and 1906*

	Liberal	*Conservative*	*Unionist*	*Independent*	*Neutral*
1901 *daily*					
½d.	5	3	1	20	6
1d.	14	7	—	9	7
2d.	—	—	—	—	1
Total	19	10	1	29	14
1901 *evening*					
½d.	42	20	1	20	10
1d.	1	1	—	2	2
Total	43	21	1	22	12
1906 *daily*					
½d.	4	3	1	16	5
1d.	12	7	—	8	8
Total	16	10	1	24	13
1906 *evening*					
½d.	41	15	3	17	7
1d.	1	1	—	2	2
Total	42	16	3	19	9

*C. Mitchell, *Newspaper Press Directory*, 1901 and 1906

the National Democratic League – was really Radical, styling itself, in the old fashion, 'democratic'. Thompson's own dispute with the Independent Labour Party made *Reynolds* only a qualified supporter of Labour, but it carried Labour news, was usually at least benevolently neutral, and was always rudely 'democratic'.[12] Of the other Sundays, the *Weekly Dispatch* had gone to Harmsworth in 1904; *Lloyds Weekly News*, even when Donald became editor in 1906 was hardly Radical; and the *News of the World*, under another of Lloyd George's friends, George Riddell, had yet to prove itself even as a Liberal force, let alone a Radical one. Only in the muck-raking sense, referred to by Labouchere, could any of these be reckoned Radical before 1906.

Despite the gloomy views of some contemporaries, the provincial picture was rather brighter. Although Liberal press losses between 1901 and 1906 were numerically small, they included the important Radical *Newcastle Daily Leader*, and the *Liverpool Mercury*, which was merged with the *Liverpool Daily Post* edited by Rosebery's confidant, Sir Edward Russell. Furthermore, many Radical papers were becoming weaker in the face of competition with the growing commercial chains. This deterioration was most marked in the major cities of the North and the Midlands, areas to which Radicals would increasingly turn for votes.

It was in the most crucial of these areas that the most respected Radical provincial paper, the *Manchester Guardian*, was situated.[13] Since the appointment of C. P. Scott as editor in 1872, the paper had been weaned gradually from a habitual Whiggism to a moderate Radicalism, a process accelerated by the sale of the leading Manchester Radical paper, the *Examiner and Times*, to the Unionists in 1886. Scott himself sat in Parliament from 1894 to 1906. His editorial staff, led first by W. T. Arnold and then by C. E. Montague helped by L. T. Hobhouse, built up an impressive record in the struggle for social reform during this period. There had been a campaign for old-age pensions, and much sympathy had been aroused by the informed local reporting of the miner's dispute of 1893 and the engineers' strike of 1897-8. During his coverage of the last of these Hobhouse wrote that 'the power of organised capital is the standing danger of democracy'. It was in the darkest days of the Boer War, however, that the *Guardian* became the brightest beacon of Radicalism. It had lost one-seventh of its circulation by 1902, and Manchester men tore it to shreds on the pavement, but it survived. Having first to be bought for the cotton news, it was thus able to defend its uncommercial principles.

Of the provincial penny morning press, only the *Newcastle Daily Leader* could rival the *Guardian* as a champion of Radicalism. An answer to the Imperialism of Joseph Cowen's *Newcastle Daily Chronicle*, it had been edited since 1895 by an ex-editor of the London *Echo*, Aaron Watson. His stand against the war, and his criticism of the local railway company during a strike, led Sir James Joicey, proprietor of the paper, colliery owner and director of the railway company, to sack him in 1901. After two more years Joicey decided that he could no longer subsidize a paper that was hardly friendly to his fellow Northumberland industrialists, and he closed it in October 1903.[14]

The radicals still had a halfpenny morning paper in Darlington, the *Northern Echo*, founded in 1870. A pioneer of the 'new journalism', it remained the leading voice of Northern Radicalism and in July 1903 helped Arthur Henderson to victory at Barnard Castle. By the turn of the century, however, it had run into financial difficulties. Charles Starmer, the young Liberal manager, approached Joseph Rowntree for help. Rowntree, like his fellow Quaker confectioner, Cadbury, believed in the press as a weapon of social reform. In 1904 the newly formed Rowntree Social Service Trust took over the paper in the form of the North of England Newspaper Company, chaired by Joseph's nephew, an active Liberal, Arnold Rowntree. Starmer continued as manager, and George Armstrong from the *Morning Leader* replaced Cox Meach as editor. The ubiquitous Ernest Parke was involved as adviser, and the *Leader* and the *Echo* thereafter ran in close harness. Not the least significant aspect of the *Echo* was the mere fact of its survival. Under Starmer's expertise it actually proved a profitable venture, thus constituting an important, if unusual, lesson for gloomy Radical journalists.[15]

Evening provincial papers were usually considered politically insignificant, and indeed the majority were dominated by sport, but there were several important Radical ones which deserve notice. In Blackburn, Ritzema's *Northern Daily Telegraph* had helped Philip Snowden considerably in his fight for Blackburn in 1900, and the paper continued to be an important Radical organ for many years.[16] Ritzema was also actively involved in another Radical paper, H. Gilzean-Reid's *North Eastern Gazette* in Middlesbrough.

At a local level, the weekly press was also important, but it was rarely advertised as 'Radical', and it is, therefore, difficult to know how numerous were such papers as the *Nelson Leader* at Clitheroe, the *Daylight* at Norwich, or the *Walthamstow Reporter*. Even allowing for such as these, however, in aggregate terms the Radical press was very small. Attempts were made before 1906 to remedy this. In 1904-5 J. E. Taylor, the proprietor of the *Manchester Guardian*, was unsuccessfully urged to obtain control of the *Leeds Mercury* and the *Yorkshire Observer* (Bradford).[17] In 1905 the Liberals made a coup by buying the Conservative *Leeds Daily News*, but this hardly altered the global picture.

Absorbed with the problem of disseminating ideas and principles, it was natural that Radicals should have looked to the serious weekly press where the object was not to sway potential voters, but to influence the decision-makers. As few of the existing weeklies were political, the competition was small. Here undoubtedly lay one of the strengths of Edwardian Radicalism. In the *Speaker* and its successor the *Nation*, and in the *New Age*, it possessed journals whose arguments carried exceptional weight amongst even orthodox Liberals.

Wemyss Reid, the father of the Parliamentary Lobby, and since 1871 editor of the *Leeds Mercury*, had launched the *Speaker* in 1890 with the financial support of Sir John Brunner. It stood for a weighty and principled Gladstonian Liberalism, which earned for it the nickname of the 'Squeaker'. As it commanded a circulation of only a few thousand, it constituted a heavy drain on Brunner's pocket. In 1899 he arranged for his secretary, J. L. Hammond, a leader writer on the *Leeds Mercury*, to take control. Hammond received support from some of his young Oxford Liberal friends, Francis Hirst, Hilaire Belloc, and J. A. Simon, and financial assistance from William McEwan, Liberal MP and proprietor of the *Edinburgh Evening News*. The Rowntrees' lawyer, E. R. Cross, was the trustee and solicitor. For the next seven years under Hammond's editorship the *Speaker* paraded the best Radical journalism. Its 'romantic Radicalism', as some thought it, was possibly closer to Cobden and Bright than to the 'new liberalism'. It has been calculated that in 1904 only 17 out of 626 pages were devoted to social reform, the rest being given over to foreign affairs and free trade. Against this, however, there was the publication of a series of its articles in book form, *Towards a Social Policy* (1905), an important discussion of the future of Radical policy in terms of the 'new liberalism'.[18]

An important complement to, but hardly the equal of, the *Speaker* was the *New Age*, edited by A. E. Fletcher, a former editor of the *Daily Chronicle*, helped by Ramsay MacDonald. Towards the end of the century A. Compton-Rickett, then moving in Fabian circles, took over, but was shortly replaced by a militant anti-war man, Joseph Clayton. In 1899 the paper had been bought by a Unitarian minister, the Rev. Harold Rylett, a Georgeite, active in the Agricultural Labourers Union, and secretary of the 1900 Stop the War Committee. The *New Age* played a part in the attempt to bring Liberals and Labour together in 1901, and more generally in Radical politics until its sale in 1907, the start of an even more Radical career.[19]

An attempt to start a new Radical weekly in 1902 failed, but in 1903 a new monthly, the *Independent Review*, appeared, edited by the legal journalist and historian, Edward Jenks, helped by Hirst, C. F. G. Masterman and G. L. Dickinson. It provided a much-needed forum for Radical debate, as the *Westminster* and the *Fortnightly* had long since departed from Radicalism.

Such, then, was the extent of the Radical press before the general election of 1906. The election was a crucial test, not only of the strength of that press, but of the conception of journalism which informed it. The electoral influence of the newspaper, an axiom of the 1860s, was already being questioned by the 1880s. Indeed, this doubt was one of the keys to the 'new journalism'. There were journalists and party organizers who were aware that the support of the press was no guarantee of votes.[20] H. M. Hyndman, as early as 1895, had called such claims 'just so much rubbish and rodomontade'.[21] The belief was slow to die, however, and although modern studies of the political influence of the press tend to confirm the sceptics' view, it would be rash to assume that the press played no part in shaping the social, and therefore the political consciousness and behaviour of the electorate. In so far as the new style of journalism was perhaps better suited to a new style of politics, with both becoming nationally rather than community oriented, and as this often entailed the simplification of ideas, the Radicals' complaint that ideas were being forced out of the press had some justification.

In this particular context the electoral victory of the Liberals in 1906 against an overwhelmingly Protectionist press[22] was undoubtedly embarrassing, not only to the Conservatives, but to the Radicals. J. A. Spender later argued that it reflected the fact that the electorate and the newspaper readership no longer shared the same opinions, were no longer the same group.[23] This was little comfort, however, to those who looked to the press to gain popular support for Radical policies. Even the notion that the press was more effective in forming opinion by the presentation of news, rather than ideas, as Herbert Stead had claimed in 1900 over the issues of old-age pensions,[24] did not rescue ideas from potential oblivion. Besides, whether electorally influential or not, the Radical press was still preoccupied with the struggle for survival. As long as it survived, and as long as elections were won, other awkward questions could be put aside.

Ironically, in the midst of the election that was to raise these doubts, a new Liberal penny morning paper was started in London, *The Tribune*. It had been devised to help the Liberals in opposition, but was now faced with the much more difficult task of advising a party in power. It was a failure. It ran through the several hundred thousand pounds bequeathed by J. P. Thomasson for its establishment, and was wound up at the beginning of 1908. At a penny, it failed to attract a large readership, it imprudently offended potential advertisers, and in the end could find no benefactor willing to subsidize it further. It had begun with perhaps the most Radical editorial staff that could have been obtained: Hobhouse, J. A. Hobson, Brailsford, Hirst, Hammond, William Archer, G. H. Perris, and the editor William Hill. For various reasons they all left the paper, and it fell back into the older, more individualistic Radicalism of its proprietor, Franklin Thomasson. It succumbed in the end to forces which threatened all the Radical press, and to which they all, in the end, succumbed.[25]

'The journalist *qua* journalist always prefers to have his party in Opposition', wrote Spender.[26] The victory of 1906 had deprived the Radical–Liberal press of precisely this advantageous position. On most of the major issues, it is true, there was no serious conflict. This was, however, to some extent the result of the closeness of the relations between Radical journalists and politicians. How far such semi-institutionalization of the Radical press tempered its Radicalism is a difficult and complex problem. Occasionally, the tensions became apparent, as when Gardiner of the *Daily News* was forced to release two chief leader writers, H. W. Nevinson and Brailsford, because of their protests at the treatment of suffragettes at a Lloyd George meeting.[27] The line of the *Daily News* and of the *Manchester Guardian* was to obtain votes for women, but without violence. Indeed, Scott in 1911 had a hand in the promotion of the Conciliation Bill. In the field of social reform there was hardly likely to be conflict in the face of the Lords' opposition, and little fear that the People's Budget or National Insurance would not be enthusiastically supported. As for Ireland, neither the *Daily News* nor the *Guardian* went as far as J. A. Hobson, for example, in urging government intervention in Ulster. In imperial affairs the Radical press was embarrassed more, perhaps, by the involvement of the Cadburys in the Portuguese colonies than by having to bring pressure to bear on the government in Natal.[28] The one area in which blows were struck was that of foreign policy. The Radical press, particularly the *Daily News* and the *Nation*, was exceptionally well-informed on foreign affairs. Given Grey's reluctance to divulge information, it enjoyed a very strong dialectical position. Its hostility culminated in the forcing of a debate on foreign policy in the Commons in November 1911. Nevertheless, it is doubtful whether it caused Grey to do more than tack successfully into the Radical wind.[29]

Considered quantitatively, the Radical press had been much reduced by 1912. The *Tribune* had gone in 1908, and the *Morning Leader* was absorbed into the *Daily News* in 1912, the two organizations having been amalgamated under the Cadbury Trust in 1910. On the brighter side, the *Daily News* had succeeded in starting a Manchester edition in January 1909, and there were repeated if fruitless discussions about a London edition of the *Manchester Guardian*. In 1907, with the help of the Rowntree Trust, the *Nation* had taken over where the *Speaker* had left off. Under Massingham's editorship it became more Radical than the *Speaker*, and its literary merits considerably increased its circulation. The *New Age* had also changed hands in 1907, when purchased by A. R. Orage and Holbrook Jackson. For a few years it tended to be rather Fabian, but by 1909 it was championing Victor Grayson, and shortly afterwards became the recognized organ of Guild Socialism.[30] The Webbs' *New Statesman*, founded in 1913, was in part a reply to this move to the left. The most striking facet of the Radical press during the period of Liberal government, however, was the degree to which its ownership had become concentrated. The Rowntrees still ran the *Northern Echo* and the *Nation*, Cadburys the *Daily News*, the *Morning Leader* and the *Star*, some former proprietors of which still owned the two leading Liberal papers in East Anglia. Sir Alfred Mond now owned the *Westminster Gazette* and the *English Review*, which had been started in 1909 as a Radical political and literary weekly. Despite this concentration, readership remained small. In 1910 the combined circulation of the *News*, *Leader*, *Star*, and *Manchester Guardian* was probably not much more than 750,000. If one added a few hundred thousand for provincial Radical papers, the total would hardly be more than the *Daily Mail* and the *Evening News* put together. *Reynolds*, and by this time the *News of the World*, were valuable assets, but in electoral terms their impact remains obscure.[31]

It was a period, however, during which relations between politicians and journalists, particularly amongst Radicals, were very close. Liberal journalists and proprietors had always been more politically involved than their rivals. In 1906, twenty-two of the thirty newspaper proprietors in Parliament were Liberals; in 1910, thirteen out of twenty-four, and these contained at least a handful of Radicals.[32] At the grass roots, journalists played an even bigger and more traditional role. In Manchester, for example, Scott was president of the Manchester Liberal Federation, and both editor and manager of the Manchester edition of the *Daily News* were prominent local party men.[33]

At the centre, by 1909, the government even had Sir Henry Norman acting for them as an unofficial press agent. Here, once more, it was Lloyd George who played the major role.[34] The *Manchester Guardian* had always been cool towards Asquith, but Scott reacted favourably to Lloyd George's blandishments. The Welshman's relations with Riddell, for whom he procured a knighthood from an unenthusiastic Asquith, are of special interest. In 1911 Riddell bought Walton Heath for Lloyd George, and arranged for Donald, Masterman and Sir John Simon to live nearby. He also gave detailed and welcome instructions on the best times to deliver speeches so as to obtain maximum press coverage. For his part, Lloyd George used Riddell in the settlement of the miners' strike in 1912. In addition to the support of Riddell's *News of the World*, Lloyd George also had his friend J. H. Dalziel's *Reynolds News*, and used to include a heavy sprinkling of journalists in his after-breakfast audiences.[35] This personal network was arguably more important than the influence exerted by the journals themselves although this would be difficult to prove. Herbert Gladstone, for example, when Governor-General of South Africa, told Massingham that he got 'much excellent information and instruction from the Nation'.[36]

It is difficult to escape the conclusion, however, that the Radical press was constrained by commercial forces to depend upon the generosity of a few rich men in order to bring pressure to bear upon a few politically powerful ones. Some Radical journalists began to urge the necessity of relying more upon the weekly press of opinion than trying to operate through the popular press. The 'Free Press', as Belloc termed it, could still triumph over the 'Official Press', because it was read carefully, rather than perfunctorily, and because it affected the small class through which ideas are spread.[37] This, indeed, had been precisely the intended role of that section of the Radical press, the Radical–Labour, Radical–Socialist, and minority papers, which reached small highly specific, audiences, whose membership to a considerable degree overlapped.[38] Some of the weeklies – there were no such dailies – certainly rivalled the Radical–Liberal press in size. The *Labour Leader*, the *Clarion*, and *Forward* were in many respects recognizably Radical, particularly on issues of foreign policy. Yet they were also distinct from the radical press as that term was generally understood. The daily paper was a political instrument which, despite its dubious electoral efficacy, retained a superior status. Hence the long-drawn-out discussion about the possibility of a Labour daily, from 1903 to 1912, culminating in the establishment of the *Daily Citizen*.[39] Even so, before 1914 the smaller papers, especially in the provinces, could still be said to have had a chance against the encroachment of amalgamation. The trends both in politics and in journalism, however, were against their survival, and the Radical press, in the form it had assumed during the nineteenth century, was the victim of these centripetal economic and political processes.

NOTES

1 Spence Watson to Ripon, 30 March 1900, Ripon Papers, British Museum, Add. MSS. 43,638 vol. 148, f. 1.
2 H. W. Massingham, 'The press and its message', *Co-operative Wholesale Societies Annual*, 1907, p. 174.
3 E. Dicey, 'Journalism new and old', *Fortnightly Review*, vol. 83, 1905, p. 917.
4 L. T. Hobhouse, 'The contending forces', *English Review*, vol. 4, 1909-10, p. 365.
5 G. G. Armstrong, *Memories of George Gilbert Armstrong*, London, 1944, pp. 75-90; A. G. Gardiner, *Life of George Cadbury*, London, 1923, pp. 216-17; Spencer Leigh Hughes, *Press, Platform and Parliament*, London 1918, pp. 21f.; C. Archer, *William Archer*, London, 1931, pp. 250-8.
6 For following account see [W. T. Stead], 'The reconversion of the *Daily News*', *Review of Reviews*, vol. 23, 1901, pp. 147-53; H. Spender, *The Prime Minister*, London, 1920, pp. 122-3; Gardiner, op. cit., pp. 211-36; P. P. Poirier, *The Advent of the Labour Party*, London, 1958, pp. 169, 176 and 200.
7 *Manchester Guardian*, 30 January 1905.
8 H. Fyfe, *T. P. O'Connor*, London, 1934, p. 138. See also S. Koss, *Sir John Brunner, Radical Plutocrat 1842-1919*, Cambridge, 1970, pp. 131 and 157-8.
9 *Truth*, 30 November 1904.

10 F. W. Pethick Lawrence, *Fate Has Been Kind*, London, 1943 pp. 57-66.
11 J. A. Spender, *Life, Journalism and Politics*, London, 1927, vol. 1, p. 102.
12 P. Thompson, *Socialists, Liberals and Labour: the Struggle for London 1885-1914*, London, 1967, pp. 171, 179 and 194-5.
13 For following account see J. L. Hammond, *C. P. Scott*, London, 1934, pp. 26-176; P. F. Clarke, *Lancashire and the New Liberalism*, Cambridge, 1971, pp. 153-97; D. Ayerst, *Guardian: Biography of a Newspaper*, London, 1971 pp. 165-319.
14 A. Watson, *A Newspaper Man's Memories*, London, 1925, pp. 183-90; M. Milne, *Newspapers of Northumberland and Durham*, Newcastle-on-Tyne, 1972, pp. 128-30.
15 Armstrong, op. cit., pp. 82-100; Milne, op. cit., pp. 87-8 and 204; E. Vipont, *Arnold Rowntree, a Life*, London, 1955, pp. 31-3.
16 P. F. Clarke, 'British politics and Blackburn politics 1900-1910', *Historical Journal*, vol. 12, 1969, p. 307.
17 Clarke, *Lancashire and the New Liberalism* (1971), p. 156.
18 Koss, op. cit., pp. 159-61; F. W. Hirst, *In the Golden Days*, London, 1947, pp. 169 and 202-4; M. Wilkinson (ed.), *E. Richard Cross*, London, 1917, pp. 12 and 23; L. Masterman, *C. F. G. Masterman*, London, 1968, pp. 58-9.
19 A. Compton-Rickett, *I Look Back*, London, 1933, pp. 12 and 90.
20 For example H. G. Reid, 'The press', in *The Civilisation of Our Day*, ed. J. Samuelson, London, 1896. p. 282; M. Ostrogorski, *Democracy and the Organisation of Political Parties*, London, 1902, vol. 1, pp. 409-10.
21 *The Times*, 31 July 1895.
22 A. K. Russell, 'The general election of 1906' (D.Phil. thesis, Oxford, 1962), pp. 415-43. For the 1910 elections see N. Blewett, *The Peers, the Parties and the People*, London, 1972, pp. 299-312.
23 J. A. Spender, *The Public Life*, London, 1925, vol. 2, p. 109.
24 Cited in Sell's *Dictionary of the World's Press*, 1912, p. 105.
25 A. J. Lee, 'Franklin Thomasson and the *Tribune*', *Historical Journal*, vol. 16, 1973, pp. 341-60.
26 Spender, op. cit. (1927), vol. 1, p. 34.
27 H. W. Nevinson, *More Changes, More Chances*, London, 1925, pp. 322-5.
28 Gardiner, op. cit., pp. 238-51.
29 J. A. Murray, 'Foreign policy debated', in *Power, Public Opinion and Diplomacy*, ed. L. P. Wallace and W. C. Askew, Durham, N. C., 1959, pp. 140-71; A. J. P. Taylor, *The Trouble Makers*, London, 1969, pp. 87-119.
30 P. Mairet, *A. R. Orage, a Memoir*, London, 1936.
31 Most estimates of circulations at this time must be treated with extreme caution.
32 J. A. Thomas, *The House of Commons 1906-11*, Cardiff, 1958.
33 Armstrong, op. cit., p. 151; *John Hugh Jones, 1883-1927*, 1930.
34 Blewett, op. cit., pp. 303-4.
35 *The Political Diaries of C. P. Scott 1911-1928*, ed. T. Wilson, London, 1970, pp. 24-32; Lord Riddell, *More Pages From My Diary, 1908-14*, London, 1934; F. Owen, *Tempestuous Journey*, London, 1954, pp. 219-20.
36 Gladstone to Massingham, 23 August 1918, Viscount Gladstone Papers, British Museum, Add. MSS. 46,042, vol. 58.
37 H. Belloc, *The Free Press*, London, 1918, pp. 81-3.
38 For an idea of the extent of this part of the Radical press see the lists in *The Reformers Year Book*, 1901-9; J. Brophy, 'Bibliography of British Labour and

Radical journals 1880-1914', *Labor History*, vol. 3, 1962, pp. 103-26; K. Snowden, 'The rise of the Labour press', Sell's *Dictionary of the World's Press*, 1914, pp. 29-32.

39 'The infancy of the Labour party', E. R. Pease Collection, British Library of Political and Economic Science.

4

LAYING THE CHARGES FOR THE LANDSLIDE: THE REVIVAL OF LIBERAL PARTY ORGANIZATION, 1902 - 1905

A. K. RUSSELL

The relationship between the leader and the led is significant in any group; but it was not until the introduction of the wider franchises in 1867 and 1884-5 that it became a crucial and inescapable factor in British party political affairs. As an upper-class party with deep roots in Parliament, the Conservative reaction was to woo and win the votes of those middle and lower classes of society without which it could no longer survive. As a mass movement reaching into Parliament, Labour emphasized the supremacy of its representative organizations. Predictably, the attitudes and reactions to organization of the Liberal party fell somewhere between these two extremes.

Many of the party's first constituency associations were élitist groups representing little but themselves. The National Liberal Federation (NLF) was set up, 'to put the management of the party . . . in the hands of the people',[1] and to present the whips, who were in charge of the Liberal Central Association (LCA), with agreed and coherent Liberal policies.[2]

> The essential feature of the proposed Federation is the principle which must *henceforth* govern the action of Liberals as a political party – namely the direct participation of all members of the party in the direction of its policy, and in the selection of those particular measures of reform and of progress to which priority shall be given. This object can be secured only by the organisation of the party upon a representative basis; that is by popularly elected Committees of local associations, and by the union of such local associations, by means of their freely chosen representatives, in a general federation.

After the Home Rule split and the move to London in 1886, the NLF entered its most definite policy-making phase, culminating in the Newcastle programme, 1891. Robert Hudson denied that the Federation had sought to arrogate to itself the party's programme-making role; but the leadership henceforth reacted sharply against any hint of mass policy-determination. In the difficult and divided years that followed, Robert Spence-Watson as president, deliberately and wisely encouraged the NLF to become an open forum where differences could be aired rather than policies prepared. Aided by close, cordial relationships between Spence-Watson and Hudson and the chief whips, Ellis and later Herbert Gladstone, the NLF's initial role as a pressure group was modified.

This comfortable reaction almost went too far. When he became Chief Whip in 1899, Herbert Gladstone quickly saw that if the local organizations had become ineffective, it was largely because they were impoverished and half-asleep. Canvassing and registration work were poor, candidates slow to come forward, and money often short. To establish the facts, and to make proposals, Herbert Gladstone appointed a small committee representing both the official and representative organizations of the party. It was strictly consultative, since Gladstone took the view that it could neither relieve him of his responsibility to the party leader nor 'in any way fetter [his] absolute freedom of action'.[3] But its terms of reference were broad:[4]

> to go through the whole of the constituencies of the country [in England], to consider the position of local organisations, to concert measures for finding suitable candidates and for fixing them in constituencies to the best advantage, and generally to consider such other matters and to take such action as may be found desirable.

It was, furthermore, backed by a sub-committee to examine the special problems of the metropolis, where the Liberals had won only ten out of seventy-five seats in 1895. Neither committee was able to submit its report in time for action before the 'Khaki' election in October 1900; but on 25 October 1901, Herbert Gladstone wrote to Campbell-Bannerman underlining his determination to 'set [their] house in order after the fray'.[5]

The committee finally decided that the country should be divided into three new organizational areas. Herbert Gladstone was unconvinced. Always opposed to the multiplication of federations and officials, he feared the effect of interpolating an additional level between the LCA and the constituencies. Knowing that financial limitations would make it essential to be selective, he concentrated on the revival of existing regional and local bodies – e.g. the Home Counties Liberal Federation – and on the sub-committee's recommendation that a new London Liberal Federation should be established to take over the propaganda and organizational work of the moribund London Liberal and Radical Union.

Gladstone, predictably, did not commit himself to precise schemes of financial assistance. He believed that – within the limitations of its budget – the LCA should continue to provide the various associations with the necessary finance for registration and similar work,[6] and said as much to Tweedmouth.[7]

> The best solution will be to reserve all finances [to the LCA] and to arrange with the [National Liberal] Federation that they shall be a formally accredited branch. The Federation as such, with their own staff, would not just work London, they would have to do it – as in reality they deal with Leeds, Manchester and other big towns – through the local affiliated Associations. London being by far the largest must have a larger local association of necessity more on the outline of a branch than the organisations of provincial towns. That branch would have to carry on political propaganda, it would raise a certain amount of money for its own purposes, but it would have to come to the whip for contributions to organisations and registration in the same way as all other English constituencies.

In this way he considered that the associations would retain a measure of independence, whilst their dependence on LCA finance would preserve a sufficient degree of central control.

On the basis of the London proposals, Herbert Gladstone formulated a scheme which involved:

1 the creation of the London Liberal Federation (LLF), with responsibility for both registration and propaganda work;
2 the adoption of the new boroughs as registration areas;
3 the employment, wherever possible, of professional agents to act as constituency secretaries as well as Registration Agents, and to make good 'the lack of organized workers', which was 'the supreme weakness of the Liberal party in the metropolis';[8] and
4 a six-point basis for co-operation to ensure close LCA/LLF co-operation and *in practice* firm LCA control.

This scheme was substantially, if not entirely, implemented between 1902 and 1905. The LLF set about its work with energy and enthusiasm. It was never able to raise all the money that it required, but helped by a £1000 p.a. LCA grant, and seven or eight new agents, Liberal performance sensibly improved before the Revising Barristers – the officials charged with periodic review of the registers.

TABLE 4.1 *London reorganization, 1902-1905*

Area	No. of seats	*Gladstone's priorities*			*No. of agents under alternative schemes*	
		A *Likely to be won*	B *Possible*	C *Unlikely*	1 £5000 *p.a.*	2 £3300 *p.a.*
Poplar & Hackney	5	4	1	—	2	1
Stepney	5	5	—	—	2	1
Bethnal Green & Shoreditch	4	4	—	—	2	1
Finsbury & Islington	6	5	1	—	2	1
St Pancras	4	3	1	—	1	1
Camberwell & Lambeth	7	2	2	3	2	1
Bermondsey & Southwark	6	5	1	—	2	1
Deptford & Greenwich	2	—	2	—	2	1
Kensington & Paddington	4	—	2	2	1	—
Other London seats	18	—	—	18	—	—
Total	61	28	10	23	16	8

Since the Liberals won all but two of Gladstone's category A and B seats, and made 15 per cent of their total gains (31:216) in the 11 per cent of London seats (61:567 England, Scotland and Wales), their efforts seem to have been well rewarded.

This reconstruction of the party's organizations in London was the major single structural change in the years between 1900 and 1905. But it was only part of a wider movement towards organiza-

TABLE 4.2 *Major officers in the Liberal organizations**

Liberal Central Association	
Chairman (& Chief Whip)	Herbert Gladstone
Hon. Secretary	R. A. Hudson
Secretary (Chief Agent)	Jesse Herbert
Assistants	Henry Norman
	J. A. Pease
National Liberal Federation (& Branches)	
President	Augustine Birrell
Secretary	R. A. Hudson
Secretary, London Liberal Federation	J. R. Seager
Secretary, Home Counties Liberal Federation	W. M. Crook (assisted by L. Harcourt & A. Ponsonby)
Liberal Publication Department	
(Which was 'under the joint control of the National Liberal Federation and the Liberal Central Association')	
Chairman	Augustine Birrell
Secretary	Charles Geake

**The Liberal Magazine*, 1903-6

tional renewal over which Gladstone, Hudson, and their colleagues presided.

Housed in the same set of offices, these men worked as a team and reports of organizational improvement were legion throughout the years 1903-5, from places as wide apart as Oxted, Exeter and Shropshire. In May 1905, R. V. Wells reported to Crook that the Fareham party was 'doing splendidly in organising the [South Hampshire] constituency'.[9] A month later Henry Norman wrote to Gladstone that in both Wolverhampton and Brighton – where the party won a sensational by-election victory in April – their agents had done 'marvels with the organisation'.[10] The *Daily Express* observed that the Liberals had employed 'a far more intelligent, enterprising and altogether better type of agent' than their opponents, and had honeycombed the constituencies with centres of work.[11] In Scotland the party had 'a special organiser . . . in nearly every constituency'.[12] In the management of the English and Welsh seats, the NLF and the LCA worked in close personal and political accord. This was nowhere more evident than in the flow of good-quality propaganda material – much enhanced by the wit and skill of the cartoonist F. Carruthers Gould – from the joint Publication Department of the NLF and LCA. But it also included an element of secret LCA financial support, to give the NLF the 'financial lever' that it sought over the constituencies.[13]

Herbert Gladstone had a hard time providing financial support because the Liberal party's income was so slight. The party had suffered a serious loss of upper- and upper-middle-class support as a result of the Irish Home Rule split and had had no patronage for the best part of twenty years. The situation was further aggravated by the party's Boer War divisions. Although most Liberals supported Campbell-Bannerman, those who disagreed with him were, as Herbert Gladstone complained, 'strong in ability and money'.[14] Consequently, a decline in the number of contributors was accompanied by a steady fall in the average size of contribution, from around £2000 to nearer £1000.[15] In 1903, for instance, the Leeds association obtained three-quarters of its income from a mere twenty people. In the two years thereafter, Herbert Gladstone had to face a rising crescendo of local complaints about shortage of funds.

It was only by dint of great personal effort that Herbert Gladstone succeeded in raising about £225,000 during the five years between the elections of 1900 and 1906. The central organizations necessarily were run with great economy on a paid staff of five or six. Table 4.3 shows how exiguous the budget was in the not untypical year of 1903.[16]

TABLE 4.3 *LCA expenditure, 1903*

	£s (rounded)	*% (rounded)*
Registration and reorganization	4410	32
By-elections	3860	27
Staff salaries	2600	19
Miscellaneous	1300	10
Liberal Publication Department	800	6
Whips' Department	750	5
Total	13,720	99

This left an average of £30,000 a year for help to individual constituencies. It is not therefore suprising that on the eve of the Liberal–Labour pact in 1903 Jesse Herbert described the LRC's £100,000 election fund as 'the most significant new fact in the situation'.[17] It promised, not only the hope of working-class support but the avoidance of expenditure in thirty to forty Conservative-held seats.

The unexpectedly long-drawn-out demise of the Balfour administration aggravated the situation. In anticipation of an early election, a large proportion of Liberal candidates – 75 per cent in Yorkshire – had been selected by the end of 1903, and their demands on LCA and LPD resources were heavy. A Hampshire Liberal wrote in to the Central Association on 1 May 1905 asking for the money to pay a party worker. He would 'lament a fiasco after so much labour for the sake of a somewhat larger grant called for simply by the delay'.[18] In addition to this, the by-elections constituted a 'great drain'[19] as the number of contests and Liberal candidates increased. For the Conservatives, Acland-Hood told a colleague in 1905, 'it [was] well that this drain on the financial resources of [their] opponents should continue'.[20] This was a contributory factor to Balfour's retention of office for some months more, 'behind the barricades of the Septennial Act' as Birrell put it, 'mocking [Liberal] pomp and grinning at by-elections'.[21]

TABLE 4.4 *No. of by-elections and Liberal candidatures 1900-1906*

Year	*United Kingdom*	*England, Scotland and Wales*	*Liberal candidatures (England, Scotland and Wales)*
1900 (Oct.-Dec.)	2	1	1
1901	11	9	9
1902	19	13	11
1903	25	17	16
1904	24	21	19
1905	21	17	17
Total	102	78	73

The Liberals made a virtue of necessity. They gained 21 out of the 78 English, Scottish and Welsh seats they contested in by-elections (see Table 4.4), in the process greatly strengthening their registration and propaganda work. The organizing committee for East Scotland reported in November 1905 that, like the LLF, they had been 'very successful with ordinance and lodger claims'.[22] Acland-Hood confessed to Balfour late in 1905 that the old register was 'not the advantage it used to be as [he knew] the radical Agents had been most active in tracing removals'.[23] Furthermore, the delay gave the Liberals the opportunity to strengthen many important ancillary organizations. The National League of Young Liberals, formed in 1903, by 1905 had established 300 branches and brought the organized enthusiasm of youth to bear in a way unmatched by the Tories. Similarly, the Women's National Liberal Federation and Women's Liberal Federation extended their registration and propaganda work respectively, quite outstripping the Primrose League on which, originally, they had been based.

Even more important, particularly to the by-election results, was the emergence between 1903 and 1906 of a large number of *ad hoc* bodies set up to defend the Free Trade interest. Herbert Gladstone was quick to appreciate the importance of establishing a 'half-way house to which the Unionist Free Traders could go without incurring . . . local political odium'.[24] The Free Trade Union (FTU) was formed in 1903 under his close personal supervision. In January 1904, he told Asquith:[25]

> My plan for establishing Free Trade bodies in every county on a new political basis was set on by everyone, [but] after much valuable time . . . lost, the Lancashire men are doing the very thing I proposed and I want the FTU and the Free Traders to co-operate in actively backing my movement.

In fact the FTU quickly became one of the most influential pressure groups in the country. It may have had only 10–20 per cent of the money available to the Tariff Reform League, but its election fund of £20,000 was not insignificant by Liberal standards, and the FTU became well integrated into the organizational effort of the Liberal party. Following a Unionist by-election defeat at Barkston Ash in October 1905, Sandars wrote ruefully to Balfour, 'the Radicals practically had two armies . . . , their usual political army [and] the Free Trade Union with its own special staff and workers, bring[ing] none of its election expenses into account and operat[ing] as a voluntary organisation'.[26] The important thing was less that there were two armies – the Conservatives and Unionists had at least that number! – but that these two were marching as one.

The long delay therefore brought organizational benefits as well as financial trials, and forced the adoption of some tough, but cost-effective, rules for LCA financial help:

1 no money to be promised until candidates had been adopted by the local constituency associations;

2 toughness with men who got themselves adopted, and then immediately asked for money;
3 requirement of a £ for £ contribution, wherever possible from the local candidate or constituency; and
4 avoidance of waste on newspapers: 'it never answers', Herbert Gladstone wrote, 'unless for temporary purposes in connection with local organizations'.[27]

The result was that money went where it was most needed and did most good. When the spendthrift Medway Association asked for £1500 plus £1000 a year, the reaction of Gladstone's Home Counties aide was very unsympathetic. 'The proper way to cure them', he wrote, 'would be to run a Labour candidate there.'[28] The LCA was similarly 'flinty' with the Hammersmith candidate (Blaiklock), who sought financial help in manoeuvres against an unofficial Labour rival, and with an impecunious, unprepossessing candidate in the Kent constituency of St Augustines. On the other hand, it continued to provide assistance for poor but promising progressives like C. F. G. Masterman in West Ham, and 'deliberately . . . inaugurated [a] policy of paying election expenses on a generous scale . . . where men of small means but real ability were willing to come forward as Liberal candidates'.[29] The LCA was responsible for introducing over 50 per cent of the candidates who finally ran in 1906 By a careful process of selection and distribution – e.g. £350 for Winchester with 2681 voters and £2330 for Romford with 29,316 – Herbert Gladstone concentrated over half of his total election resources on only about 20 per cent of seats (see Table 4.5).

TABLE 4.5 *Overall allocation of Liberal funds (England, Scotland and Wales)*

No. of seats	*Total financial aid (£)*	*Average size of contribution (£)*
150	nil	nil
250	4800	160
118	5200	440

The work of the LCA did not go unchallenged in the constituencies. Many local associations expressed indignation at the degree of central intervention, and at the 1905 conference the NLF saw fit to reaffirm the principle of local autonomy. But the co-ordination proved invaluable in reducing inter-party divisions at the constituency level to two (North Lambeth and South Hackney) and in keeping the activities of the potentially divisive Liberal League – 18 of whose 41 candidates received LCA financial assistance[30] – well in check. Gladstone's negotiating skills were, moreover, of great value in dealing with the challenge of Lib–Lab and LRC candidatures. He secured Liberal concessions to the miners in Yorkshire and Durham and, as Ramsay MacDonald testified, 'did his best to coerce rich Liberals who wanted to place Liberals in the field of opposition to LRC candidates'.[31] In Bradford, Dewsbury, Merthyr and a handful of other seats he was unsuccessful, but his adroit handling of delicate situations ensured that the number of Liberal–Labour conflicts was minimized.

In the autumn of 1905 Acland-Hood recorded icily that 'certain of [the Unionists'] defeat, [the Liberals had] manned the constituencies with a tribe of "carpet-baggers" '.[32] But, as Table 4.6 shows, Herbert Gladstone's work led to a far fuller constituency coverage than for many years before. Augustine Birrell had good reason for reporting to the 1905 NLF Conference that '[their] excellent candidates had, in the great majority of instances, been a long time before their constituencies . . . , were well known, [and had] held an unparalleled number of meetings'.[33]

TABLE 4.6 *Candidates and constituency coverage by parties 1906*

Party	*No. of candidates*	*Seats covered in 1904*	*Seats covered in 1906*
Liberal	539	414	535
LRC	50	15	50
Nationalist	87	86	84
Unionist	574	534	553
Others	23	7	22

Consequently the Liberals went into the 1906 election in a high state of morale, and benefiting in many ways from the long preparatory years. The correlation between lodger votes and swing was almost as marginal – even in London where it was plus 4 per cent – as the correlation of ownership votes and Unionist performance. But there can be little doubt that party organization contributed as much as political enthusiasm to the high – 84 per cent – poll that underwrote the Liberal victory. In the first place, their election material was based on the best of the election songs, slogans and symbols, and was 'infinitely superior' in quality.[34] Secondly the Free Trade Union, Free Trade Leagues and Associations not only rallied the faithful, but sowed confusion in the Unionist ranks. Thirdly, the WNLF and WLF, because they sank their differences over the suffrage issue, brought the meaning of this election home to women more clearly than on any previous occasion. The *Daily Telegraph* commented sourly, on 19 January 1906, that 'fears about prices had . . . great weight in influencing the ignorant female mind'.

It would be wrong to give the impression that, once the election campaign began, the well-oiled Liberal band-wagon simply rolled, if only because the well-planned organization of Liberal speakers throughout the country made its own campaign contribution. Whilst Campbell-Bannerman took the west route to Scotland through Cheshire and Lancashire, Asquith went by way of Yorkshire up to Fife, Lloyd George concentrated very largely on Wales, Churchill on Lancashire, and Burns on London and the Midlands. No part of the country was left unvisited by one or other of the party's leading men. Furthermore, once the Liberal tide really began to flow with the Lancashire results on 15 January, the more popular Liberal demagogues, like Churchill and Lloyd George, moved round as many unpolled constituencies as possible. By contrast, the Unionist leaders hardly moved outside their own constituencies, either because – like Austen Chamberlain – they were 'disabled by sciatica and filial duty', or – like Arnold-Forster and Brodrick – they were 'so unpopular that they did more harm than good when they did so'.[35]

The Liberals also exploited to good effect, that 'important [new] adjunct . . . of electioneering work', the car.[36] Only 20,000 cars were used by all parties, but it was symptomatic, as much of existing Liberal organization as of future trends, that so many constituencies and associations put so much effort into acquiring and using them. Liberal organization, in brief, neither slackened in the campaign itself nor fell short of the most modern tendencies of the time. It carried the party through, from the selection of candidates and the registration and lobbying of voters, to the provision of speakers and of cars for the poll.

Much in the position and performance of Liberal organization in 1905 and 1906 was of course transient. It is always difficult to retain efficiency at a peak: when the particular issues around which enthusiasm has been generated have been settled and appear safe, or become irrelevant, it is impossible. Just as the Free Trade Union depended on the continued argument over tariffs remaining at the heart of British politics, so the continued co-existence of the WNLF and WLF depended on a suspension of belief about the women's suffrage issue which had become increasingly difficult to sustain. The spur, or threat, of the Labour alliance would never be quite the same again. The contrast of a declining and divided opposition organization would never again be so acute. Furthermore, the problem of finance had not been solved, merely held at bay. Who could be sure, as Gladstone moved in 1905 to other ministerial duties, what problems the future might hold? And yet, when all is said, a party without organization can no more catch a mood than a sailor without a boat can catch a tide. The apt and artful management of the Liberal organization between 1900 and 1905 made a vital contribution to electoral success in 1906.

There was a price, rightly or wrongly, paid. Lowell was not far wrong when, in 1908, he described the mass organizations of the Liberal party as 'an opaque sham'.[37] It is arguable that success was bought at the price of independence and democratic participation. The old arguments about caucus and control had been set aside rather than resolved. But they have not been solved any more effectively since, either by the Conservative party or by the Labour party. The sense of trust that Hudson and Herbert Gladstone engendered under Campbell-Bannerman's leadership, was perhaps a better basis for agreement than any number of more formal arrangements.

NOTES

1 H. J. Hanham, *Elections and Party Management: Politics in the Time of Gladstone and Disraeli*, London, 1965, p. 133.
2 Ibid., p. 138.
3 Viscount Gladstone Papers, British Museum Add. MSS. 46,105, ff. 215-32 and 234-6.
4 Viscount Gladstone Papers, BM. Add. MSS. 46,105, ff. 1-50.
5 Quoted in A. K. Russell, 'The General Election of 1906', D.Phil. thesis, Oxford, 1962, p. 127.
6 Sir Charles Mallet, *Herbert Gladstone: a Memoir*, London, 1932, pp. 190-2 and Viscount Gladstone Papers, BM. Add. MSS. 46,105, ff. 208-10.
7 Viscount Gladstone Papers, BM. Add. MSS. 46,022, ff. 34-5.
8 Ibid., f. 232.
9 Viscount Gladstone Papers, BM. Add. MSS. 46,024, f. 203.
10 Viscount Gladstone Papers, BM. Add. MSS. 46,042, ff. 141-2.
11 *Daily Express*, 19 January 1906. See also Balfour Papers, BM. Add. MSS. 49,797, ff. 115-59.

12 *Daily Telegraph*, 14 April 1905. See also A. K. Russell, *Liberal Landslide: The General Election of 1906*, Newton Abbot, 1973, p. 40.
13 R. A. Hudson to Herbert Gladstone, 9 March 1898; and Herbert Gladstone's reply. Viscount Gladstone Papers, BM. Add MSS. 46,020, ff. 11-16 and 154.
14 Sir Charles Mallet, op. cit., p. 184.
15 Viscount Gladstone Papers, BM. Add. MSS, misc. ff.; and private information A. F. Thompson.
16 Sir Charles Mallet, op. cit., p. 194; and Viscount Gladstone Papers, BM. Add. MSS. 46, 109, misc. ff.
17 Frank Bealey and Henry Pelling, *Labour and Politics, 1900-1906. A History of the Labour Representation Committee*, London, 1958, p. 143.
18 R. J. Wells to Crook, 1 May 1905. Viscount Gladstone Papers, BM. Add. MSS. 46,024, f. 203.
19 Arnold Morley's words. Viscount Gladstone Papers, BM. Add. MSS. 46,022, f. 227.
20 Balfour Papers, BM. Add. MSS. 49,771, ff. 53-6.
21 R. Spence-Watson, *The National Liberal Federation, from its Commencement to the General Election of 1906*, London, 1907, p. 296.
22 *Minutes of the Scottish Liberal Association, 1903-1906*, p. 225.
23 Balfour Papers, BM. Add. MSS. 49,771, ff. 53-6 and 65-7.
24 Dickson-Poynder to Asquith, 18 December 1903. Asquith Papers (Bodleian Library).
25 Herbert Gladstone to Asquith, 11 January 1904. Asquith Papers (Bodleian Library).
26 Balfour Papers, BM. Add. MSS. 49,764, ff. 52-7.
27 Viscount Gladstone Papers, BM. Add. MSS. 46,105, f. 9.
28 Viscount Gladstone Papers, BM. Add. MSS. 46,023, f. 221.
29 Sir Charles Mallet, op. cit., p. 195; and see Viscount Gladstone Papers, BM. Add. MSS. 46,023, ff. 187-8.
30 Viscount Gladstone Papers, BM. Add. MSS. 46,107, ff. 16-24 and 46,021, ff. 167-8.
31 Frank Bealey and Henry Pelling, op. cit., p. 259.
32 Balfour Papers, BM. Add. MSS. 41,210, f. 50.
33 *Proceedings in connection with the Twenty Seventh Annual Meeting of the National Liberal Federation*, p. 40.
34 *Daily Express*, 19 January 1906. See also W. J. Fisher, 'The Liberal party and the press', *19th Century*, July 1904.
35 Iwan-Muller, post-electoral memorandum. Balfour Papers, BM. Add. MSS. 49,797, ff. 109-10.
36 *Minutes of the Scottish Liberal Association, 1903-1906*, pp. 239-49.
37 R. T. MacKenzie, *British Political Parties. The Distribution of Power within the Conservative and Labour Parties*, London, 1955, p. 581.

Note: The author wishes to acknowledge David & Charles (Holdings) Ltd, for permission to reproduce some material from his book, *Liberal Landslide: The General Election of 1906*, Newton Abbot, 1973.

5

1906: REVIVAL AND REVIVALISM

STEPHEN E. KOSS

'There is no getting away from the fact that ours is a Nonconformist Party, with Nonconformist susceptibilities and Nonconformist prejudices', Edwin Montagu stiffly rebuked H. H. Asquith, who had committed the indiscretion of inviting a lady of dubious virtue to a reception at Downing Street.[1] The point was no less well taken for the fact that Montagu had been born a Jew and Asquith a Congregationalist.

Liberalism and Nonconformity each enjoyed unanticipated revivals in the early years of the century, then swiftly declined in terms of adherents, political strength, and, some would argue, contemporary relevance. Surely this was no coincidence. Always a major component in the Liberal tradition, Nonconformity came to acquire an unprecedented dynamism that, if it does not in itself account for the party's spectacular performance in the 1906 general election, none the less goes far to explain the character and extent of that victory. And the Nonconformist contribution was nowhere more apparent than among the Radicals who crowded the back benches of the new Parliament.

It was understandable that Free Churchmen should assume credit for single-handedly delivering the massive Liberal majority. 'It may be said', Augustine Birrell wrote with philosophic detachment, 'that just as Free Traders are perhaps too apt to attribute all increase of material prosperity to the open market and to forget railways and electricity, so the zealous Christian sometimes places to the credit of his faith the whole of the humanitarian movement.'[2] To an extent, Free Churchmen were encouraged in their self-delusion by tariff reformers, anxious to divert attention from the adverse electoral effects of their own doctrines. While it is clear that Nonconformist militancy was only one of several factors that fortuitously coalesced to produce the 1906 result, it cannot be denied that Nonconformists infused the campaign with a moral fervour, giving secular issues an evangelical appeal that proved irresistible. Free trade, for example, was espoused not so much as an economic theory as an article of faith; the importation of Chinese labour to the Transvaal was decried as an affront to God; and, not least of all, the 1902 Education Act was attacked on neither pedagogic nor administrative grounds, but essentially on spiritual ones.

Distracted by their grievances, Nonconformists saw none of the virtues of the Balfour government's education policy. Most galling was the requirement that they contribute through their rates to the maintenance of Anglican schools from which Nonconformist teachers were often barred by tests. The problem was most acute in rural districts, where Anglican control was usually exclusive. And, as if to add insult to injury, Roman Catholic schools also received a generous measure of preferential treatment.

It was not, as one historian has suggested, simply a matter that Nonconformists feared 'the subtle and pervading influence of Anglicanism' on the minds of their young.[3] Rather they were inclined to dismiss Anglicanism as too negligible a creed to be capable of pervading anything. To an extent which cannot be exaggerated, Nonconformists were reacting to a threat, half real and half imagined, of a Roman Catholic menace, which they saw everywhere and, particularly, in the higher reaches of the Establishment. The fear was constant, but never more intense than when educational proposals were periodically debated. W. E. Forster, who had brought down the wrath of Nonconformists by his 'erastian' Act of 1870, sadly concluded that 'the only belief much felt is that we are not and will not be papists'.[4] It is significant that Forster made his complaint to Archbishop Tait, himself a vigilant opponent of ritualist tendencies in the late-Victorian Church. If the Archbishop of Canterbury saw cause for alarm, can one blame the spokesmen for Nonconformity?

Although they had moved with the times to the extent that they now preferred to call themselves 'Free Churchmen' – which had a more positive ring than 'dissenter' – Nonconformists remained children of the seventeenth century. In recent years, they had become more self-consciously anti-sacerdotal, while the Established Church had become less distinctly Protestant. True to their heritage, they fretted about the undisclosed number of monks and nuns who stealthily slipped across the Channel. They helped to circulate chilling accounts of a new Popish Plot, which, had it not been foiled, would have planted a Catholic pretender on Edward's throne. Rarely did Nonconformist divines miss an opportunity to deplore 'the progress which continues to be made in the Romanising of the Church of England', or to join publicly 'in prayer to the "Father of lights" that He would prevent the darkness of Mediaevalism from returning upon our land'.[5] Proposals were mooted for a watchdog committee to uncover Catholic subversion and to recommend parliamentary counter-measures. John Morley was among those who remained sceptical. 'As far as any designs to make old John Bull R.C.,' he remonstrated with R. W. Perks, Liberal MP for Louth and a leading Wesleyan, 'you will not, I think, persuade me either that they are seriously entertained, or that they can ever have a single atom of success.'[6] But agitated Nonconformists were not likely to take reassurance from Morley, who, during his celebrated editorship of the *Fortnightly Review*, had printed 'god' with a small letter and 'Gladstone' with a capital.

In terms of organization and propaganda techniques, Nonconformists had much to learn from those whom they most distrusted. 'We Free Churchmen are only gradually awakening to the value of the press', observed the Rev. Hugh Price Hughes, the first president of the National Council of Evangelical Free Churches; 'the Roman Catholic Church with its usual astuteness has set itself to train journalists . . . We shall have to do the same.'[7] The later years of the nineteenth century and the early years of the twentieth witnessed a dramatic rise in the number and quality of left-wing religious journals, as well as the conversion of London's *Daily News* into an avowed organ of Radical Nonconformity. In the same period, a number of missions were opened, principally in the greater London area. These institutions, headed by men who appeared prominently in the denominational press and on Liberal platforms, combined social and spiritual ministration with unabashed political activity.

But the best gauge of renewed Nonconformist vitality was provided by the 'simultaneous' or 'united' evangelical tours, which were inter-denominational ventures under the auspices of the National Council. In the spring of 1900, preliminary plans were laid for a 'national mission . . . to reach the masses' that opened early the following year.[8] In London alone, attendance was estimated at 200,000, and the intensive campaign yielded a gratifying number of conversions and temperance pledges. Village missions, usually featuring local preaching talent, and house-to-house visitations were undertaken in the smaller towns of England and Wales.

Special missioners were dispatched to conduct rallies and 'open-air work' in approximately a hundred of the larger urban centres. Enthusiasm reached so high a pitch that even *The Times* could not fail to be impressed. 'The organisers of the movement', it wrote with unaccustomed warmth on 2 February 1901, 'speak with excusable pride of their achievements.'

The individual entitled to take greatest pride was the Rev. Thomas Law, 'organising secretary' of the National Council. He employed the service of a trio of itinerant evangelists – Rodney (better known as Gipsy) Smith, W. R. Lane, and the Rev. J. Tolfree Parr – who continued on circuit after the 1901 'simultaneous mission' was officially brought to a close. Three years later, there was another 'simultaneous mission', reportedly even more successful. The Rev. F. B. Meyer, whose 'Letter to Missioners' set the standard, was himself active, as was Dr Robert Forman Horton, whose 1905 'presidential campaign' took him on four-day visits to eight strategically placed cities. From farther afield, Dr R. A. Torrey and Charles M. Alexander arrived from Chicago in January 1903 for a three-year tour of the British Isles.[9]

The most phenomenal results of Edwardian revivalism came in Wales, and with no appreciable stimulus from the National Council. Indeed, if local accounts are to be believed, the Welsh revival of 1904-5 was the gift of God and owed little to any earthly agent. Thomas Law, Gipsy Smith, and W. T. Stead journeyed like the Magi to Cardiff and marvelled at what they beheld. Stead, 'a child of the Revival of 1859-60', described how Evan Roberts, a twenty-six-year-old blacksmith's apprentice, could weld an audience of a 'thousand or fifteen hundred persons . . . into a myriad-headed but single-souled personality'.[10] Chapel membership soared throughout the principality, with the greatest gains registered by the Baptists, the sect 'perhaps least curbed by ecclesiastical formalism'.[11]

Admittedly envious, English Free Church leaders met in the 'closing hours' of 1905 to consider the 'spiritual awakening in Wales' and the 'possibility of its spreading to London and the rest of England'. But what could be done to influence events which were 'entirely independent of man'? Trust soon gave way to impatience. 'Is it too much for us to seek that tens of thousands may be converted to God in London, as has been the experience in Wales through the great outpouring of the Holy Spirit?' demanded the Rev. J. H. Shakespeare, president of the Metropolitan Federation of Free Churches. Although the National Council received persistent reports that 'waves of spiritual blessing' had begun to roll upon various provincial towns, England proved stubbornly resistant to the Welsh variety of evangelical enthusiasm.[12]

Doubtless it was asking too much of English Nonconformists that they should deliver themselves to Christ with the same communal abandon. Dr G. Campbell-Morgan, who conducted English-style revivalist meetings at Christ Church in Westminster Bridge Road, 'did not propose to have his regular services broken up by anyone save God alone'.[13] And yet it would be a mistake to conclude that a genuine revival eluded English Free Churchmen, whose contribution to the overall increase in communicants was not insubstantial. Theirs was a commitment that manifested itself less often in conversions at revivalist sessions than in Liberal votes in a succession of dramatic by-elections and in the general election of 1906.

An increase in communicants is more easily ascertained than the secular repercussions of evangelical activity. Few, however, would dispute F. B. Meyer's contention that 'every great revival of religion has issued in social and political reconstruction'.[14] Again, Wales proves the point most conclusively: swept by religious fervour during 1904 and 1905, its thirty-four seats were swept by the Radicals in the next year's election. From the first, the Rev. H. Elvet Lewis explained, the spiritual revival in Wales was stimulated and sustained by a national revolt: 'The Revolt without the Revival might have become too political; the Revival without the Revolt might have become too pietistic.'[15] Although English Nonconformists obviously lacked a comparable sense of national resentment, they too saw themselves as the victims of an alien administration. In response, Nonconformity temporarily overcame its parochialisms: Wesleyans made common cause with Baptists, Welshmen with Englishmen, pro-Boers with Imperialists, and plutocrats with trade unionists.

Always a force to be reckoned with in modern British politics, if only in isolated localities, Nonconformity achieved now a truly national dimension. Four days before Sir John Gorst announced the provisions of the 1902 Education Bill to the Commons, R. W. Perks invited Lord Rosebery to preside at a massive demonstration at the Queen's Hall on 10 June. The Rev. John Scott Lidgett, another Wesleyan and a pillar of the National Council, helped Perks to assemble an array of speakers as diverse as Asquith, Sydney Buxton, David Lloyd George, Dr Horton, Dr J. Guinness Rogers and Dr John Clifford. Rosebery, who did not seem to Perks 'quite [to] appreciate the intensity of the Nonconformist feeling', was given a lesson in tactics. '*Possibly* the Bill may be made to work,' Perks conceded, 'but 9 Liberals out of 10 don't *believe* so: & it is hardly our business, I think, to stem the torrent of popular hostility against the Government.'[16]

As the Queen's Hall demonstration symbolized, education was as yet one of those rare issues that permitted Liberals of different persuasions to join in concerted activity. Sir Henry Campbell-Bannerman instructed Herbert Gladstone, the party's chief whip, to sound out prominent Imperialists so that the front bench might 'take such a line on the 2nd R[eading] as may furnish a united attack'.[17] Liberals, who had recently dissipated their energies and often their credibility in internecine strife, now joined to denounce the few hapless Nonconformists who sat on the government benches, or, better still, the Irish Nationalist MPs who supported the Bill as Catholics instead of rejecting it as allies of British Radicalism.[18]

The leaders of the Nonconformist community knew better than to put too much trust in professional politicians, even those with whom they consorted on campaign platforms. Their own response to the Education Act was a passive resistance movement, conducted with a zeal worthy of the seventeenth-century commonwealthmen from whom they claimed descent. To be sure, only a small minority of the nation's Nonconformists had the courage as well as the conviction to defy the law. But those who passively resisted tended to be ministers and other men of station, who commanded the respect of their neighbours. Duly warned, they were visited by the local sheriff, who impounded some possession – usually a silver inkstand or tea service – estimated as equal in value to the unpaid rates. The merchandise, put up at public auction, invariably found its way back to its owner through the good offices of friends, members of the same chapel, or, if all else failed, a servant dispatched to tender a discreet bid. The passive resister thereby managed to keep his principles, while his account was settled for him. But one would not wish to suggest that the protest was a charade: often those involved were summoned before the magistrates, fined or imprisoned. The *British Weekly* brought its readers 'News of the Persecutions', and, each October, a National Passive Resistance Day was celebrated at London's City Temple, where the Hampdens and Eliots of the previous year were applauded.

The initiative for the movement came from 'Alderman' George White, a Baptist shoe manufacturer who became MP for North West Norfolk in 1900.[19] Its moving force was, without question,

Dr John Clifford of Westbourne Park Chapel, Paddington, who combined Hampden's fidelity to principle with a Cromwellian sense of vengeance. The Rev. C. Silvester Horne, newly appointed to head Whitefield's Mission in Tottenham Court Road, wore the mantle of Ireton, although one can detect traces of Lilburne in the *Crusader*, the penny journal which he edited first as a monthly and, from October 1903, as a weekly.

The Baptist and Congregational unions gave their emphatic endorsement to passive resistance. The National Council of Evangelical Free Churches, whose officers occupied key places on the National Passive Resistance Committee, helped with organization. By the end of 1903, a network of some 430 citizens' leagues and committees operated throughout England and Wales. The object was not so much to incite others to rebellion as to publicize and justify the actions of those whose consciences had impelled them to rebel. Nonconformity, its sense of mission and identity weakened by the concessions it had won during the mid-Victorian period, had again to be taught to defend its own vital interests. For this reason, Dr William Robertson Nicoll was not perturbed when passive resisters were disenfranchised as criminal offenders: 'Where one vote is lost,' he reasoned, 'at least ten will be gained by the public demonstration thus afforded of the iniquities and injustices of the Act.'[20]

What did the passive resisters hope eventually to accomplish? There are indications that, at least initially, they acted more out of desperation than out of any belief that they could achieve positive results. Obviously, they could not expect to bankrupt the exchequer by non-payment of rates. Nor was there much chance that they might reverse the policies of a government whose tyranny they likened to that of Strafford and Laud. They were not especially sanguine about the Liberal Opposition. The *Crusader* asked its readers:[21]

> Is there anyone optimistic enough to believe that the swing of the pendulum would be so great as to enable the Liberal Party to go back to power with a majority, independent of the Irish, sufficient to secure the repeal? And, even granting that, is the great Committee of the Anglican Church (as Dr Clifford aptly styled the House of Lords) to be overthrown?

Within three years, the Liberal party was returned with a huge majority; and, within a decade, the House of Lords was shorn of its powers. Yet these developments, to which Free Churchmen contributed significantly, failed to bring them the benefits which they were entitled to expect.

Even before the Education Bill had passed into law, Liberal candidates began to score handsome successes at by-elections. In May 1902, Bury was wrested from Tory hands by George Toulmin, a journalist of Wesleyan background. His strong views on the education issue may have had no direct bearing on the situation at Bury, where there were no board schools. But Bury's Nonconformist community would not have been indifferent to the plight of their brethren elsewhere, and, in any case, would have reacted against the presence of a large and well-organized Roman Catholic population. In July, North Leeds fell to the Liberals, and here the Nonconformist factor was even more pronounced. Perks rejoiced 'that the victory [of R. H. Barran, a local Methodist] is that of the Nonconformists & school board advocates. It is the first time for 35 years that the chapel bell has rung.' Horne and Clifford were equally exultant.[22]

More incredible in its way was the outcome in August at Sevenoaks, always considered one of the safest of Conservative seats, where a Baptist stood in the Liberal interest and was returned on a 24.1 per cent swing. Despite the constituency's unlikely social composition, the education controversy was described as 'the main topic' of the campaign.[23] Joseph Chamberlain, who nursed profound misgivings about the education policies of the government to which he belonged, took fright. 'I do not think', he advised the Prime Minister, 'that any seat, where there is a strong Nonconformist electorate, can be considered absolutely safe.'[24] That winter brought further Liberal gains at Newmarket and Rye, both traditional Tory strongholds with Nonconformist entrenchments. Perks confided to Lord Rosebery that there were certain problems posed by the fact that C. D. Rose, the candidate at Newmarket, had (like Rosebery) connections with the turf. None the less, Nonconformists there were 'working hard for Rose "regarding him not so much as a man as the embodiment of a principle"!'[25]

Campbell-Bannerman, taking the waters at Baden-Baden, had ample time to consider the situation. While he had no wish to appear intractable, he shared James Bryce's view that Liberals should resist any compromise which, one way or the other, would deprive them of militant Nonconformist support. He found it impossible to understand why the government had decided to 'meddle with this hornet's nest' instead of applying itself to pressing problems of higher education and technical training.[26] Not for the last time, he gave his opponents credit for a strategy which they did not have. Balfour, never a particularly good judge of popular opinion, took for granted that the Nonconformist 'fever will be allayed in twelve months',[27] and expected that the Act would be vindicated by its efficient implementation.

There was serious apprehension among Nonconformists that they might be sold short by their parliamentary allies, whose vision often did not extend beyond Westminster. Bryce, speaking more as a Baptist than as a member of the party hierarchy, communicated to Clifford his 'impression that Liberals outside Parliament, especially Free Churchmen, are clearer and stronger in this matter than many Liberals in Parliament, and that outside opinion might . . . have the greatest weight'.[28] The education committee of the National Council, taking a similar view, 'resolved to recommend the [local] Councils to make Education a test question at all elections and to carefully watch the selection of candidates'.[29] More directly, Nonconformists applied pressure by sending deputations to wait upon Campbell-Bannerman and Lord Spencer, leader of the Liberal peers. They sponsored public meetings and rallies, culminating on 23 May 1903 in a demonstration in Hyde Park. And, most frequently, they called at the office of the Liberal chief whip.

It was on the golf links that Horne asked Arthur Porritt, a writer for the *Christian World* and later its editor: 'Don't you think the Free Churches ought to put up a hundred candidates at the next election?' It was not enough to elect a Liberal Parliament; it had to be a Parliament that contained a healthy complement of Free Churchmen who conceived of themselves as such. At Horne's suggestion, Porritt went on 16 July 1903 to see Herbert Gladstone, who 'was not enthusiastic', and who made brutally clear that 'he did not want to be encumbered with men with bees in their bonnets over one issue'.[30] Where, it was asked, were a sufficient number of qualified candidates to come from, and who was to finance them?

In the cramped pages of his diary, Gladstone pretty much answered his own questions. On 17 June, for example, he had seen James Gibb, who was soon adopted to stand successfully at Harrow in the next election. Willing to 'put down a certain amount' for his campaign expenses, Gibb was typical of many Nonconformists who, though they had always taken a keen interest in politics, 'never before thought of standing but Educ^{n}. and F[ree] T[rade] bring (him) out'.[31] Other Nonconformist hopefuls, less able to pay their own way, were promised support from a fund raised by the National Council in collaboration with the *Christian World*. With landed wealth solidly behind the Tories, and trade union subscriptions diverted to Labour candidacies, Herbert Gladstone was in no position to spurn an offer of Free Church support. Besides, from the little that we can piece together about Liberal party finances, he already depended heavily on the generosity of Nonconformist businessmen.

Gladstone 'encouraged [the] proposal for a Noncon. Com. (Silvester Horne, Guinness Rogers, etc.) to put pressure on desirable men to fight constituencies'.[32] But the constituencies he had in mind were those 'forlorn hope seats', as Porritt called them, which no one else would have wished to fight. Further meetings followed between Gladstone and the Rev. Thomas Law, whom some partisans have cited as the real architect of the 1906 Liberal victory.[33] There can be no doubt, however, that Law was no match for Gladstone, who always had the better of him. On 11 August, Law proposed names which Gladstone agreed to consider for possible vacancies. But, on the morning of 23 September, Law and three other Free Church leaders complained bitterly to Perks 'that Herbert Gladstone had given them 25 hopeless constituencies to fight with Nonconformist candidates (if they can be found)'. For Rosebery's amusement, Perks recounted how the four 'reverences' had explained that W. P. Hartley, the Primitive Methodist jam manufacturer, 'has given them £5000 provided I will do the same – & they said if I would do this they saw their way to another £10,000'. Instead Perks rebuked them for taking 'Herbert Gladstone's leavings . . . They . . . admitted they were "like children" at the business, but were supremely anxious to put into line all the fighting forces of dissent, and then to see that they are not thrown overboard as in 1870 when the battle is won'.[34] Rebuffed by Perks, Law returned to Gladstone's office, hat in hand. Asked to allocate £25,000 for the promotion of Free Church candidacies, Gladstone 'undertook to contribute' no more than £5000, and that in several instalments. 'Much satisfied with this arrangement', he minuted, and he had every right to be.[35]

Any evaluation of the Nonconformist effort must take into account the question of tariff reform, which intruded in the spring of 1903. Chamberlain admitted that he had propounded his scheme with a view to winning back support alienated by the government's education policy. As Lord George Hamilton, his erstwhile Cabinet colleague, put it: 'If we had had no Education Bill of 1902, we should have had no Tariff Reform in 1903.'[36] Historians, much like contemporaries, have heatedly debated whether the Liberals owed their eventual success more to outraged Nonconformists or to steadfast free traders. Campbell-Bannerman, for one, was firmly of the opinion 'that Education is far before Tariffs in the public mind. Tant mieux!'[37]

There was the distinct threat that Chamberlain, himself the product of a dissenting background, might outbid his Liberal rivals for Nonconformist support. In a previous incarnation, 'Radical Joe' had led the assault against the 1870 Education Act. It was not inconceivable that some Nonconformists would accept tariff reform as the price of his explicit promise to work for a repeal of the 1902 measure. 'Law gave me a hint', Perks wrote nervously to Rosebery, 'that Chamberlain has been making some overtures to the Free Church Federation re Education of a somewhat advanced nature. Protection & Disestablishment would sound curious.'[38] Not so curious, some Nonconformists might have retorted, as the combination of free trade and 'protected' schools. It was subsequently feared that R. J. Campbell of the City Temple had 'completely gone over to Chamberlain', who was allegedly 'quite ready to give to the Nonconformists what they want'.[39]

The Liberal leaders were in a dilemma. Chamberlain's latest tack made it both logical and expedient for them to strike an alliance with Free Traders on the Unionist side; unfortunately, several of their potential allies were infamous defenders of the Education Act. However dexterous, Liberals could not pick up the support of Unionist Free Traders without dropping their Nonconformist parcels. On this score, Perks and Lloyd George stood in rare agreement: 'It is the bounden duty of the Nonconformists, thru every agency in their power, to oppose every candidate be he Unionist Free Trader or anything else who will not accept our Education policy.'[40] Gladstone hoped that they might be induced to give ground, but Asquith, who had personal experience to guide him, was doubtful. 'The Nonconformists are in a difficult mood & require special handling', he observed. 'They don't sufficiently realise that it is all important to defeat J.C., & for the moment to concentrate on that.' Gladstone broached the subject at a meeting with Law, who went so far as to say that each case 'wd. be considered on its merits. Eg. He wd. support Winston [Churchill] against a Tory', provided that Churchill 'stepped forward on Temperance & on Educ[n]. accepted Public Control & No Tests'. At Gladstone's suggestion, Campbell-Bannerman deputed Bryce, a former president of the Nonconformist Union at Oxford, to 'try to feel the pulse of the Non Cons' and to convince 'Clifford & Co. . . . that this is as much their game as ours'. Bryce accepted the assignment, but not without demur: 'We must . . . be careful not to arouse a suspicion that the N.C. grievance is being sacrificed for the sake of Free Trade', he warned. 'It would not do, when we are going into battle, to blunt the edge of the Puritan sword.' Bryce put the case to Clifford, who consulted 'several friends' and replied in terms so stringent that the matter was dropped.[41]

Largely ignorant of these top-level deliberations, Nonconformist candidates prepared for the fray. They were armed with copies of *The Education Act: A Handbook for Free Church Workers,* which contained facts and figures culled from the *Daily News* by Law and was published under the imprint of the National Council of Evangelical Free Churches. In the closing days of 1903, Fred Horne, Silvester's brother, made an unsuccessful attempt to revive Liberal traditions in the Ludlow division of Shropshire. It was not a constituency in which Nonconformity particularly thrived, but Horne, a local farmer, was virtually the only man both willing and able to take the field. Incurably optimistic, Free Church spokesmen assured an incredulous Gladstone that even Rutland where no Liberal had stood in the last four general elections, 'can be won on the Educ^{n}. question!'[42] Their self-confidence was more justified in the case of several more imminent contests. J. Williams Benn, the son of a Congregational minister, took a seat at Devonport by a majority of 1040 votes; Philip Stanhope, not himself a Nonconformist, increased the Liberal vote at Harborough in Leicestershire by capitalizing on the 'strong feeling in many of the villages about the Education Acts'; and J. S. Higham, a Congregationalist married to Hartley's daughter, romped home at Sowerby by 'put[ting] the Education Act and its repeal in the front of his election address, and refus[ing] to vote for a Roman Catholic University'.[43]

On 2 February 1905, Jesse Herbert, secretary to the chief whip, calculated that the Liberals had won no fewer than sixteen seats and had lost only one since the introduction of the Education Bill. The most recent breakthrough had come at North Dorset, where A. W. Wills had professed 'strong Nonconformist sympathies' and was accordingly rewarded by the Free Churches with 'substantial aid in canvassing and on the platform'. An even greater upset occurred in April at Brighton, where E. A. Villiers, a renegade from Anglican orders, declared himself 'in favour of vitally amending the Education and Licensing Acts'. The local Free Church council rendered him stout assistance, and Villiers self-consciously ascribed his surprise victory to 'fear of Protection and the Priest'. His Tory opponent was even more explicit that the 'crusade against the Education Act [was] one of the chief causes of his defeat'. In June, Noel Buxton became the first Liberal to sit for Whitby, his candidacy actively supported by Dr Clifford and the Rev. J. Hirst Holloway. During the same week, the Conservative majority at Chichester was sharply reduced by J. E. Allen. The election committee of the National Council was gratified to report that its agents 'had been in full evidence at . . . Brighton, Whitby and Chichester. Leaflets had been delivered throughout each constituency and cartoon-posters used in connection with each election. The candidates had testified to the fact that the co-operation of the Free Churches and the help they gave on the Education question had been a powerful factor in the elections'. Within weeks, East Finsbury and Carlisle were both captured from the Conservatives: the former by J. Allen Baker, a Quaker; the latter by F. W. Chance, whom the Free Church Council prodded to take a more vigorous stand on the education issue.[44]

Where did the Nonconformists obtain the funds to carry out their ambitious programme? The *Christian World* had proposed to raise £50,000, but receipts fell far short of this goal. On 4 February 1904, Law revealed that £10,629. 6*s*. 6*d*. had been pledged, of which only £1566. 9*s*. 6*d*. had been collected. Arthur Porritt told the committee that 'as far as the "Christian World" was concerned the fund could not be regarded as having been successful'. Within a fortnight, prospects had improved. George Cadbury gave £2500, subsequently increased by a further £1000, and Hartley promised '£5000 if £20,000 were raised or ten per cent on all sums up to £50,000'. Appeals were henceforth addressed to wealthy individuals instead of to congregations. There are also indications that, as the Nonconformists proved their usefulness, the Liberal whip became more open-handed. Gladstone was willing to put up as much as £400 if Silvester Horne could be persuaded to beard the Chamberlain lion in his den at West Birmingham.[45]

The longer Balfour clung to office, the greater the likelihood that the Nonconformist offensive would lose steam or turn against its Liberal allies. One may safely assume that such possibilities entered into his calculations. True, his 1904 licensing proposals – scorned as 'the Brewers' Endowment Bill' – intensified Nonconformist hostility to the Unionists. But, throughout 1905, the Nonconformist –Liberal alliance was subjected to increasing strain. J. F. Cheetham, a Methodist trying to tip the scales in a January by-election at Stalybridge, complained to Bryce that the party's line on education was costing him support. Might he perhaps 'hint at exceptional treatment for Catholics and Jews'? Bryce vetoed the suggestion, but, writing to Herbert Gladstone, betrayed a consciousness of the responsibilities that would soon devolve upon him: 'Whatever course we may ultimately have to take, promises made now would make great trouble with the N.C.s. . . . They would think we were deserting them'.[46] Lloyd George, another Liberal politician on whom Free Churchmen relied, was even more intoxicated by the scent of impending office. In March 1904, he privately communicated to a meeting of Free Church leaders the terms of an 'educational compromise' which he had negotiated with the Bishop of St Asaph. It was denounced as 'a surrender that would take the heart out of the Dissenters'.[47] A year later, he gave his proposals a second airing in an interview with Porritt in the *Christian World*. Nonconformists, he prophesied, would have to make some concession on the crucial question of clerical instruction during school hours, and furthermore could not expect complete redress from any future Liberal administration. His remarks created such an uproar that Lloyd George claimed that he had been misrepresented and obtained 'clarification' in the next issue. Porritt, who insisted that Lloyd George had tacitly approved a proof of the article, kept his distance from the 'Welsh Wizard' for the next quarter-century.[48]

The chief whip's office, which had never taken enthusiastically to doing business with the Free Churches, resented the way that Law and others arrogated the right to speak for the party. Nonconformists, on the other hand, considered themselves 'the predominant partner in the Liberal firm' and uniquely equipped 'to save Liberalism from its peril'. On 21 September 1905, Perks joined Clifford, Law, and others at a Cheltenham rally. 'There were 3000 people present', he told Rosebery. 'Evidently these worthy Nonconformist divines mean to give the next Liberal Government a pretty lively time.'[49] Not that there was any serious threat that Nonconformists would gravitate to the other side. There existed a Nonconformist Unionist Association, but even the Unionist chief whip dismissed its members as 'mostly a self-advertising lot'.[50] But, as the general election drew closer, Free Churchmen served notice that they were not to be taken for granted. According to Law, the National Council required 'a very clear and definite understanding with the Liberal leaders' on education before it would consent to throw its weight behind them.[51]

In October, the Congregational Union met at Leeds, and delegates divided their time between the sessions there and the by-election campaign nearby at Barkston Ash. Silvester Horne delivered fifteen speeches, five of them from Liberal platforms. 'Let the Liberal leaders go back on their word in regard to the [Education] Act,' he warned, 'and I for one will be the first in the new revolt. And if we leave the ship because she has turned back on her course, . . . we will fire the torpedo which will blow the Liberal Party sky-high.' The Rev. J. H. Jowett, chairman-elect of the Congregational Union, echoed these sentiments: 'Freedom of Trade is important,' he acknowledged, 'but it is infinitely more important that we should have free communion with the Highest without the intervention of any priest.' Horne subsequently revealed that he and Jowett received 'some mild rebukes' for the 'threats' they had uttered at Leeds, but he insisted that it would do the Liberal leaders no harm to hear the truth: 'To be forewarned is to be forearmed.' Clifford, too, saw no reason to mince words. Although he welcomed Campbell-Bannerman's 'lucid and decisive' statement on 16 November, he deplored the fact that 'there are some Liberals so faithless to the central principle of Liberalism as actually to say that the Roman Catholics must have preferential treatment'.[52]

Barkston Ash, which the Liberals had previously contested only twice, was a great victory. In Lloyd George's opinion, the Education Act 'did more to win [it] than any other single cause'.[53] The Free Church performance was notably more restrained at Hampstead, which the Tories held in November with a diminished majority. Local factors were largely responsible, but the estrangement between party and Nonconformist leaders played its part. As the days passed, it became increasingly probable that Balfour would resign office, leaving his Liberal successor with the unenviable task of forming a government before an election. Gladstone, among others, advised Campbell-Bannerman that acceptance of office under such circumstances 'wd. bring upon us all the difficulties which we are entitled to avoid. Labour men, Irishmen, cranks of all sorts, & last but not least the *Noncons* wd. hammer at you & all our candidates to extort their pounds of flesh'. He instructed Robert Hudson, secretary of the Liberal Central Association, to gather opinions from '15 or 20 of the most representative men' who were 'in touch with the constituencies & with the Noncons. . . . The Clifford school I suspect wd. be for acceptance'.[54] In case Nonconformists required any further proof of Gladstone's sentiments, he was heard to speak of the education question as a '2½*d.* one'. Small wonder that Clifford admitted to Perks 'that he sincerely distrusts Gladstone, & that he belives C.B. will not go straight on Education'.[55]

To the relief of the 'Clifford school', Campbell-Bannerman not only accepted the king's invitation to form a Cabinet, but also filled ten of its nineteen places with reputed Nonconformists. Although Free Churchmen had expressed a preference to have either Bryce or Lloyd George at the Education Office, they were more than satisfied with Birrell, a Baptist minister's son who had lost the habit of chapel-going as a Cambridge undergraduate. Lloyd George, after a dutiful reference to Welsh disestablishment, went to the Board of Trade. Perks congratulated the Prime Minister on assembling 'a very powerful government'. Clifford, unable to contain his enthusiasm, exclaimed 'I almost feel as if I were in the Cabinet myself'.[56] There was something pathetic about the tendency of Nonconformist spokesmen to embrace Cabinet ministers as fellow-communicants: Asquith, Burns, and even Morley showed up on various lists of 'Free Church statesmen'.

Gladstone need not have worried. Nonconformists had waited too long to stint their labours. 'The opportunity of the Passive Resister and the Free Churchman has come!', the *Crusader* trumpeted on 14 December. Everything depended on the new government amassing a majority 'absolutely independent of Unionist and Irish votes'. Sir Edward Grey, who usually held aloof from domestic controversy, shared the 'hope [that] the size of the majority . . . will be large enough to carry a reform of the Education Act; if we aren't strong enough to do that we shall do very little good'.[57] To this end, the National Council of Free Churches implemented plans which had been held in readiness for years. Its fifty-one district federations and nearly 900 local councils were hives of activity. Some of the most celebrated names in Nonconformity took to the road on motor tours; in more remote villages, their disembodied voices were heard giving 'phonographic speeches'. Quantities of literature were distributed by local councils, which excelled at canvassing. 'The contribution of the Free Churches is magnificent', the *Daily News* wrote on 6 January 1906. 'It is not only the Education Act that will be discussed. The message will also include a statement of the entire case for a purer, better informed, less unscrupulous national life.'

There were some Nonconformist clergymen who thought that the pulpit and denominational press had become too blatantly partisan, and that the National Council had been reduced to 'an adjunct of the Liberal Party'.[58] Their complaints were not without foundation. Reports proliferated of 'unscrupulous' divines who led their congregations in prayer for the defeat of sinful Tories, and who proclaimed that 'in voting for the Liberal . . . electors would be voting for Christ Himself'. Still, as one historian has cogently argued, Nonconformists' 'passionate moral fervour exalted the election more than their bigotry sullied it'.[59] To what degree, if any, did either their fervour or their bigotry have an effect?

Regarding the outcome in certain areas – Wales, the West Riding, and Northumbria – as 'a foregone conclusion', the National Council concentrated its effort 'upon the weaker places'.[60] Occasionally, the results were negligible. Accompanied by the Rev. J. D. Jones, Silvester Horne conducted a motor tour through Buckinghamshire, Shropshire, and East Anglia, speaking on behalf of many candidates, not one of whom won.[61] In the Birmingham area, which was Chamberlain's fief, the Unionists professed abiding sympathy with Nonconformist grievances and held their ground.[62] It has been said that the Liberals owed their phenomenal success in Lancashire to free trade, which they emphasized to the exclusion of other issues; but Nonconformist spokesmen there pointed proudly to the fact that A. A. Haworth, 'the only out-and-out evangelical Free Churchman in the field', garnered a majority at Manchester South that exceeded any other in the city.[63] Certainly there is no denying the fact that, whatever issue dominated attention, 'Nonconformity formed the backbone of Liberalism' in Lancashire.[64]

Elsewhere the Nonconformist factor shows up more clearly. The Rev. G. Campbell-Morgan toured the eastern counties and Lincolnshire with Dr Clifford, and, in 'four-and-twenty years . . . of religious campaigning' had never experienced anything 'more deep and remarkable'. The Liberals swept all but two of the seats in the area. Hull and Spalding gave particular satisfaction to the Passive Resistance League. Richard Winfrey, a self-styled 'political dissenter' and another passive resister, became the first Liberal to sit for South West Norfolk. And, more astoundingly, the eccentric Arnold Lupton was returned at Sleaford. 'We didn't win it', Lupton's agent told those who proffered congratulations; 'it was an act of God.'[65]

It was the authoritative opinion of C. F. G. Masterman, who entered Parliament as Liberal member for West Ham North, that protection was probably not 'in any degree responsible for the winning of London'.[66] The Metropolitan Free Church Federation was unremittingly active, drawing its support from 843 chapels organized into 65 local councils. Gipsy Smith had been conducting missions in the weeks that preceded polling, and the revivalist spirit ran strong. In addition to Horne and Clifford, there were a number of Radical divines, including the Revs C. Ensor Walters, Alexander Connell, and Thomas Phillips. Whitefield's Mission, where the *Crusader* and the *Signal* had their editorial offices, attracted thousands to its open meetings. A virtual campaign headquarters, it was the scene of frenzied jubilation on the night the first returns poured in.[67]

By attracting countless middle-class Nonconformists back to the Liberal fold, the education issue 'helped to turn the balance in many [London] constituencies, and in a few, such as Brixton, East Islington and North Hackney', provides 'the most convincing explanation for the Conservative defeat'.[68] Whitefield's took an especially keen interest in the contest at South St Pancras, a constituency which the *Daily Mail* had had the effrontery to label a 'Tory pocket borough'. The Liberal challenger was P. W. Wilson, labour correspondent for the *Daily News*, who belonged to Horne's congregation and contributed his talents to the *Signal*. The professionals gave him little chance, but he confounded them with a majority of 61. 'I could have fought Wilson,' his defeated opponent stated, 'but I could not fight Whitefield's.'[69]

When the dust had settled, somewhere between 180 and 200 Nonconformists had been elected, not a few to their own astonishment. They could not agree among themselves on an exact number: some included Unitarians and/or Scottish Presbyterians in their tallies; most chose to ignore the presence of a half-dozen or so dissenters, mostly Unitarians and Wesleyans, on the Unionist side. Arthur Porritt, who based his count in the *Christian World* on a questionnaire he had addressed only to prospective Liberal and Labour candidates, acknowledged the imperfections of his method: 'Men who had always relied on their wives' church membership to get them into heaven woke up to the political advantage for the moment of having some slender link with Methodism, or Congregationalism, or Presbyterianism.'[70] Nevertheless, Porritt's figures are as good as any and better than most. All that he – or anyone – could say with precision was that fifteen passive resisters had won seats.

The return of a sizeable phalanx of Free Church MPs had been assumed. Sixty-five Nonconformists were defending English or Welsh seats which they, or, in a few cases, their party had won in the 1900 general election or in by-elections since. With few exceptions, these constituencies were classified by the chief whip[71] as 'certain wins', and were located in traditional areas of Nonconformist electoral strength. The remarkable results were achieved by the 112 Nonconformist candidates who were not incumbents. Fifty-five of them, including all five who stood in Wales, were reckoned by Gladstone to have an even chance or better: 'certain win', 'probable win', or, most usually, 'possible win'. Of the remaining fifty-seven, eight do not appear in Gladstone's forecast: six candidates for Scottish or Irish seats, and, inexplicably, two in England. Seventeen Nonconformist challengers were given an 'off chance' of success, seven were regarded as probable losers, and twenty-five were written off as certain casualties.

Thirty Free Churchmen, whose candidacies Gladstone had dismissed more or less as exercises in futility, won majorities, some of them quite respectable: they included no fewer than ten of the twenty-five from the 'certain loss' category. Forty per cent of Nonconformist candidates in this bottom group therefore attained success, as compared with only 22 per cent of other 'certain loss' Liberals, who won in eighteen of the remaining eighty-one contests. Was it that they were carried along by the Liberal landslide, or do they deserve credit for helping to create that landslide? Would they have offered themselves, sometimes standing where no Liberal had previously dared, without an indomitable belief in the righteousness of their cause? Could they have roused the electorate with anything less than their messianic zeal?

'We have been put into power by the Nonconformists', averred Campbell-Bannerman.[72] Making due allowance for the fact that he was attempting to fend off an importunate Roman Catholic prelate, his statement carries a fair measure of conviction. Admittedly, the Liberal party would have enjoyed a comfortable majority without thirty additional backbenchers, and Free Church leaders would have been no less entitled to boast that the 1906 Parliament contained a greater number of chapel-goers than any since the days of Oliver Cromwell. But the parliamentary party would have differed in spirit and, to some extent, in social composition without the membership of men whose own inconceivable success inspired the belief that the promised land lay within reach. Having arrived in office, Liberal Nonconformists soon learned that, in other respects, they had not yet left the wilderness; but that is the denouement to a longer and sadder story.

NOTES

1 Quoted in S. D. Waley, *Edwin Montagu, A Memoir and an Account of his Visits to India*, Bombay, 1964, p. 30.

2 Birrell, 'Patriotism and Christianity', *Contemporary Review* (1905), pp. 193-4.

3 R. B. MacCullum, *Asquith*, London, 1936, p. 47.

4 Forster to Tait, 14 July 1874, quoted in P. T. Marsh, *The Victorian Church in Decline*, London, 1969, p. 111.

5 Minutes of the annual meeting of the General Body of the Three Denominations, Memorial Hall, London, 28 March 1901 and 30 March 1905 (Dr Williams's Library, London); minutes of the organizing committee, 7 October, 18 July 1904, Free Church Federal Council archives, London (hereafter FCFC).
6 Morley to Perks, 27 March 1905, Perks Papers (courtesy of Sir Malcolm Perks).
7 Quoted in Arthur Walters, *Hugh Price Hughes, Pioneer and Reformer*, London, 1907?, p. 92.
8 Minutes of the general council, 5 February and 11 June 1900, 7 October 1901, FCFC; *Daily News*, 3 October 1900; *The Times*, 28 January and 2 February 1901.
9 Minutes of the general council, 28 March 1905, FCFC; *Examiner*, 6 February 1905; W. T. Stead, *The Revival of 1905*, London, 1905, p. 77; *British Weekly*, 30 November 1905.
10 *Daily Chronicle*, 13 December 1904; also C. R. Williams, 'The Welsh religious revival of 1904-5', *British Journal of Sociology*, III (1952), pp. 242-59.
11 K. O. Morgan, *Wales in British Politics, 1868-1922*, Cardiff, 1963, p. 217.
12 *Examiner*, 5 January 1905; Shakespeare, letter to the editor of the *Christian World*, 9 February 1905; *Free Church Yearbook, 1906*, pp. 168 ff.
13 *Christian World*, 5 January 1905.
14 Presidential address, ninth annual meeting of the National Council, 1904, quoted in Stead, op. cit., p. 12.
15 Lewis, 'The revival in Wales', *British Weekly* (supplement), 7 December 1905.
16 Perks to Rosebery, 3 and 20 May, 24 July 1902, Rosebery Papers, vol. 10,050 ff. 249, 256-7, and 282 (National Library of Scotland, Edinburgh).
17 Campbell-Bannerman to Gladstone [4 May 1902], Viscount Gladstone Papers, BM. Add. MSS. 45,988, f. 14.
18 Perks to Rosebery, 31 May 1902, Rosebery Papers, vol. 10,050, f. 262; also 'Sketches from Westminster', *Manchester Guardian*, 9 May 1902.
19 T. H. Darlow, *William Robertson Nicoll: Life and Letters*, London 1925, pp. 378 ff.
20 Quoted in the *Crusader*, 15 May 1903.
21 *Crusader*, 15 February 1903.
22 Perks to Rosebery, 30 July 1902, Rosebery Papers, vol. 10,050, f. 286; W. B. Selbie, *The Life of Charles Silvester Horne*, London, 1920, pp. 130-1; Henry Pelling, *Social Geography of British Elections, 1885-1910*, London, 1967, p. 255.
23 Beaumont Morice, celebrating his victory, expected it to 'put another nail in the coffin of the Education Act on which the battle was fought'. *The Times*, 23 August 1902.
24 Quoted in Julian Amery, *Life of Joseph Chamberlain*, London, 1951, vol. 4, p. 495.
25 Perks to Rosebery, 24 December 1902, Rosebery Papers, vol. 10,051, f. 46; minutes of a joint meeting of the legal and organizing committees, 15 December 1902, FCFC.
26 Campbell-Bannerman to Bryce, 23 September 1902, Bryce Papers (Bodleian Library, Oxford).
27 Balfour to Devonshire, 4 June 1903, quoted in B. Holland, *The Life of Spencer Compton, 8th Duke of Devonshire*, London, 1911, vol. 2, p. 308.
28 Bryce to Clifford, 2 October 1902, quoted in Sir James Marchant, *Dr John Clifford, C.H.: Life Letters, and Reminiscences*, London, 1924, pp. 123-4.
29 Minutes of the education committee, 7 April 1903, FCFC.
30 Porritt, *The Best I Remember*, London, 1922, pp. 51-2.

31 Diary entry for 17 June 1903, Viscount Gladstone Papers, BM. Add. MSS. 46,484, f. 44.
32 Diary entry for 16 July 1903, Viscount Gladstone Papers, BM. Add. MSS. 46,484, f. 49.
33 Cf. E. K. H. Jordan, *Free Church Unity: A History of the Free Church Council Movement, 1896-1941*, London, 1956, p. 104.
34 Perks to Rosebery, 23 September 1903, Rosebery Papers, vol. 10,051, ff. 134-5.
35 Diary entry for 29 September 1903, Viscount Gladstone Papers, BM. Add. MSS. 46,484, f. 53.
36 Hamilton, *Parliamentary Reminiscences and Reflections*, London, 1922, p. 317.
37 Campbell-Bannerman to Vaughan Nash, 26 September 1903 (copy), Campbell-Bannerman Papers, BM. Add. MSS. 41,237, ff. 168-70.
38 Perks to Rosebery, 21 December 1903, Rosebery Papers, vol. 10,051, ff. 171-2.
39 Perks to Rosebery, 1 April and 8 July 1904, Rosebery Papers, vol. 10,051, ff. 205-8.
40 Perks to Rosebery, 23 December 1903, Rosebery Papers, vol. 10,051, f. 173; Perks to Asquith, 23 December 1903, Asquith Papers, X, f. 118 (Bodleian Library).
41 Gladstone to Asquith, 24 December 1903, Asquith Papers, X, f. 120; Asquith to Gladstone, 27 December 1903, Viscount Gladstone Papers, BM. Add. MSS. 45,989, f. 98; Campbell-Bannerman to Bryce, 15 January 1904, Bryce Papers; Bryce to Campbell-Bannerman, 16 January 1904, Campbell-Bannerman Papers, BM. Add. MSS. 41,211, ff. 269-70; diary entry for 13 January 1904, Viscount Gladstone Papers, BM. Add. MSS. 46,484, f. 61; Gladstone to Campbell-Bannerman, 18 January 1904, Campbell-Bannerman Papers, BM. Add. MSS. 41,217, f. 82; Clifford to Bryce, 2 February 1904, Bryce Papers.
42 Diary entry for 14 March 1904, Viscount Gladstone Papers, BM. Add. MSS. 46,485, f. 3; also Herbert to Gladstone, 29 October 1903, Viscount Gladstone Papers, BM. Add. MSS. 46,026, ff. 11-12; Selbie, op. cit., pp. 185-6.
43 *Crusader*, 23 June and 7 July 1904.
44 Herbert to Gladstone, 2 February 1905, Viscount Gladstone Papers, BM. Add. MSS. 46,026, f. 103; *Christian World*, 2 February, 13 April, 1, 8 and 15 June, 13 and 20 July 1905; minutes of the general committee, 5 June 1905, FCFC.
45 Minutes of the finance and education sub-committee, 4 February 1904, and minutes of the election campaign committee, 23 September 1904 and 20 January 1905, FCFC; diary entry for 16 February 1905, Viscount Gladstone Papers, BM. Add. MSS. 46,485, f. 23.
46 Bryce to Gladstone, 27 December 1904, Viscount Gladstone Papers, BM. Add. MSS. 46,019, f. 95.
47 The words were Perks's, who reported that Joseph Compton-Rickett, Albert Spicer, Percy Bunting, Dr John Massie, Clifford, and others 'all agreed with me'. Perks to Rosebery, 1 April 1904, Rosebery Papers, vol. 10,051, ff. 207-8.
48 Porritt, *The Best I Remember*, pp. 96-7; *Christian World*, 2 and 9 March 1905.
49 Perks to Rosebery, 22 September 1905, Rosebery Papers, vol. 10,052, f. 83; *Examiner*, 10 August 1905.
50 Acland Hood to J. S. Sandars, 23 September [1905], Balfour Papers, BM. Add. MSS. 49,771.
51 Minutes of the general council, 25 September 1905, FCFC.
52 *Daily News*, 12 October 1905; Arthur Porritt, *John Henry Jowett*, London 1924,

p. 116; *Examiner*, 19 October 1905; *London* (*Whitefield's*) *Signal*, November 1905; *Crusader*, 23 November 1905.

53 *Crusader*, 26 October 1905; *Daily News*, 16 October 1905.

54 Gladstone to Campbell-Bannerman, 25 November 1905 ('secret'), Campbell-Bannerman Papers, BM. Add. MSS. 41,217, ff. 279-80; Gladstone to Hudson, 27 November 1905, Viscount Gladstone Papers, BM. Add. MSS. 46,021, f. 89.

55 Perks to Rosebery, 4 December 1905, Rosebery Papers, vol. 10,052, f. 110.

56 Perks to Campbell-Bannerman, 11 December 1905, Campbell-Bannerman Papers, BM. Add. MSS. 41,238, f. 170; *British Weekly*, 4 January 1906.

57 Grey to Perks, 18 December 1905, Perks Papers.

58 J. C. Carlile, *My Life's Little Day*, London, 1935, pp. 114-15.

59 A. K. Russell, 'The general election of 1906', Oxford D. Phil. thesis, 1962, p. 387.

60 *Free Church Yearbook, 1906*, p. 187.

61 Jones, *Three Score Years and Ten*, London, 1940, pp. 227-30; Selbie, op. cit., pp. 194-5; *Examiner*, 25 January 1906.

62 Russell, op. cit., p. 295.

63 *Free Church Yearbook, 1906*, p. 196.

64 P. F. Clarke, *Lancashire and the New Liberalism*, Cambridge, 1971, pp. 56 and 267.

65 *British Weekly*, 25 January 1906; Sir Richard Winfrey, *Leaves from My Life*, King's Lynn, 1936, p. 151; Philip, Viscount Snowden, *An Autobiography*, London, 1934, vol. 1, pp. 309-10.

66 Quoted in the *National Review*, February 1906.

67 *Daily News*, 25 November 1905; *London* (*Whitefield's*) *Signal*, January 1906; Horne to his wife, 14 January 1906, quoted in Selbie op. cit., pp. 196-7.

68 Paul Thompson, *Socialists, Liberals and Labour: the Struggle for London, 1885-1914*, London, 1967, p. 168. London Nonconformity had the further grievance of the 1903 London Education Act, which Lloyd George thought 'altogether worse than 1902'. Minutes of the education committee, 7 April 1903, FCFC.

69 *London* (*Whitefield's*) *Signal*, November 1905; *British Weekly*, 25 January 1906.

70 Porritt, *The Best I Remember*, p. 52.

71 Gladstone put each English and Welsh constituency into one of six categories: 'certain win', 'probable win', 'possible win', 'off chance', 'probable loss', or 'certain loss'. The present calculations are based on his list of 21 November 1903 (Viscount Gladstone Papers, BM. Add. MSS. 46,106, ff. 43-62), which tends to be more complete than subsequent lists and gives a better picture of the situation that prevailed when most candidates were adopted.

72 Quoted in *The Times*, 17 June 1931.

Note: The author gratefully acknowledges the support of the John Simon Guggenheim Memorial Foundation, which has made his research possible.

6

H. G. WELLS AND THE FABIAN SOCIETY

MARGARET COLE

This essay is concerned with H. G. Wells, principally as he appeared during the short years of his membership of the Fabian Society and the much-publicized row between him and the leaders of the Society, in which he was decisively defeated. Most of the socialist writers and social historians who have dealt with this struggle have accepted the episode as a clear case of good fighting evil, with Wells as the genuine and generous Radical whose ideas were shipwrecked on the reactionary rock of the Fabians, particularly Bernard Shaw, Sidney and Beatrice Webb and Edward Pease. This version of the story is far from correct. The first reason why it held currency so long is that Wells, who had become the darling of the younger Radicals when he graduated from being one of the best English writers of science fiction and novels like *Kipps* to a position as persuasive prophet of great changes in society, was very angry at his defeat (though, as he recognized years afterwards, it was largely his own silly fault) and took revenge, in the political novel called *The New Machiavelli* (1911), by a savage satire on the Webbs and their 'hard little house on the Embankment' where they ensnared and ruined honest Radical politicians. The novel was serialized also in the *English Review* and so secured its author plenty of publicity at a time when the popularity of the Webbs had sunk very low. The second reason is that Pease, who wrote the official *History of the Fabian Society*,[1] was an uncritical admirer of Webb and all his works, going so far as to admit, in an essay written after Webb's death, that he considered him to have 'a perfect character'.[2] His complacent account of what he plainly believed to be an unimportant fracas, with its reiteration of the phrase 'so the Old Gang triumphed', convinced many that it was nothing but a biased and unreliable piece of special pleading. Wells, at the end of the second of his 'prophetic' books, *Mankind in the Making*, published in 1903, well before the row began, had written this call to the generation which was coming to maturity in the years before the Great War:[3]

> Without the high resolve of youth, without the constant accession of youth, no sustained movement is possible in this world. It is to youth, therefore, that this book is finally addressed, to the adolescents, to the students, to those who are yet in the schools and who will presently come to read it, to those who, being still plastic, can understand the infinite plasticity of the world. It is those who are yet unmade who must become the makers.

He had appealed to the young generation, and, as Shaw wisely pointed out in a letter to Beatrice Webb, they rose to his appeal even if they did not carry the day for him. To understand properly, however, the real story of the dispute, which is much more interesting than the *simpliste* version, it is necessary to know something of the nature and background of the protagonists and something of the affairs and climate of the time.

The battle of H. G. Wells and the Fabians coincided nearly though not quite exactly with the years of Campbell-Bannerman's government after its huge and startling election victory at the beginning of 1906. A great deal has been written about the various issues and slogans of that election; but in sum there is little doubt that the main reason for the size of the vote was the feeling of revolt against the stale Tory government and its works, many of the voters feeling shame at the image of Britain projected during the South African war – an image not simply of an oppressor but of an *incompetent* aggressor – and of shame, also, at the revelation of poverty and preventable misery exposed in studies like Charles Booth's impressive *Life and Labour of the People of London*, coupled with an increasing sense of revolt against the traditions of repression and hypocrisy in Victorian society. Let Robert Ensor, who was himself a young Fabian at the time, bear witness:[4]

> Radicalism and socialism alike, released from the suppressions of two decades, were radiant with sudden hopes of a new heaven and a new earth. No leader not alive to that *morning glory* [my italics] could have carried the House with him; and that was where Campbell-Bannerman in his kindly and generous old age gave the parliament an incomparably better

start than the efficient but earth-bound Asquith could have done.

Ensor is good evidence of the Radicals' state of mind; and though the morning glory was to fade before very long, for the moment the hope was to convert it to high noon, and so to proceed to large-scale reorganization of society. And there was no lack of guides. Besides the group of thirty or so MPs belonging to the young Labour party, there were several Radical and/or socialist societies all equipped with programmes and busy recruiting. Even the little Fabian Society, barely recovered from the set-back which it had suffered from its indecision over the South African war and its support of the 1902–3 Education Acts, was enjoying what Mrs Sidney Webb rather patronizingly called 'a little boom', and already in its ranks was Herbert George Wells, by then a well-known writer and poised to spell out to his fellow-Fabians exactly what they ought to do.

It is nicely ironical that it was the Webbs themselves who in the early months of 1903 had recruited Wells. Beatrice seems to have been the prime mover: she had come across him at meetings of a club called the Coefficients, which for all that Wells later scorned it as a mere talking shop had then a number of well-known and intelligent persons on its membership list. She had listened to him expounding some of the ideas which he put into the first of his 'prophetic' books, *Anticipations*, which she read and found really exciting – her mind was always more imaginative than her partner's. She was also, as it happened, interested in a dispute in which Wells was currently engaged with the borough of Folkestone and the urban district of Sandgate. The question was of the distribution of powers; and Wells, generalizing (as he so often did) from his own personal experience, seized the occasion to formulate, and to expound to her, a plan for the reorganization of the whole of English local government on a regional basis. This scheme he christened, harking back to Anglo-Saxon history, the New Heptarchy. The Fabian Society subsequently endorsed the idea and planned to expound it in a series of *Fabian Tracts*; some were in fact produced and published, though the series was abandoned after the quarrel. Wells explained part of his idea to the Fabian membership in a lecture with the forbidding title, 'The Question of Scientific Administrative Areas in Relation to Municipal Undertakings', delivered, as Pease unkindly recorded, 'in a low monotonous voice addressed to a corner of the Hall'.

The Webbs would not be put off by unappetizing titles – see some of those which they chose for their own books – or by low monotonous voices. They were not, in fact, by any means always safe judges of individual personalities; it was one of their weaknesses as politicians. But at the time they were very much impressed, not only by Wells's apparent interest in the machinery of government but by his quickness of thought and power of leaping in a flash to conclusions and suggestions. They, at least Beatrice, thought he would be a valuable acquisition for the Fabian Society, in which Shaw was perhaps too much of a sceptic and iconoclast. Wells, for his part, was delighted with them. He had recovered from the unfavourable impression he had gained of the Fabians in the mid-eighties when he had attended evening lectures by Shaw, Graham Wallas, William Morris and others at Morris's Kelmscott House on Hammersmith Mall. Then he had found them a disappointing lot, Protesters rather than Planners, incapable of working out guidelines for a changeover to the profitless society which they advocated or of finding 'a competent receiver' – a phrase of which he became more and more fond – to supervise the process.[5] But when he met the Webbs again he was struck with their precision, their grasp of detail, and above all by their capacity for hard continuous work in the public interest. He accepted their invitation with genuine gratitude, not realizing what very different sorts of animal he and they had been brought up to be.

The Fabians, as Shaw many times pointed out,[6] belonged for the most part to the educated middle classes, enrolling a high proportion of professionals of one kind or another. In the very early days they shed their anarchist or, as Shaw called them, 'impossibilist' members. They were now concerned to bring about a socialist society a bit at a time, by making proposals that were practically possible and could be shown to be so by *argument*, by the marshalling of undeniable facts in cool and reasonable language. *Pas de zèle,* a hasty observer might have said of them, though not truly, for almost all of them, including Shaw himself, had plenty of zeal and were prepared to work long unpaid hours in 'speaking and debating, or in picking up social information in the most dingy and scrappy way . . . on squalid little committees and ridiculous delegations to conferences of the three tailors of Tooley Street'.[7] But they were averse to highly charged emotional appeals; they criticized one another sharply if sometimes humorously; they believed in 'the inevitability of gradualness' forty years before Sidney Webb formulated it in a presidential address to the Labour Party Conference; and they did not enrol, or after the foundation of Keir Hardie's Independent

Labour Party of 1893 even seek to enrol, any large number of the proletariat or the really downtrodden poor. They were a homogeneous group, largely London-based, with a good deal of interest in the details of London government; their approach was intellectual and altruistic.

The approach of Wells was very different. He came of the lower middle class, and of that part of it, moreover, which appeared to be sinking into the proletariat in accordance with Karl Marx's predictions. His father was an unsuccessful gardener who became an unsuccessful shopkeeper, broke his leg and lived his life out supported by Wells's mother, who had returned to domestic service as housekeeper at the big house of Up Park. An uncle was head of an unsuccessful small school; of his mother he said, not very kindly, that she was 'the kind of woman who is an incorrigibly bad cook'. His childhood home was ugly, noisy and insanitary, and his education cheap and uninspiring except for one wonderful year when as a 'teacher-in-training' at eighteen he was able to study biology at South Kensington under Huxley. He left school at the earliest legal age and became, first a very inefficient shopboy, then a not-very-good teacher. Having muddled himself into marriage with an ill-matched cousin with whom he came to have less and less in common, in 1894 he ran away from her to live with a pupil of his, Amy Catherine Robbins, who became his second wife. Very shortly afterwards, almost by chance, he leapt to fame and comparative affluence as a journalist and writer of science fiction.

This sort of background meant that Wells had very little direct knowledge of the sort of people who had built up the Fabian Society. It comes out quite plainly in the characters found in his novels. What he knows well, and can make very real to his readers, are the incompetents of society, the 'general little misfits', as he describes himself in his shopboy days, the failures, like Kipps and Mr Polly, who, nice as they are, are exploited through their own weaknesses as he and many of his friends and relations had been; and by contrast, people like the hero of *Tono-Bungay* who become suddenly well-off and well-known, as he had done. He cannot describe convincingly an ordinary employer or an ordinary workman; nor, more important for his own theories of the future, does he appear to understand the civil servant or other 'bureaucrat' who would be required in such large numbers to run the kind of society he was envisaging.

For as soon as he was both happily married and set to become quite comfortably off without having to work desperately hard – and incidentally to enjoy far better health than in his youth – his energetic mind set itself to imagining, and very soon to expounding in detail, the possible creation, speedily and with the minimum of fuss, of a society more rational, juster, more efficient and more productive than the muddle in which he had grown up. And, having thought, he wasted no time before starting to preach. His message, during the period of which I am writing, was delivered in four books, as well as incidentally in many articles and excursuses in other productions. As Desmond MacCarthy wrote of him after his death, his mind was like a cart filled with miscellaneous products, whose tailboard he would suddenly let down, overwhelming you with the load. These books were *Anticipations* (1901), *Mankind in the Making* (1903), *A Modern Utopia* (1905) and *New Worlds for Old* (1908); and we should possibly add *Ann Veronica* (1909), though that is more concerned with the social and sexual emancipation of women and so is less all-embracing than the others.

It is no use the reader expecting to find, even after careful study of these four or five books, a complete and precise definition of what Wells meant by a socialist state of society, and the means by which he proposed to attain it. Not only did his views change even in that short space of time, as they were to change again and again as he grew older, but a vision of the future, such as he expounded in *A Modern Utopia* – rather lengthily, it must be admitted – could not be expected to be quite the same as the picture drawn in *New Worlds for Old*. This last is really a giant propaganda pamphlet advocating massive immediate changes which he was just beginning to see would not be achieved through the activities of the Fabian Society. There is not, however, save for the institution of the Samurai mentioned below, any great difference between them, so one may fairly safely look in brief at the main propositions laid down in *New Worlds for Old*, and compare them with the views of the Fabians.

Wells assumed, as the basis of his new society, the communal ownership of 'the great common services of land control, mining, transit, food supply, the drink trade, force supply, and the like', this to be secured by the 'peaceful and systematic taking of them over from private enterprise' and by forbidding any new private development of the kind. Here he was broadly in line with the Fabian leadership, though inclined to go further in the list of activities suitable for *immediate* nationalization or municipalization. On the other hand, he was somewhat to the right of them – if 'right' be the proper word – in insisting on adequate compensation for those whose right to profit was thus extinguished. The Fabians, though on the whole they agreed, were a good deal more hesitant on the question of compensation versus partial confiscation. Both parties were at one in calling for scaling down what remained to the wealthy by means of taxation and inheritance duties, and both would confine future property rights to personal possessions, though Wells, rather surprisingly, was inclined to be more tender to a man's concern for the well-being of his family after his death.

This derived perhaps from Wells's strong concern with the welfare of children in general, on which, at least in 1908, he laid very much more stress than did the Fabians. He advocated, again and again, generous endowment of motherhood by money paid direct to the mother 'so long as [the child] is kept clean in a tolerable home, in good health, well taught and properly clad' – a fairly sweeping proviso. It was in this connection that he asked for a full state medical service, which suggestion was taken up by Lawson Dodd, the future treasurer of the Society, only after Wells had left it; and for a 'root and branch' reform of all education, public and private, in which subject the Fabians of the day seem to have been singularly uninterested. It may be that the Fabians – always excepting Shaw, with his denunciations of 'boy-prisons' – half-thought that all that was necessary had been secured by the Education Acts for which Sidney Webb had campaigned so strongly. It may be, also, that Webb and Shaw felt that Beatrice's work on the Poor Law Commission, which had begun sitting in December 1905, relieved other Fabians from immediate responsibility. Certainly, the *Minority Report of the Commission* when it appeared contained a great deal of what Wells had asked for, though by that time Wells was cross enough to call it a miserable hotch-potch. His own specific policies on education were not by then fully developed – his sons were perhaps not yet old enough.[8] But, in a rather vague discourse upon the need for *assuming* 'full employment' – a topic which the Fabians had scarcely discussed at all – he included an intelligent passage on the necessity, not properly realized even today, of retraining men and women whose skills and abilities have become obsolete.

This, though a small point in itself, illustrates fairly well a certain difference of emphasis and of approach between Wells and some other socialists. He insisted that any new society must be scientifically based and must always be ready to develop in the direction in which science was leading; it must never be static. But this involved, not simply a great expansion of research, of museums and libraries, etc., but, together with the enormous increase of communal services predicted, a vast army of properly trained communal servants, and what almost amounted to a caste of specialist persons to guide the whole system. These were the Samurai of *A Modern Utopia*. The idea of the Samurai, obviously, came straight from that of the Guardians in Plato's *Republic*. They were to be a dedicated order of volunteers subjected to a stern entry test and bound to adhere to a common rule which, as in the *Republic*, called for abstention from a good many things which ordinary people enjoy. They were to be committed to the many disciplines and services set out in the pages of the book in which they are described. 'Practically the whole of the responsible rule of the world is in their hands'; all the upper executive jobs are held by persons drawn by lot from their ranks. There is no need, today, to reproduce Wells's lengthy elaboration of his scheme: one need only observe that it is sketching a model for world political society – the Samurai and the Others – which would certainly not have been acceptable to the Radical democrats of his own day. Yet Sidney Webb, coining the phrase *a discreetly regulated freedom*, does not sound so very far from Wells's outlook, if we remember that the latter was writing of the future. Shaw, of course, soon went very much further than Wells in his mistrust of the political capacity of the common man.

There does not, then, appear to be a great deal of difference, so far as general propositions were concerned, between Wells and the leading Fabians of the day. Wells went into much more detail than any Fabian could be expected to subscribe to; and there was certainly food for disagreement about timing and what we now call 'priority'. But, on a general view, neither was more radical than the other.

What, then, *was* the difference between them? What gave Wells his very strong appeal to the young? What was it all about? It is easier to try and find, first, the answer to the second question, which is twofold. It lies in Wells's enormous and vivid imagination, and his eager anticipation of the possibilities opened up by scientific discovery – the great debt which he owed, both in thought and in actual concrete earning capacity, to the years he spent at South Kensington. One might also include his impatience, a characteristic which has appealed to youth in any and every generation; though this accounts more for his failure than for his appeal.

Everyone who reads or re-reads Wells today, bearing in mind the time which has elapsed since the books I have mentioned were written, must be astonished to discover the wide sweep of his imagination, the extent to which he anticipated changes which did not come about for many years, the uses to which scientific discovery could be put, and the effect which it could have on human conditions. Even where his vision was wrong or inadequate – and no prophet can be right all the time – his hearers were not to know that, only to feel the burning inspiration of what he had to suggest to them. Without going into full detail, which would take up many pages, since at that stage in his life Wells could hardly open his mouth without making some futuristic suggestion, we can look for a while at a few of the sparks of both kinds which he threw out. Many of them came from the first book of the series, *Anticipations*, of which he wrote in his autobiography, 'I became my own first disciple.' It is in that passage that he demands – looking well forward to our own time – the creation of professorships of human ecology, of which he would gladly have held the first.

His primary emphasis was first upon the need for a modern utopia, whatever it was called, to be *flexible* and not static, and open to continuous development as the economic and biological conditions changed. 'The statesman's conception of social organisation', he wrote in a singularly perceptive sentence, 'is no longer stability but growth'. His second assumption was that this made imperative continuous planning, in the first instance for the nation, meaning Britain as a whole, and in the later stages for the world as a whole – 'no less than the whole planet will suffice'. He never quite faced the practical difficulties involved in combining these two concepts, only murmuring in a sort of aside that 'Utopia will be saturated with consideration' – as indeed has proved to be the case in many modern societies which are very far from Utopia. Furthermore, he fully grasped, at a time when the petrol-driven engine was only in its infancy, the fundamental importance of what he called 'locomotion', what we should now call transport and communication. In a brief but pregnant account of railway history he pointed out that the development of locomotion had been 'completely independent of most of the other great movements', leaving the narrow-gauge railway lines cramped by 'the ghost of a superseded horse'. He foresaw the coming of the motorized truck, the motor-bus, with the privately owned motor car covering *three hundred miles in a day* (!) and proceeding 'with a pleasant hum' along segregated arteries, very wide, one-way, and beautifully engineered, crossing one another by similarly well-engineered bridges. For those unable to use cars or buses, Wells envisaged their own traffic facilities – tramways which will be 'a triumph of design', and walkways moving at differen speeds so as to make it easy to progress by stages from the very slow to the speediest track. Railways, he assumed, would still carry the major part of the bulk traffic in goods, but with reasonable foresight he warned that 'the wider the affluent arteries become, the more terrible the battle of the traffic' between the huge modern cities, up to 100 miles in radius though far better built and developed, which he foresaw. This would seem to be today's epigram that 'a motorway is the shortest route between two traffic jams', enunciated seventy years ago.

Telephones he thought would develop rapidly, notwithstanding 'that unmitigated public nuisance, the political control of our post office by non-dismissible civil servants' appointed very young. This rather characteristic grumble of his was to be partly met by the reorganization of the Post Office more than half a century later. It is a little odd that radio, so soon to catch Crippen on the high seas, never seems to have attracted his attention. The Babble Machines in *The Sleeper Wakes*, bellowing out announcements in public places are only huge gramophones centrally connected; and even after the war all he could say about radio was that it ought to supersede incompetent school teachers. On transport by sea and air his predictions were less happy. He had nothing particular to say about ocean-going ships, and he believed that submarines would suffocate their crews and founder at sea. As for aeroplanes, though he thought that perhaps '*before* 1950 a successful aeroplane will have soared and come home', he wrote in *Anticipations* 'I do not believe that aeronautics will ever come into play as a serious modification of transport.' Civilian transport, that is; under war conditions things might be very different.

Reflection on the possibilities of large-scale war, which Wells at that time hoped would not come about, nevertheless stimulated his imagination to a quite exceptional degree, as can be seen from the following vivid picture of, not the war which came in 1914, but of the other which was to follow it twenty-five years later.

> Once the command of the air is obtained by one of the contending armies, the war must become a conflict between a seeing host and one that is blind . . . the moral effect of this predominance will be enormous. All over the losing country, not simply at his frontier but everywhere, the victor will soar. . . . By day the victor's aeroplanes will sweep down upon the apparatus of all sorts in the adversary's rear, and will drop explosives and incendiary matter upon them, so that no apparatus or camp or shelter will any longer be safe. At night his high-floating searchlights will go to and fro. . . . And now

men on the losing side will thank God for the reprieve of a pitiless wind, for lightning, thunder and rain.[9]

'Locomotion' and war were only two of the many fields in which Wells's lively mind played its torch around, giving much delight to his audiences, and displaying the same kind of mixture of prophecy, sense and undoubted error – and also an individual quirkiness, a propensity to hope for the banning or disappearance of anything which he personally found disagreeable, which might have given rise to sharp criticism but was in fact generally received with tolerant amusement as indicating that whatever he might say about the inescapable necessity of firm planning on a wide scale, free play was to be allowed for at least his own individuality. Playing cards, public sport, horses, household pets, patent medicines, polishing of boots, mowing of lawns, ornamental 'bedding-out' of flowers and plants, individual private kitchens, the 'time-wasting antics' of the House of Commons, female fashions and 'bizarre contours' in the female sex – all these he hoped never to see in his new-made world. He also combined a confident trust in his elite Samurai with an equal mistrust of all monarchs and the trappings of monarchy. 'So long as you suffer a man to call himself your shepherd,' he summed it up at a later date, '*sooner or later you will find a crook around your ankle.*'

But he had a good many more positive and pregnant suggestions to make: that there should be a wide variety of 'marriage relationships', for example; that the processes of education should be reformed so that 'cycle-menders' would develop into 'educated mechanics' rather than old-style craftsmen, and be better and more rounded beings. He thought, and was to think more fiercely in his later years, that Marx's theories of class were out-of-date (and Marx himself a dyspeptic bearded old horror) and that society would make progress by distinguishing types of mind and ability rather than economic and social classes – therein getting fairly near to Michael Young's conception of a meritocracy. He envisaged the growth of a great variety of 'non-productive but active men who are engaged in more or less necessary operations of organisation, promotion, advertisement and trade. There are the business managers, public and private, the political organisers, brokers, commission agents, the varying grades of financiers down to the more greedy camp-followers of finance, the gamblers pure and simple, and the great body of their dependent clerks, typewriters, and assistants.' All these, he asserts in a sweeping condemnation, are concerned mainly with the shifting, uncertain prejudices and emotions of the general mass – and so will find themselves in opposition to the technologists, the engineers and their kin, who are working consciously or unconsciously for growth and the improvement of civilization. As to agriculture, he finds a population of small agriculturists as hopelessly immoveable a thing as possible. He foresees – and who shall question his foresight? – an enormous system of index cards for everyone, classifying an incessant stream of information – '*organised clairvoyance*' he calls this system and seems to regard it as a pleasing prospect.

On the social side of civil life, he is unquestioningly in the permissive camp: he writes that 'vice and depravity, in every form that is not absolutely penal, will be practised in every grade of magnificence and condoned'. It is not perfectly clear what the last sentence (quoted from *Anticipations*) means; but it certainly does not mean harsh treatment for those whose depravity is not 'condoned'. For in *A Modern Utopia* we find the rather charming suggestion that those who are quite unable to conform to society's view of proper conduct should be banished in perpetuity to one of a set of remote Alsatias where they could live without further penalty with their mental kin, for example in the Island of Incurable Cheats, with exiles from Park Lane and Petticoat Lane living cheek by jowl.

There are only two cold-water comments which need to be made on this cornucopia of ideas: the first, and much the less important, being that the whole conception, and the assumed scale of values, are predominantly middle-class – and educated middle-class at that. This fact becomes apparent at a dozen or more points, especially, perhaps, in the frequent references to the need for *quiet* living conditions, for efficient, plentiful and courteous communal service, for all the amenities usually associated with a first-class club (see the description of the Modern Utopian train, with its shelves of books, its bathrooms, hairdresser, etc.); and the confident remark that the more intelligent will be a very *moral* people, linked by 'great and sober papers' like (of all things) the *British Medical Journal*. Though this is not a very large matter, it does at least raise some queries as to what the millions, given the freedom on which Wells so strongly insists, and the economic security which he almost casually predicates, will in practice ask of their new society. The second criticism, however, is more serious.

Wells's vision of future society was not democratic but élitist. More than that, it was highly Malthusian, quasi-imperialist, and racialist. While rejecting, partly on individualist grounds, the proposals of the eugenists of his day for the 'scientific' breeding of human populations, and making, as we have seen, vast claims for the most up-to-date and scientific treatment of children from the moment of birth, he yet swallowed whole the thesis of Malthus in the *Essay on Population*, and further declared fiercely that[10]

> it has become apparent that whole masses of human population are, as a whole, inferior in their claim upon the future, to other masses, that they cannot be given opportunities or trusted with power as the superior people are trusted, that their characteristic weaknesses are contagious and detrimental in the civilising fabric, and that their range of incapacity tempts and demoralises the strong. To give them equality is to sink to their level, to protect and cherish them is to be swamped in their fecundity.

One would like to think that this outburst was a single aberration. But it was not. In the preceding chapter of the same book, Wells in the course of an attack on nationalism predicted the emergence of a white English-speaking federation centred in North America which would [my italics] '*protect or dominate or actively administer* most or all of the non-white states of the present British Empire, *and in addition much of the South and Middle Pacific, the East and West Indies, the rest of America, and the larger part of Black Africa*'.[11] This was going much further than Shaw, impatient of small nationalities and of the attempt to push the Fabian Society into pro-Boer proclamations, went a year or so later in the Tract *Fabianism and the Empire.* Wells emphasized it by writing, in the final pages of *Anticipations.*[12]

> And for the rest, those swarms of black and brown, and dirty-white and yellow people, who do not come into the new needs of efficiency? . . . They will have to go . . . So far as they fail to develop sane, vigorous, and distinctive personalities for the greater world of the future, it is their portion to die out and disappear.

Radicalism, indeed! but it was not this racial-imperialism that he was trying to force the Fabians to swallow. It may be, indeed, that he had half forgotten it himself. In *A Modern Utopia* both nationalism and colour have ceased to have any relevance, and it is not mentioned in *New Worlds for Old.*

What, then, *was* the quarrel about? Essentially, it was about style –

and method. After a couple of years, Wells had, it seems, become thoroughly *bored* with the Fabian Society, its membership and its activities. We do not know much about what he was doing, but in February of 1906 – it should have been a month earlier but was postponed owing to the general election – he read to a general meeting of members a paper entitled 'The Faults of the Fabian', which made the crowded gathering gasp. For 'the Fabian' seemed, in Mr Wells's eyes, to have scarcely anything but faults.

The Society had had a good past, he admitted; but in the present it was no good. It was small, shabbily poor and collectively inactive; it lived in a dismal basement, tested applicants savagely instead of welcoming them in, made them sign a stupidly drafted Basis of Faith, and when they had signed set them to rubbishy tasks like writing letters to the local press. Most irritating of all its defects was the tendency of its members to have private jokes: their supreme delight was to *giggle*, and they permeated English society with their ideas about as much as a mouse may be said to permeate a cat. They would not get anywhere, he went on to say, unless they changed their mode of life altogether, went all out to get a large membership, taxed members in proportion to their incomes, moved to 'a light, beautiful and hopeful office', engaged a large, paid staff, organized a vast number of branches and published a wide selection of brilliant brightly written pamphlets. The meeting became very excited; the Executive committee, keeping its head, suggested the appointment of a special committee to discuss ways and means of increasing 'the scope, influence, income and activities of the Society', and proposed that Wells should nominate anyone he chose, 'up to a reasonable number', to sit on that committee with its own nominees. Wells refused to co-operate unless he were allowed to choose the Executive's representatives as well as his own, and the Executive, after a little protest, gave way. Wells then departed on a lecture tour of the United States, leaving the special committee to deliberate without him, though he had agreed to serve on it. The other members were Mrs Bernard Shaw, G. R. S. Taylor, and the Rev. Stewart Headlam from the Executive, and from outside, Sydney Olivier, a past member of the Executive, Dr Stanton Coit, W. Arthur Colegate, Dr Haden Guest, Mrs Pember Reeves, and Mrs Wells, who acted as secretary.

By October Wells was back, and the committee had finished its labours, producing an expansionist report which said much the same things as Wells had said in his paper, though of course, being the work of a committee, it expressed them in much less lively language.

It was printed and circulated to all members with a reply from the Executive written by Bernard Shaw. In this reply Shaw in effect asked the special committee to be its age and face the facts of life. The Executive, he said, welcomed criticism and would endeavour to make the Society more efficient, broaden the membership, and remove unnecessary restrictions. As to the more colourful recommendations, they would be only too delighted to publish brilliant new Fabian Tracts, as soon as the brilliant writers turned up to write them; and to acquire handsome new offices and a large staff, as soon as somebody could tell them where the money was to come from. The two reports were then discussed at various meetings, of which the most significant was that held on 14 December 1906 when Wells in effect turned an amendment supporting the special committee's report into a motion of no confidence in the Executive. Shaw, late in the evening, replied in a Second Reading type of speech. The result was a foregone conclusion. Let Wells speak for himself:[13]

> On various occasions in my life it has been borne in on me, in spite of a stout internal defence, that I can be quite remarkably silly and inept; but no part of my career rankles so acutely in my memory with the conviction of bad judgement, gusty impulse and real inexcusable vanity, as that storm in the Fabian tea-cup . . . the crowded meetings in Cliffords Inn – the old radical veterans and the bubbling new young people; the fine speeches of Shaw; Sidney Webb with his head down talking fast with a slight lisp . . . myself speaking haltingly on the verge of the inaudible, addressing my tie through a cascade moustache that was no sort of help at all, correcting myself as though I were a manuscript under treatment, making ill-judged departures into parenthesis.

In fine, he was nowhere near up to Shaw's fighting weight in a debate, even when he had more right on his side than on this occasion. As Shaw said, 'he annihilated himself', and withdrew his amendment to save himself from being badly beaten. In March 1907, the Fabian membership, still registering belief in his ideas though less in his methods, elected him to the Executive, in a very high poll, fourth on the list below Shaw, Webb and Pease. He was elected again in the following year; but even though the enlarged Executive, which contained members from both camps cheerfully collaborating, had put into effect several of the minor changes for which he had asked originally, he liked the Society no better than before. 'Wizened already, though not old', he called the body in which he had once hoped to find 'the beginnings of an order akin to the Samurai'. He attended committee meetings rarely, and in September 1908 sent his resignation to *Fabian News* in a muddled letter whose clearest sentence said that the opportunity for propaganda to the English middle classes was now over.

So the persistent advocate of socialist planning marched angrily out of the only group of socialist planners available at the time because he didn't like their faces – or, to put it more solemnly, because he could not manage to work with them. It did not make the breach any more friendly that he underlined, as it were, the difference between his way of life and that of most of them by running off and living for a while with the daughter of two prominent Fabians. But the breach itself was no isolated action. In later years he resigned, just as hurriedly and just as indignantly, from the Labour party, the League of Nations Union, and other less impressive organizations. He was fundamentally a natural anarchist who, while calling loudly for a Plan, was constitutionally incapable of the kind of consistent and considerate collaboration with others without which no planning is practicable. Hence he was driven back to belief in what he called the Open Conspiracy – a kind of cosmic movement of the minds of all intelligent persons which would force them jointly to create a socialist utopia without being at any time fully aware of what they were doing. This may be utopia, in the true sense; nevertheless, it enabled him to keep his mind free of the web of dogmatic detail in which so many groups trying to work out plans for the future have entangled themselves, to remain an inspiration – and a romantic.

For it seems undeniable that the intellectuals whom we have been looking at, whether they thought of themselves as advocating slow changes or fast changes, were at heart romantics as much as William Morris – who did in fact think that his own utopia would be preceded by a not-very-well-realized civil war. They had experienced, in England, domestic quiet for so long. As Chesterton, in some ways more realist than any of them, said of a minor Tory politician, 'From his first hour, in his expensive cot, He never saw the tiniest viscount shot.' They believed, all of them, that reason, argument, combining with the Spirit of Progress, sooner or later (in Wells's mind probably sooner!) would carry the day. So to us, who know what was coming to them, their discussions and antagonisms are bound to have something of the airborne quality of sixth-form debate; but this does not mean that their fundamental desires have any less validity for today.

NOTES

1 E. R. Pease, *History of the Fabian Society*, London, 1916, revised edition, 1925, reprinted, 1963.
2 E. R. Pease, 'Webb and the Fabian Society', in Margaret Cole (ed.), *The Webbs and their Work*, London, 1949, pp. 17-26.
3 H. G. Wells, *Mankind in the Making*, London, 1903.
4 R. C. K. Ensor, *England: 1870-1914*, Oxford, 1936, p. 391.
5 Wells, *Experiments in Autobiography*, London, 1934, pp. 238 ff. It should be noted, however, that this book was published nearly fifty years after the event and Wells's memories have a good deal of hindsight about them.
6 Notably in *The Fabian Society: What it has done and How it has done it*, Fabian Tract no. 41, 1892; and in the Introduction to *Essays in Fabian Socialism*, London, 1932; where Tract no. 41 is reprinted with its more familiar title, *The Early History of the Fabian Society*.
7 *Essays in Fabian Socialism*, London, 1932, p. 145.
8 See *Joan & Peter*, London, 1918, for what Wells really wanted and how he failed to get it.
9 Wells, *Anticipations*, London, 1901, pp. 195-6.
10 Ibid., p. 289.
11 Ibid., p. 261.
12 Ibid., p. 37.
13 *Experiments in Autobiography*, p. 660.

7

SOCIALISM AND PROGRESSIVISM IN THE POLITICAL THOUGHT OF RAMSAY MACDONALD

RODNEY BARKER

Ramsay MacDonald has been accused of many things, but seldom of being a Radical. Put simply in these terms, the description is absurd since what distinguished him amongst the Labour pragmatists and Lib-Labs of the prewar Parliamentary Labour party was his possession of a distinctive socialist rhetoric and vision. His skilful manipulation of its resonances gave him a special place within the new party and enabled him to give some sense of identity to a body which would otherwise have been fragmented and incoherent. It was natural that when W. T. Stead published his series of *Coming Men on Coming Questions*, MacDonald should be asked to write on the Labour party, that he should write on *Socialism* in 1907 for Smeaton's *Social Problems* series, and on the *Socialist Movement* in 1911 for the Home University Library. He was, as Hardie flatteringly put it, 'the biggest intellectual asset which the Socialist movement had in this country today'.[1] He was the man who, *par excellence*, spoke for the new party and the peculiar beliefs associated with it, and he was recognized both within it and outside it as being distinguished by this special position: 'when the man in the street thought Socialism', as Elton put it, 'he inevitably thought MacDonald'.[2]

Yet if it would be perverse to view MacDonald as a Radical, there is still something to be gained from beginning an examination of the political arguments he wielded by looking at what he owed to that form of Radicalism which its exponents variously called 'Social Radicalism' or 'New Liberalism', and to progressivism, its broader context, and by examining how he exploited his inheritance, and how he marked himself off from it. Such an inquiry is required both because MacDonald's political beginnings lay as much in Radicalism and progressivism as in socialism and because progressive Liberalism and socialism were not at the time separated from one another with the simplicity and clarity with which they have retrospectively been segregated.

MacDonald's eclectic political experience reflected that of the party he was to lead. As a young man in Lossiemouth in the 1880s he seems to have been involved in the campaigns of two Liberal parliamentary candidates, one a Chamberlainite Radical, the other a home ruler who advocated the payment of MPs, reform of the land laws, free education, and one man one vote. In 1885 MacDonald joined the Bristol branch of the Social Democratic Federation and became its librarian, and in London the following year he joined the Fabian Society. In 1888 he was honorary secretary of the Scottish Home Rule Association, and became private secretary to Thomas Lough, Liberal candidate for West Islington. Lough's chief interest was Irish affairs, but he later declared his enthusiasm for the Newcastle programme and for what he called 'labour reform'.[3] In 1892 MacDonald himself made preliminary moves in the direction of a parliamentary candidature in Dover under the title 'Labour'. In 1894 he joined the Independent Labour party, and the following year, having failed to secure Liberal nomination, contested Southampton as an independent labour candidate. In the mid-1890s he was active in the progressive Rainbow Circle, and by 1898 in the Ethical Movement. With the formation of the Labour Representation Committee in 1900, he became its secretary, and in 1911 was elected chairman of its parliamentary party.

The context of MacDonald's political activities was not socialist but progressive. His encounters with Radicalism and socialism did not involve mutually exclusive sympathies, for although differences were accepted between them, and between Liberal and Labour, it was possible to view them as all, or potentially all, part of a single broad progressive movement. Appealing to the electors of Southampton in 1895, whilst describing the departure of his trust in the Liberal party, MacDonald boasted that he had ten years previously in Scotland assisted a Radical candidate 'against a Whig landlord'. He complained, not of progressive politics, but of 'the good faith and soundness of old progressive politicians'. The electors of Southampton were not convinced, and he wrote dismally to Herbert Samuel of the obviously parlous state of 'the party of progressive ideas'.[4]

Just what sort of a party he thought this was – and it was considered a party, not a Party – is revealed in his association with the

Rainbow Circle. This group encompassed a variety of opinions of a general progressive bent and would, in the words of a preliminary memorandum signed by MacDonald, William Clarke, Herbert Burrows and J. A. Hobson, amongst others,[5]

> provide a rational and comprehensive view of political and social progress, leading up to a consistent body of political and economic doctrine which could be ultimately formulated in a programme of action, and in that form provide a rallying point for social reformers, so much needed in the present chaotic state of opinion.

This rallying point would constitute a 'New Radicalism', and many members of the group were quite content with the term 'New Liberalism' as a sufficient description of its character. Though to at least one of his colleagues in the circle MacDonald appeared more of 'an independent radical with Socialist sympathies', he seems to have been happy to regard himself as part of its progressive consensus. When it was decided to 'propagate those doctrines that were held in common',[6] MacDonald was secretary of the venture, aptly titled the *Progressive Review*. The journal, MacDonald informed his colleagues, would provide a forum of debate 'to the progressive movement in all its aspects' and the unsigned editorial articles 'will not so much represent the opinions of a writer as the ideas of a school'.[7] What 'the ideas of a school' were was illustrated in the first number of the review. Readers were told of the need to synthesize progressive forces and Liberal politics, and of the necessity for a positive interpretation of Liberalism, in terms not of the absence of restraint but of the presence of opportunity. Broad sympathy was expressed both for 'social radicalism' and for 'experimental collectivism'. The review was to investigate[8]

> how far, how fast, in what directions, and by what instruments, the public may rightly assert its paramount interest in and authority over agriculture, the railways, banking, and the other foundations of industry without impairing the effective stimulus of private skill and enterprise.

For Herbert Samuel, who was a member of the Rainbow Circle, the purpose of the review was to prevent a Labour–Liberal split which would aid the Conservatives, and 'to forestall such a disruption of the progressive forces in British politics'. Its penultimate issue contained an article by Clement Edwards proposing railway nationalization as a means of securing harmony between, amongst others, the Liberals and 'the great Collectivist Labour element'.[9]

The Rainbow Circle was only one forum for MacDonald's involvement with the movement of progressive opinion of the 1890s. From 1898 he was active in the Ethical Movement, a late Victorian attempt to translate the moral purposes of evangelicalism in a manner which freed them from a Christianity which was unacceptable without losing a respectability which was essential. MacDonald joined J. A. Hobson and Dr Stanton Coit, one of the leaders and founders of the movement in England, in signing the manifesto of the Society of Ethical Propagandists which aimed at promoting 'a fully conscious recognition among Labour men of the moral implications of their economic revolt'.[10] His participation in the movement allowed him to develop the blend of civic concern, political radicalism, and moral exhortation which was his particular style. MacDonald was fluent in translating religious sentiments into secular messages. He told an audience in 1913 that the decline in chapel attendance need not alarm them, for outside the churches and chapels,[11]

> in great secular movements, in movements that are independent of what we would call organized Christianity, there is a life of hope, of aspiration, of belief, of faith that holds up even higher than ever the flag of Christian fellowship and of Christian belief.

On that occasion he modestly refrained from identifying these great movements, but with other audiences, he was less reticent: 'the individualist morality of evangelicism is the basis of the social morality of socialism'.[12]

The Ethical Movement encompassed an even greater variety of opinion than the Rainbow Circle, ranging from Bernard Bosanquet who occupied its staider suburbs, to J. A. Hobson in its wilder fringes. The variety of advanced thought, and the diversity of progressivism, presented several claimants for leadership. The chief contenders were the New Liberals, at a political level attempting to ally the movement for labour representation with their party, and at an intellectual level trying to secure the position of Radical sentiments in the vanguard of progressivism. R. B. Haldane hoped that socialism could be incorporated as a kind of progressive ginger group, and the two strains came especially close together in the efforts of C. P. Scott in Manchester, where a political effort to create a progressive party based on a Liberal–Labour *rapproche-*

ment was matched in the columns of the *Manchester Guardian* by L. T. Hobhouse's interpretation of a Liberalism appropriate to a collectivist age.[13] Hobhouse recognized that his views were sufficiently different from those of most of his party, to be surprised when they did not disqualify him as hopelessly socialistic.[14] But he recognized the need to describe the new emphasis on social reform in a way which pinpointed its liberal character, and marked it off clearly and unequivocally from socialism. The idea of Liberal progressivism represented a desire to establish the broadest possible electoral alliance under the Liberal aegis, to utilize labour representation and head off any challenge it might pose to the traditional Liberal appeal to working-class voters, to provide an account of policy which would justify and explain new directions in terms of both old principles and new aspirations, and to distinguish socialism from Liberalism in a way that made the former either an aberration or an error.

But the claim which the New Liberalism presented was equally a threat to the elucidation of a credible version of socialism. In Hobhouse and Hobson it had formidable propagandists who could not only resist the claims of socialism but oust socialism from any serious position in the progressive movement of ideas. Hobson's tactic was to swallow socialism whole, spitting out the bad bits, and incorporating what was left in social radicalism. Reflecting on the general increase in the role of the state in promoting the well-being of its citizens, he commented, 'such measures and the policy of public finance which they involve are correctly designated as "socialistic" in their character'. But he distinguished between 'practicable Socialism' which was a kind of 'Socialism in Liberalism', and 'full or theoretic' Socialism. The former[15]

> aims primarily not to abolish the competitive system, to socialize all instruments of production, distribution, and exchange, and to convert all workers into public employees – but rather to supply all workers at cost price with all the economic conditions requisite to the education and employment of their personal powers for their personal advantage and enjoyment.

Hobhouse was less inclined than Hobson to draw subtle distinctions. At times he was prepared simply to include socialism as a camp follower, even perhaps as an ally:[16]

> The Liberal stands for emancipation and is the inheritor of a long tradition of men who have fought for liberty, who have

> found law or government or society crushing human development, repressing originality, searing conscience. Against this repression the Liberal is for the unimpeded development of human faculty as the mainspring of progress. The Socialist, or if the vaguer term be preferred, the Collectivist, is for the solidarity of society. He emphasises mutual responsibility, the duty of the strong to the weak. His watchwords are co-operation and organization. The two ideals as ideals are not conflicting but complementary.

And if they could be complementary, then a form of Liberalism might be possible which incorporated the better part of socialism: 'Socialism has many meanings, and it is possible that there should be a Liberal Socialism, as well as a Socialism that is illiberal.' Illiberal socialism included 'mechanical' and 'official' socialism, which were spat out, like Hobson's 'theoretic' brand.[17] MacDonald, and his political aspirations, were in danger of becoming the pip in the New Liberal orange.

The Liberal bid for the leadership of the progressive movement thus had two aspects: the patronage and assimilation of labour representation, and the intellectual hegemony of social radicalism. From 1895, when he had contested Southampton as 'independent labour' candidate, MacDonald concentrated his efforts for progressivism and socialism in the field of independent labour representation. This was in the first place a tactical decision, rather than a choice of principles or programme. His ILP endorsement only followed a failure to secure Liberal approval and he could still write jokingly at about this time, 'Socialism might inspire me were it not for Socialists'.[18] The labour tactic was no more than a tactic, the socialism a tentative gloss on progressivism. Two kinds of distinction therefore need to be made: between electoral action through the Liberal party or by independent labour candidatures, and between the Liberal and socialist versions of progressivism. There was no necessary coincidence between tactical and intellectual positions. As M. A. Hamilton put it, 'in these years Socialists still believed in the Liberal Party – mainly because, politically, there was nothing else to believe in'.[19] But if social radicalism, the New Liberalism, or Liberal progressivism on the one hand, and socialism on the other, were differing emphases in a common frame of mind, and if there were those, like Hobhouse or Hobson, who were ably campaigning to secure priority and leadership for the former, then socialism either had to give way or assert its own special claims.

In an attempt to make this assertion in an article published in the *Nineteenth Century* in January 1899, Keir Hardie and MacDonald sought to create an explanation of the state and direction of English politics which would both vindicate the claims of socialism to be the true champion of the progressive cause and establish the special position of some form of independent labour representation as the political vehicle for this championship. Clearly they could not argue that in terms of actual proposals the Liberal party did not contain at least the hopes of progress. Their own proposals in the article were hardly such as to mark them off as revolutionary or even as very different: abolition of the House of Lords; an eight-hour day; nationalization of railways, canals, and mining royalties; taxation of ground rents; and a special tax on wealth to be used to finance a scheme of old-age pensions. It was appropriate to argue therefore that though progressive ideas might be found within the Liberal party, the character and spirit of the party were such as to give them no lasting prospect there. The old parties had fulfilled their purpose, and though there might be intimations of the future in both of them, these new intellectual stirrings could not flourish in old bodies. The New Liberalism could not grow in a party whose 'day of historical fitness had passed away'. What was needed therefore was to 'form a new party from the sympathetic elements of both the existing camps'. Those readers who could not guess which party this might be were not left in suspense for very long. 'The Independent Labour Party is in the true line of the progressive apostolic succession. It alone is able to interpret the spirit of the time.' This was not the rhetoric of revolution, but of rebellion. Socialism was being used not to supplant Liberalism, let alone to replace progressivism, but to seize the leadership of the progressive cause. The special claim of Liberalism to have fathered the new intellectual mood was countered by the assertion that both the old parties contained sympathizers. No attempt was made to criticize Liberalism or the New Liberalism. On the contrary, it was argued that they led naturally into socialism and that socialism was worthy of support from their advanced supporters. The unoriginality of the actual legislative proposals put forward by Hardie and MacDonald thus became an advantage in the attempt to tap the forces of Liberalism, since socialists were not threatening to do anything that Liberals might not well have done themselves. The proposal for a statutory eight-hour day was supported by the modest argument that,[20]

In this again we are in the apostolic succession and can claim no

> more originality than that of having seen an underlying philosophy in a series of somewhat disconnected attempts that reformers have been compelled by circumstances to make in the past, and of applying that philosophy to the questions of the present day.

One theme of MacDonald's political argument as it had emerged by the end of the 1890s was thus the attempt to establish socialism as the vanguard of progressivism. The case was well made, but the rival claimant was supported with equal ability and, after the general election of 1906, was in a position to give legislative evidence of the soundness of its case. Hobson was able to argue, in terms strikingly like those employed by Hardie and MacDonald ten years earlier, that the New Liberalism would arise when Liberals reflected on their achievements, grasped the principles underlying them, and then used those principles to guide and inspire further advances.[21] The argument was particularly challenging at a time when the Labour party had established an encouraging toehold in Parliament. A firm lead to progressivism from the Liberal party might either make Labour superfluous or assimilate it. Neither of these alternatives was attractive. The dilemma was highlighted by remarks such as those of Arthur Henderson who asked an audience in 1909 how they could go on fighting 'a Government that has passed such a great social reform'.[22] It was necessary to gain widespread currency for the belief that the[23]

> Socialist idea of the use of wealth, of the position of classes in society, of the relation between the individual and the community, is the only possible basis for a progressive party in an epoch when a nation is solving the problems of wealth distribution, communal responsibility, and social morality.

This necessity provides one of the two keys to the role of MacDonald's socialism. It has been customary to dismiss his political writings as either mere verbiage or calculated duplicity. The reasons for this are familiar: MacDonald was the man who betrayed the party in 1931, and as an increasingly overburdened scapegoat has been loaded with the responsibility for all Labour's failures before that date and even for some of them thereafter. Those who have commented on his political arguments have tended either to dismiss him as an empty windbag and to throw up their hands with incredulity that the party took him seriously; or to see him as insincere, a man who 'never really accepted the Socialist faith';[24] or to treat his political arguments as a diagnosis of the sickness of politics and society and a prescribed course of treatment which, being incorrect, led to the continuing ill-health of the patient and the unimpressive career of his medical advisers. Part of what is assumed here is no more than that politicians are concerned to persuade. But a further assumption underlies these criticisms: that when MacDonald wrote about socialism he was engaged in more than simple political persuasion. He is taken to have philosophical aspirations, and to be providing an analysis of the nature and development of society, state, and economy from which a guide to both strategy and tactics could be and was deduced. This view can gain some support from his own writings. The socialist, he said, 'is like a man in a tangled wood' of perplexing problems and idiosyncratic situations. But he is 'guided all the time by a compass and a general map of the country he is traversing. The others are like the same man similarly beset, but without compass or map.'[25] But the writings of other English politicians have not usually been accorded such lofty status, and the very scorn with which MacDonald's critics have dismissed his performance may suggest that he never really occupied such a position, and that his arguments are better seen in more commonplace terms.

There is a sense in which MacDonald's contribution was in the sphere of myth. It contained an account which justified, sustained, and encouraged activity rather than precisely defining or guiding it. It served rather 'as the orthodox expression of revolt, and as a serviceable cry, than as a well-considered programme of reform'.[26] The importance of this mythical, because persuasive rather than prescriptive, element in MacDonald's work is perhaps some explanation of the vigour with which he attacked Georges Sorel. Sorel's use of the myth of the general strike came at times very close to MacDonald's use of socialism. When MacDonald complained that the general strike 'may never really happen, but it will be the delusion which will be the cause of whatever does happen'[27] he might have been talking about arguments nearer home. He himself described socialism as a historical goal to be slowly pursued, not a policy to be immediately implemented.

MacDonald was well aware of the mythical elements in political argument, of the way in which rhetoric could serve to enhance the sense of identity and direction. Writing to Enid Stacy in the summer of 1894 he said of the ILP: 'the socialist conversion was not primary . . . but secondary, as a necessity imposed upon the new party to find a sufficiently ample basis for independent existence'.[28] 'Apocalyptic visions as an impetus to effort' had their place in the early days of a movement. Even the more mundane work of organization was sustained by 'a faith in eternal purposes'.[29] It was the power of words, phrases, ideas, to create effects quite distinct from their simple literal meaning which led him to attack the 'draughts of intoxicating strength . . . borrowed from Hegel through Marx'.[30] There could be no rival myth.

The function of MacDonald's political writings and speeches was to give the new party, and the socialism with which it was associated, a vivid sense of identity, to distinguish socialism from other forms of progressivism, and to show, at the same time, how it incorporated everything that was best within them, that it was the truest form of progressivism, and its vanguard. In terms of actual achievements this was clearly impossible. The Parliamentary Labour party was not distinctive in any way flattering to itself and in terms of legislative achievements and ambitions was little more than a diminutive shadow of the Liberals. There was a need for an account of its character and eschatology that would give it an identity which its behaviour denied it. This identity had to be one that would attract and encourage all the party's supporters, a task which, if anything, became more difficult as the numbers of MPs grew. The problem that MacDonald and Hardie had faced on behalf of the ILP became more complex when taken up for the Labour party. Labour had always been ideologically heterogeneous, and the decision of the miners' MPs to adhere to it, whilst increasing its parliamentary strength, hardly helped its political coherence. Both as a political myth and as a rhetorical umbrella, MacDonald's account of socialism was admirably suited to this situation.

The image which he created consisted not of an argument or an analysis – though it often appeared to be this – as much as of a series of impressions and invocations. This image of socialism as the rational co-ordination of the life of society, the full assertion of public rights, and the ending of private and discordant privilege, was offered in order to justify the socialist claim to speak for labour and the labour claim to the political leadership of progressivism. The argument was initially a negative one. The Liberals did not or could not, as a party, understand and promote the interests of the working man: 'The wants of Labour were ill understood in Parliament street.'[31] Consequently labour required its own representatives who would serve its interests, but who would do so in the light of a full understanding of the national interest and of the growth of the whole society: 'An infusion of labour class representation into the

House of Commons would therefore not result in class, but in national legislation'.[32] The socialist claim to Labour, and the Labour claim to the working class had to be made good on a number of fronts. There were a number of suitors with imperfect manners and traces of foreign ancestry – syndicalism and Marxism, doctrines of class war and revolution – who had to be seen off before an appropriate courtship on proper English lines could be conducted. Belief in class war both as a historical fact and as a political method would have rendered the parliamentary politics of the Labour party nugatory, while discrediting any claim it might make to be the natural successor and unspectacular next stage of Liberalism. Consequently, in *Socialism and Society* MacDonald took care to employ the analogy of society as an organism, of which he was so fond, to attack Marx and to argue that a political method based on crisis or conflict was misconceived. In 1912 he attacked syndicalism, and in particular Sorel's variety, as both unrealistic and undemocratic, reacting particularly strongly against the Sorelian discussion of myth, and attacking it as a reliance on feeling at the expense of thought.[33] Such versions of socialism both threatened the hold of socialist progressivism on the Labour party and on its working-class clients and equally, indeed more important, presented a sensational vision of the new party to those whom it wished to attract – the progressives and working men who were still, though temporarily, within the Liberal fold. To protect their sensibilities, MacDonald was always most careful to deny any suggestion that socialism or Labour involved a threat to established parliamentary methods, to religion, or to the family.

The Labour claim to speak for more than those who at the time supported it was central to MacDonald's case, and had been so ever since his earliest involvement with the progressive movement. Once the claim to be part of a broad movement cutting across party boundaries had been made, Labour had either to be a subordinate part of that movement, or to lead it, 'assimilating and not being assimilated'.[34] There was no middle way. His often decried comment that socialism was an ultimate goal, not an immediate possibility, and that hence the appropriate means of working towards it was 'the creation of a political party that is not Socialist but only Socialistic – like our Labour Party'[35] may be seen as not primarily a qualification of socialist zeal. What was presented was a portrait of the progressive labour movement which opened it up to advanced Liberals whilst presenting no obstacles to its own parliamentary socialists, 'Socialism, the stage which follows Liberalism, retains everything that was of permanent value in Liberalism, by virtue of its being the hereditary heir of Liberalism.'[36] The journey was to be the same for socialists and advanced Liberals, but since the socialists were going to the end of the road they were likely to move with greater purpose.

In so far as progressivism as a whole could be accommodated, so far also was the problem solved of providing a coherent basis for the diverse strands within the Labour party. The problem was not one of formulating doctrines or analysing capitalism, but of giving an account of socialism which would enable both supporters and potential supporters to recognize their own political aspirations and to be encouraged in support of a common image. 'All barrier phrases and sectional dogmas must be removed from Socialism', argued MacDonald, and 'the basis of the movement must be such that everyone sharing in the disturbed promptings must be included'.[37]

This involved ambiguity in the character of the socialist goal, and a resolution of the difficulties raised by Liberal individualism. The ambiguity was necessary because the function of progressive socialism did not end when it had attracted socialists by its statement of distinctive and rousing principles. It had to attract Liberals also by describing historical goals and political directions in such a way that there was no immediate breach in the continuities of practice and belief, but simply a revised picture of the eventual destination:[38]

> We have to preach Socialism and familiarise the public with our opinions and general standpoint, on the one hand, and on the other we have to convince the genuine progressist who is not an out-and-out Socialist that in our hands the minor, as we think, reforms are quite safe.

Lastly, practical trade unionists had to be attracted, by providing them with a non-Liberal rhetoric for the pursuit of reforms in whose execution the Liberal party seemed untrustworthy.

The organic analogy proved its usefulness here, inspiring courage by its sense of inevitability, and soothing caution by its assurance of continuity. It was not, of course, an original creation of MacDonald, and even within progressive circles was quite common. Hobson employed it, as did Stanton Coit, and Clement Edwards had warned readers of the *Progressive Review* that the Liberal party must respond to the changing needs and directions of the social organism, or perish.[39] However, biological analogy was not for MacDonald a contribution to political thought, but a device in political argument. He could be amusingly frank about this:[40]

> In order to live you summon more angels from heaven who come with advanced copies of human evolution in the pages of which you read of the doom of John Burns and the *Daily Chronicle* and the divine calling of yourself and Fabian Questions for Poor Law Guardians.

When other metaphors were more appropriate, they were employed instead (a most orthodox application of evolutionary principles). The language of Idealism, and the names of its exponents, could be employed just as readily as could biological reference. They were particularly useful in reconciling sectional aims with national purposes, and in resolving the antagonism between liberal individualism and socialist collectivism. A socialist party and a partial approach to public policy were not incompatible with the highest national good, because the real will 'is not that which is expressed in one mood or moment, but that co-ordinated with other expressions of the will and also with the social will'. Similarly socialism, by using the state to create positive opportunities for individual freedoms, pursued the true individualism: 'Self and government are but aspects of the same individuality'.[41] In none of this was MacDonald being in any way original: he was simply drawing on familiar progressive arguments, and doing a job which Hobhouse, on the other side, did very much better. But when it is said that his argument was 'much more pedestrian than Hobhouse's',[42] a strength, not a weakness, has been identified. He was in part aiming his arguments at that quintessential pedestrian, the man in the street.

The biological metaphors and the philosophical allusions, by sustaining the impression of the naturalness of socialism, also assisted the idea of its rightness. The final strand in the argument was a moral one, and MacDonald's experience in the Ethical Movement had shown his ability to develop such sentiments. The political revolt of labour occurred 'not because they were covetous, or greedy, or wicked, but because they felt they were wronged'. The claim to public ownership, intervention, or control could be strengthened by adapting the efficient or evolutionary arguments for growing state co-ordination into a description of the naturalness and rightness of such a process, and the fecklessness of the rich advanced as a reason for depriving them of their stewardship.[43]

MacDonald was a great name-dropper, for ever ready to buttress a modest argument with a major authority, and some sport has been had with the manner in which he flashes the credit cards of his intellectual and scholarly respectability. But to treat him as if he were an academic writer, and then charge him with superfluous reference and undue and sometimes unacknowledged reliance on secondary sources, is to miss the point of what he was doing. He was contributing to a political debate, and using ideas, books, thinkers, analogies, as tools in that debate. Seen in this light, his initially bewildering transition from organic metaphors to Idealism and from Idealism to the indictment of social injustice becomes explicable in terms not of logical coherence, but of argumentative intention. The conclusions did not follow from the apparent premises of idealism and biology, but were sustained by them, and given credibility and a sense of historical purpose, ethical substance, and intellectual significance. His political arguments helped to create for progressive socialism a reputation for respectability, radicalism, distinctiveness, reasonableness, scientific authenticity, and relevance both to the problems facing the nation and to the political aspirations of the heterogeneous adherents of the Parliamentary Labour party. The eclecticism of his references became, in this context, an advantage rather than a flaw, for it broadened the appeal of his writing to potential supporters who were united in their imprecise adhesion to a progressive labour policy, but were ideologically diverse and incoherent.

Several problems remained for MacDonald once he had established his portrayal of socialism, particularly that of the relation between this portrayal and the actual business of politics. Certain things were proscribed: syndicalism, class war, parliamentary scenes. What was recommended, apart from parliamentarianism and patience? Very little, for it was precisely because any immediate proposals on which parliamentary labour might have been able to agree were so undistinctive that the stress needed to be laid elsewhere: on the direction, not on the *ad hoc* arrangements. Similarities between Liberalism and socialism and Liberal and Labour at the level of practice needed to be overcome by a stress on differences of the spirit. The purpose of the myth was to be an incitement to action and a creator of images, rather than to provide a doctrine or a programme. MacDonald was aware of this problem, and an early experience in his Fabian lecturing days gave it vivid illustration. He arrived at Oxford station one night and found himself immediately embroiled with a young crowd of aspirant luggage carriers:[44]

> A crowd of ragamuffins surrounded me and a Dutch bargain immediately began. Said I: 'Bag-carriers and fellow citizens, read the *Clarion* and the *Labour Leader*. Having given that general advice let me come to particulars. My bowels yearn with the thought of your degradation, but until the means of prod: dist: and exch: are nationalized – well, gentlemen, I can but address meetings and split the Liberal vote. Fellow workers, I am a Labour candidate, and I am shocked at this unseemly wrangle. I was born to be sacrificed for Democ. My clothes hang loosely upon me. Distribute them amongst you, and when you have relieved me of all my exterior impedimenta conduct me please to a respectable inn.' Of course when brought to the scratch the loafers would not work and I marched to the Wilberforce.

If the seeker for programme in the pages of MacDonald was equally left to carry his luggage, how was he to be satisfied? Even to the annual conference of the ILP MacDonald was ready to admit that the 'mere principles of Socialism do not carry us very far, because they are capable of application in so many different ways, and their meaning in relation to existing things is so very general'.[45] The answer was that socialism was a matter of direction, and particular actions must therefore be decided *ad hoc: solvitur ambulando.*[46] Labour, he told the audience of Stead's *Coming Men* series, 'has hitherto refused to compile a programme, for the very sufficient reason that a Party is not created upon a programme, but upon a point of view. Not pledges but standpoints gain the confidence of the people'.[47] This was a much more convincing statement of the position than the idea of a 'general map' which he employed in *The Socialist Movement*. Even the qualifying word 'general' does not make this satisfactory because maps are maps and help to tell you where you are, how far that is from where you are going, how much farther there is to go, and what obstacles lie along the way. MacDonald's socialism created a general sense of a distinctive direction necessary to a party, but it did not chart the direction in detail: a compass, perhaps, but not a chart. The Labour party, he wrote, was not 'the embodiment of a political dogma'. Nor was it 'founded on the rock of first principles', but was rather 'the temporary exponent of a method', 'constantly in a state of flux and flow', 'a barque floating upon currents and moving with the stream'.[48]

In 1915 the Labour party moved into a new phase. Before that date MacDonald's political arguments had provided, in a way that no other version of socialism did, a necessary means both of unity and of broadening appeal. The foundations were already laid, by the outbreak of the world war, for the accession to the party of disillusioned Liberals who were to find in socialism, as described by MacDonald, a political sentiment which promised integrity and purpose in the pursuit of policies which their own party no longer seemed capable of developing. Their change of alliance was eased by the ark of MacDonald's eloquence, which carried them over the flood and set them down again on increasingly solid parliamentary ground. And if they seemed to be standing on the same shore from which they set out, this was in part because although they had deserted Liberalism, socialism had, by default, captured progressivism.

NOTES

1 *Independent Labour Party Annual Conference Report 1909*, p. 48.
2 Lord Elton, *The Life of James Ramsay MacDonald (1866-1919)*, London, 1939, p. 155.
3 Elton, op. cit., p. 35; W. T. Stead (ed.), *Coming Men on Coming Questions*, no. xii. London, 1905, p. 219; *Dod's Parliamentary Companion*. It is unclear precisely whose campaigns he worked for, and when, and different accounts occur in Elton and Stead..
4 J. R. MacDonald, *Southampton Parliamentary Election, Work and Vote for James Ramsay MacDonald*, etc., Southampton, 1895; in Viscount Samuel, *Memoirs*, London, 1945, p. 27.
5 Samuel Papers, quoted in Bernard Porter, *Critics of Empire*, London, 1968, p. 164.
6 Samuel, op. cit., pp. 52, 51 and 24.
7 Private circular, and circular dated August 1896, Samuel Papers, quoted in Porter op. cit., pp. 164-5 and 166 n. 2.
8 'Introductory', *Progressive Review*, vol. 1, no. 1, October 1896, pp. 5 and 6.
9 Samuel, op. cit., pp. 24-5. Clement Edwards, 'Progressive unity and railway nationalization', *Progressive Review*, vol. 2, no. 11, August 1897, *passim* and p. 438.
10 Elton, op. cit., p. 95.
11 MacDonald, *Adult Schools and Democracy*, London, 1913, p. 6.
12 MacDonald, *Socialism and Society*, London, 1905, p. 165.
13 R. B. Haldane, 'The New Liberalism: I', *Progressive Review*, vol. 1, no. 2, November 1896; P. F. Clarke, *Lancashire and the New Liberalism*, Cambridge, 1971.
14 Clarke, op. cit., p. 157.
15 J. A. Hobson, *The Crisis of Liberalism: New Issues of Democracy*, London, 1909, pp. 133-4 and 172-3.
16 L. T. Hobhouse, *Democracy and Reaction*, London, 1904, pp. 226-7.
17 L. T. Hobhouse, *Liberalism*, London, 1911; New York, 1964 ed., pp. 87-91.

18 MacDonald to Enid Stacy, n.d., quoted in Anne Fremantle, *This Little Band of Prophets*, London, 1961, p. 132.
19 Mary Agnes Hamilton, 'Rt. Hon. J. Ramsay MacDonald, MP., Labour's first prime minister' in Herbert Tracey (ed.), *The Book of the Labour Party*, London, 1925, vol. 3, p. 128.
20 Keir Hardie and J. R. MacDonald, 'The Liberal collapse, III: the Independent Labour Party's programme', *Nineteenth Century*, vol. 45, no. 263, January 1899, *passim* and pp. 24, 25, and 31.
21 Hobson, op. cit., pp. vii-xiii.
22 Arthur Henderson, reported in the *Manchester Guardian*, 17 December 1909, quoted in Clarke, op. cit., p. 360.
23 MacDonald, 'The Labour party and its policy', *Independent Review*, vol. 8, no. 30, March 1906, pp. 265-6.
24 L. MacNeill Weir, *The Tragedy of Ramsay MacDonald, a Political Biography*, London, 1938, p. xi.
25 MacDonald, *The Socialist Movement*, London, 1911, p. 157.
26 Herbert Samuel, 'The Independent Labour party: II', *Progressive Review*, vol. 1, no. 3, December 1896, pp. 256-7.
27 MacDonald *Syndicalism*, London, 1912, p. 20.
28 Quoted Fremantle, op. cit., p. 125.
29 MacDonald, *Socialism and Government*, London, 1909, vol. 1, pp. xxx-xxxi.
30 MacDonald, *Socialism and Society*, 1908 ed., p. 116.
31 MacDonald, *The New Charter, a Programme of Working Class Politics*, Dover, 1892.
32 MacDonald, *The Labour Party*, London, 1905, p. 7.
33 MacDonald, *Socialism and Society*, London, 1905; *Syndicalism*, London, 1912.
34 MacDonald, 'Socialism and politics. A reply to Dr. Beattie-Crozier', *Fortnightly Review*, vol. 33, no. 498, June 1908.
35 MacDonald, *Socialism and Society*, 1908 ed., p. 191.
36 Ibid,. 1905 ed., p. 164.
37 Ibid., p. 146.
38 Report in *Rochdale Labour News* of speech in October 1896, quoted in Elton, op. cit., p. 89.
39 Hobson, op. cit., Chapter 4; Stanton Coit, Address to West Kensington Ethical Society, reported in *Labour Leader*, 6 December 1899, quoted in Porter, op. cit., p. 163; Clement Edwards, 'Progressive unity and railway nationalization', *Progressive Review*, vol. 2, no. 11, August 1897.
40 MacDonald to Enid Stacy, n.d. quoted in Fremantle, op. cit., p. 126.
41 MacDonald, *Socialism and Government*, London, 1909, vol. 1, pp. 9-10, vol. 2, p. 155.
42 Peter Weiler, 'The new liberalism of L. T. Hobhouse', *Victorian Studies*, vol. xvi, no. 2, p. 157, n. 51.
43 MacDonald, *The Social Unrest, Its Cause and Solution*, London and Edinburgh, 1913, pp. 33 and 35-8.
44 MacDonald to Enid Stacy, n.d. quoted in Fremantle, op. cit., pp. 126-7.
45 *Independent Labour Party Annual Conference Report 1907*, p. 3.
46 '*Solvitur ambulando*, not *sic volo*', *Socialism and Society*, 1905 ed., p. 179.
47 *The Labour Party*, p. 8.
48 *Socialism and Society*, 1905, ed., p. 142.

Note. The author wishes to thank Dr G. W. Jones for his comments on a draft of this essay.

8

CHARLES TREVELYAN AND TWO VIEWS OF 'REVOLUTION'

A. J. A. MORRIS

Charles Trevelyan was born in October 1870, the eldest of the three sons of Sir George Otto Trevelyan – Liberal politician, historian, and squire of Wallington in the county of Northumberland. The Trevelyans were members of that well-defined, small yet politically influential upper middle class of Englishmen, with their own special aura of country gentry. Sir George, in different Liberal governments, had been Irish Secretary, Chancellor of the Duchy of Lancaster, and twice Scottish Secretary. From the first it was assumed that the eldest son should follow in his father's political footsteps.

Educated at Harrow and Trinity College, Cambridge, in October 1892 Charles Trevelyan began his formal political education when he was dispatched to Dublin Castle as private secretary to Lord Houghton, the newly appointed Liberal Lord Lieutenant of Ireland. It was not a happy experience for Trevelyan. He was bored by the lack of work, contemptuous of the show and superficiality of Dublin Castle etiquette, and amazed to discover that, himself and Houghton apart, there was hardly a Home Ruler in the administration. By turns he became disappointed, angry, lonely and depressed. Most of all, he despised the way Dublin Castle administrators betrayed the trust and duty they owed to 'the people'.

> By God, I will have my revenge one day upon these supercilious gentry. They don't know the flimsy platform they stand upon. . . . It will be a pleasant day when we can pull away the props.
> *This* I shall have learnt to serve me through life: that courtiers are the most narrow, the most ignorant of all men, the most weak because they do not count the strength of their enemies.

Trevelyan returned from Ireland in September 1893. That same month the Home Rule Bill passed the Commons only to be rejected by the Lords. Trevelyan now began in earnest his preparations to fit himself for, and to secure, election to the Commons. Though only twenty-three, he enjoyed advantages that allowed him confidently to expect swift recognition and election. His social and political credentials could not have been better. All the most important considerations were satisfied: he was a committed Liberal; his father enjoyed considerable influence in that party; and, most important, he was rich. This last was crucial at a time when most members were expected not only to support themselves but by generous contribution to swell party and constituency funds. Merely to fight an election was a costly business. In addition to his own contribution, the six electoral campaigns Trevelyan fought between 1895 and 1910 cost his father £6000.

Though at first he called himself a Liberal Radical, at this time neither by intellect, intuition nor inheritance was Trevelyan disposed to adopt a radical stance in politics. He talked frequently of 'revolution', but in his political vocabulary this was merely a synonym for 'change'. The greatest single outside influence upon his early political thinking was John Ruskin. It was not Ruskin's 'sincere love of Kings' that attracted Trevelyan, but the ideal of the hero striving in true chivalric spirit to serve the poor, weak and oppressed. The rhetoric of heroism compensated for a guilty consciousness of the unnecessary suffering of so many people. Trevelyan's understanding of Ruskin provided him with the broadest possible philosophy of purpose in politics. It was the Webbs and George Bernard Shaw who first afforded some precision and direction to his political aims.

In his novel, *The New Machiavelli*, H. G. Wells, through his hero, Remington, explains why the Webbs were such an important influence on a whole generation of young Liberal politicians. 'They seemed to stand for the maturer, more disciplined, better informed expression of all I was then urgent to attempt to do.'[1] Trevelyan's contact with the Fabians brought a new dimension to his social as well as to his political experience. He wrote to tell his father how he was now seeing 'a good many people from the other side of the political picture', a side to which he had never before been admitted. 'The conventionality and narrowness of people are exposed often by contact with Shaw and his friends.' Shaw's ebullience, and Beatrice and Sidney's ready analyses and remedies for all known social, political, even dietary, problems, were in marked contrast to the

Liberal leaders in Parliament who seemed, to Trevelyan, 'content merely to twiddle their thumbs'.

Socialism had been a much-discussed subject when Trevelyan had been a student at Trinity. On one occasion, after meeting and talking with Tom Mann, the dockers' leader, he wrote to his father: 'I always thought that Socialism was essentially destructive, but all the ends and proposals of Mann are the very reverse and essentially constructive.' That was an uncomfortable conundrum to have to solve. For the time being, Trevelyan ignored it. He was an optimist and believed in progress. But he was not convinced by 'the Socialist doctrine of a regenerated society'. As long as the Liberal party was 'imbued with a deep and democratic conviction', then it would remain the 'best *immediate* instrument for securing progress'. Addressing Liberal meetings in the late 1890s, Trevelyan scorned the idea that socialists ought to be treated as enemies.

> Their complaints, activities, passion and polemic are creating the sort of opinion reformers want. They hammer the evils that surround us into people's minds better than we Liberals. I want the Liberal party to throw itself as heartily into reform.

Commented the *Manchester Guardian*, 'He talks much of "equality of opportunity". Fabianism all over – and not very shocking either.'[2] Trevelyan confined his real dissatisfaction with socialist ideas to his private journal.

> The trouble with Socialism is that it is put before the world as a gospel of the weak and unfortunate. The English see themselves as a strong and fortunate race, and take their pride in it.

The role he assigned to socialists was that of ally. The prime instrument of reform should be Liberalism in Parliament: not an outdated Liberalism that placed an undue emphasis upon *laissez-faire* individualism, but a Liberalism that would embrace and welcome new ideas.

Trevelyan finally entered Parliament in 1899, as the Liberal member for the Elland division of Yorkshire. Rapidly he acquired a reputation as a man of independent views with the courage to voice them. A Radical newspaper commented, with evident satisfaction,

> He is neither a political adventurer, a party hack, nor a seeker after any of the desirable pickings which reward diligent drudgery in the Tom Tiddler's ground of St Stephens.

> Beating the party drum is necessary work, there are times when it must be done, and they also serve who only stand and beat. But Mr C. P. Trevelyan is not cut out for tasks of that kind.

Many informed Liberals had supposed that Trevelyan would be given junior office when the Liberals returned to power in December 1905. However, he was not given junior rank until October 1908 when he was appointed Under-Secretary at the Board of Education. This position he kept until his resignation on the outbreak of war with Germany in August 1914.

In 1908, soon after Asquith succeeded Campbell-Bannerman as Prime Minister, many political pundits were confidently predicting imminent electoral disaster for the Liberal party. Few then foresaw the possibility that the major cause of the Liberal dilemma – the intransigent opposition of the Lords – could become a saviour of Liberal fortunes. Sir George Trevelyan, in February 1908, predicted that the future of Liberalism depended upon the party fighting the Lords, an opinion enthusiastically shared by his son. But was it realistic to expect Asquith to be bolder than his Radical predecessor? The answer was provided in the last week of the 1908 parliamentary session.

The Prime Minister was being entertained to a dinner by Liberal MPs at the National Liberal Club. Though the celebration was to compliment Asquith on his handling of the Licensing Bill, he chose the opportunity to declare war upon the Lords. In great delight, Trevelyan wrote to his father:

> I think this may be the *real* turning point. Asquith's power of leadership was at issue. If he could not fire a real load now he never would. He had a splendid audience . . . and all knowing that nothing mattered except that he should be plain spoken about the Lords. . . . He got better as he went on – every sentence interrupted by cheers, getting louder and louder until when he declared, 'I invite the Liberal party tonight to treat the veto of the House of Lords as the dominating issue in politics', we all leapt to our feet and cheered. . . . It is the step I have been longing for. There is no going back now. I have always hoped that Asquith with all his caution would be very formidable, and now he is proving it.

'Bravo Asquith!' echoed Sir George. 'We have been kicked for seventy years, for the kicking began when Melbourne was P.M. It is time to kick back.' Almost as a postscript to his speech, Asquith had added, 'The Budget of next year will stand at the very centre of our work by which we shall stand or fall, by which certainly we shall be judged in the estimation both of the present and posterity.' As Asquith's biographers commented, this prediction was to prove truer than he could have supposed at the time. The 1909 budget was to be the anvil on which the fate of the House of Lords was forged.[3]

At the opening of the new session, Trevelyan reported to his wife that he thought the party was 'in pretty good heart'. In March and early April, Parliament was fully occupied with the naval estimates and an anti-German scare – a discomforting, even hysterical, prelude to the budget. On 29 April 1909, in an inordinately long speech which Trevelyan considered 'not at all up to the occasion', David Lloyd George introduced his budget. After detailed study of the proposals, Trevelyan concluded that the Chancellor had dealt 'very fairly' with the land question, a topic in which Trevelyan took special interest as an active member of the parliamentary Land Values Group.

> Apparently all land is to be valued under the Act. So we shall be in a fair way to getting our valuation complete. Otherwise too, it is excellent . . . bold and uncompromising. The more I understand the Budget, the more it is the embodiment of all I could hope for. Certainly it will be a severe year. Now, if ever, I will stick to work with no rest till it is all over.

Writing to his mother in July, Trevelyan first mooted the idea that perhaps the true political potential of the budget did not lie entirely in its fiscal proposals, but in the passions it aroused.

> The way the landlords and peers are cursing and whining is all to the good. We shall very soon have a clear cut issue between the many and the few. I am half inclined to wish the Lords would throw it out.

Perhaps the 'Welsh Wizard' had conjured better with his budget than they all had supposed – a social and constitutional revolution in one, wrapped in a speech as dry as dust! But would the Liberal leaders seize their opportunity? 'I am convinced,' wrote Trevelyan to his wife, 'the reaction of the last eighteen months has been stopped.' Should the government have had any doubts that the budget, and in particular the land clauses, afforded enormous electoral advantage, they were soon convinced by Oswald Partington's triumphant re-election for High Peak.

> The effect of the Budget has been even more rapid than I expected. . . . High Peak was unquestionably won on the Budget and especially the Land Taxes. I frankly did not expect the win and it is a great victory. For, if we can keep that sort of seat we can keep anything!

The budget continued to make painfully slow progress through the Commons. In the constituencies Liberal morale was high. In Parliament, Trevelyan admitted, the members would have 'died of boredom but for the speculation about the Lords'. The Upper House began its proceedings in September in a suitably intransigent mood – that is, for those who, like Trevelyan, fervently desired the Lords in their rage to ignore constitutional convention and reject the budget. On 2 November, the budget was finally approved by the Commons with a majority of 230 votes. By an almost equally overwhelming majority, the Lords rejected it. Asquith responded by moving a resolution in the Commons, joyfully accepted by the majority: 'That the action of the House of Lords . . . is a breach of the Constitution and a usurpation of the rights of the Commons'.

So the battle lines were drawn, and a January general election was inevitable. The issue at debate was not the merits of the budget, but whether a Tory House of Lords should be allowed to exercise an absolute veto on legislation sent to it by a Liberal House of Commons. One thing only worried Trevelyan, as he confided in a letter to his friend Walter Runciman.[4]

> I hope all the energy and wisdom of the most important heads of the party will be devoted in the next week or two to trying to find a modus vivendi with the Labour party. It is much too big to be left to the whips who are not sympathetic enough to arrange it. In truth, Asquith and Lloyd George ought to make it their personal affair.

Trevelyan could never appreciate why Labour and Liberal should not co-operate to their mutual advantage. Personally, he was sympathetic to many of Labour's demands. He insisted, however, on the Liberals retaining their primacy as the party that represented 'the people'. When Victor Grayson won Colne Valley in July 1907 – a seat where the Liberal candidate had been returned unopposed in 1906 – Trevelyan was not offended by Grayson's reputation as an independent and revolutionary. 'I don't mind much,' he wrote to his wife, 'though the success will make the Labour men perky and they will be hard to deal with.'

> It means that you and I will have to work very hard to keep my seat safe. . . . But, the people are independent and thinking for themselves. Why shouldn't they have their own man? I dare say I should have voted for him myself. What I have to make them feel is that I am as good as any Labour man they could get. Perhaps I shall succeed.

Trevelyan chose to ignore the fact that most Liberals were too much 'individualist' of the old Liberal school to unbend easily, co-operate with Labour members, and support Labour measures. Political expediency might dictate that in times of ill fortune Liberalism in Parliament should pay court to Labour. But, at the best, it could never be more than a temporary 'marriage of convenience'.

However promising were the general prospects for the Liberal party, Trevelyan knew that this time he would have a stern personal test to face. The local ILP were threatening to put up their own candidate. For once, the Tories had a strong candidate in George Ramsden, a local man and a member of the Halifax council. He had been adopted by the Tories in 1908 and for the past twelve months had been nursing the constituency. Ramsden promoted himself as 'the worker's friend'. He recommended strenuous opposition to the budget because it was 'Socialistic'. Why should there be more taxes when they were already taxed enough? They should 'tax the foreigner instead'. Lloyd George, not Trevelyan, was Ramsden's target. Trevelyan's manifesto ignored Ramsden, concentrating an uncompromising attack upon the House of Lords. Once in his constituency, Trevelyan spent most of his invective on the Lords' hatred of the land taxes.

> Why do the Lords hate the land taxes?
> [A voice in the crowd] Because of their pockets. Hear! Hear!
> The Lords opposed the Budget because the land and their interest in it is far more important to them than the liberties of the people.

Trevelyan's meetings were well attended, his audiences enthusiastic. But, for the first time at Elland, he was heckled. The local Tory press gleefully reported that the minds of Elland Liberals were agitated by the question: 'What will the Labour party do?' Eventually, the local ILP decided that their members should vote according to the dictates of their conscience, but only after the narrow defeat of a resolution that they should support Ramsden. The Brighouse section of the ILP joined with the Spen Valley Socialists in a determined attempt to unseat the Liberal member, Sir Thomas Whitaker. Trevelyan was not unduly concerned by the machinations of the ILP. He did, however, make a point of constantly affirming that both he and his father were delighted to see more Labour members in the Commons as 'evidence of the growing support for progressive policies'. These declarations of enthusiasm for Labour were to lead to an amusing incident at a meeting at Rastrick, three days before polling. 'Is it true,' asked a man in the audience, 'that your father . . . has tried to bribe Mr Keir Hardie by offering him a safe seat in Parliament and £300 a year if he will relinquish his independence?' Trevelyan was temporarily thrown by 'this merest, wildest fabrication I have ever heard'. Obviously, it was a Tory plot! 'My father, sir, is a thorough good democrat and has always welcomed Labour members to the House of Commons.'

Trevelyan was resigned to the fact that he could not hope this time to repeat his bumper majority of 1906. Nevertheless, he still secured a comfortable majority, though losing 900 votes. Half of these were probably explained by Labour abstentions, the rest by Tory 'outvoters'. 'The Stock Exchange is in absolute consternation,' wrote Sir George when congratulating his son upon his victory. 'That shows what the Tories really think of their prospects.' For once, Sir George's electoral forecast proved incorrect. The huge Liberal majority of 1906 was steadily eroded until the two major parties were left with almost the same number of seats. Thus, Labour and Irish members held the balance.

Not in the least disturbed, Trevelyan fired off an almost violent missive to Sir Edward Grey, his Northumbrian neighbour, insisting that the government should now go for the Lords 'neck and crop'.

> We won the election on two things. First, the quite new impression that the Government was a strong Government capable of doing big things. This opinion was created by the Old Age Pensions Act, the Budget – especially the land clauses. But secondly, and immensely the most important, the political North wants to have an end put to the interference of the land owning aristocracy. Seeing their opportunity for this once, they made up their minds to trust the Liberals to deal with the Lords. . . . If we try to conciliate the South by delay or mild measures, we shall lose the North.

There was much more in Trevelyan's long letter in similar fighting vein, and Grey, though polite as always, by the very coolness and brevity of his reply implied that Trevelyan had failed to appreciate that Liberal success now depended, more than ever, upon the support of the Irish and Labour members – difficult allies at the best of times. Grey assured Trevelyan, 'There is not here . . . any disposition to underrate either the urgency or the importance of the issue of the Lords'. In fact, Trevelyan's stratagem was based upon a keen appraisal of the nature of the Liberal victory in the election. This is clear from a letter he wrote to Runciman a week earlier than that to Grey.[5]

> I do not see how any course is possible except a perfectly direct policy of attacking the Lords as if we had a majority of 250. It is obviously the only terms on which we can keep Irish and Labour support for a moment. Nor will the Northern Liberals tolerate any other course. . . . Defy the reactionaries and the nation will want to be ruled by you.

'Politics will be furiously interesting,' wrote Trevelyan to his wife at the beginning of the new Parliament. 'We may be out in a fortnight. But I think not. If we are not, the fortunes of the party will be made for a generation. The Government are going to take a very strong line.' Like any good Radical, Trevelyan would have been pleased to see the Lords replaced by an elected chamber. 'I am not certain,' he wrote to his mother, 'that the audacity of such a policy might not compensate for [the Government's] lack of audacity in their strategy.'

Through the Commons, the government passed three resolutions intended to weaken the power of the Lords. In their turn, the Lords offered two resolutions intended to modify their composition. Asquith had introduced a Bill to implement his resolutions; Rosebery, with Lansdowne's approval, intended to do the same for the Lords' resolutions. Deadlock could be avoided only by the king exercising his prerogative to create enough new peers to swamp the Tory majority. Meanwhile, the budget had been rushed through the Commons by 'squaring' the Irish and by a ruthless use of the closure. The scene now seemed set for the final denouement of the dramatic struggle between the two Houses when Parliament reassembled in May. With his customary impeccable sense of timing, however, King Edward avoided the constitutional contretemps he had so long dreaded by dying on 6 May. The Tories, never backward in making political capital out of any situation, implied that Asquith's Radicals had killed the king! Surely he did not contemplate embarrassing Edward's heir by ruthlessly pursuing the vendetta with the Lords? Behind the scenes ministers bargained with Opposition leaders; commoners and peers sought some compromise that might at least postpone the crisis. In the end, it was agreed that there should be a conference between eight principals representing the two great parties. In vain, Irish and Labour expostulated that they were being ignored. In July, Asquith announced that Parliament would suspend its meetings until November. Meanwhile the principals in conference continued their horse trading.

In June, Trevelyan had written, 'I utterly disbelieve in the Conference. . . . I don't see how we gain anything, and I fail to see what material concessions we can make without abandoning our main position.' In July, he wrote that while most Liberals were 'suspicious and uneasy about the Conference', they were not 'rebellious. Everybody is content to wait till the Autumn. The Tories are inactive.' On 10 November, it was announced officially that the conference had failed to reach agreement. 'I have seen Lloyd George and Samuel,' wrote Trevelyan to his mother. 'I gather nothing is settled yet . . . but, there will be no faltering now. Our headquarters consider themselves to be well prepared. I suppose that may precipitate an election.' Lady Trevelyan replied that she had never thought it possible that the conference would find a formula 'honourable to both sides. . . . I hope Asquith will lead well now – so much depends upon that.' Asquith received the king's private assurance that, if necessary, he would create sufficient Liberal peers to allow the Parliament Bill to become law. The way was now clear for another general election. Crewe announced the dissolution for 28 November, but already the benches of the Commons were virtually empty as members rushed back to their constituencies for the coming battle.

'Wherever I go I find the Liberals in great heart. . . . It does not look like our being beaten. Good trade has made tariff reform look foolish after the wailings in January.' Trevelyan was also confident of his own chances. Ramsden reluctantly stood against him again, but with only a week to go to the poll, Trevelyan told his mother that his constituents simply refused to get excited. 'I think they regard it as a formal election and a foregone conclusion.' On 3 December, there was a nasty jolt to Trevelyan's confidence when the Elland LRC called a conference of trade unionists, socialists, and members of the ILP. They agreed they would not support Trevelyan, but abstain – a decision the Tory *Yorkshire Post* calculated would cost Trevelyan at least 500 votes. Labour dissatisfaction should not have surprised Trevelyan. Organized Labour had been angered by the Osborne Judgment. Many Labour supporters saw in this judicial decision by the House of Lords that a trade union member could refuse to pay a political levy to his union, the end of their dream of an independent Labour party. Starved of its main revenue source, Labour would be doomed to permanent dependence upon the Liberals. This state of affairs, they not unnaturally supposed, most Liberals were only too anxious to maintain. It was true that Trevelyan had condemned the decision as 'a national disaster of the highest magnitude'. But Labour supporters, in their anger and frustration, did not pause to discriminate between one Liberal MP and another.

Trevelyan's campaign was directed at one target only – the Lords. 'This is the simplest election of our time,' he told his constituents. 'You have simply to decide whether the Parliament Bill will be passed which the Lords have refused to discuss.' But, were the Lords not prepared to reform themselves? 'Do not believe in death bed repentance,' counselled Trevelyan. 'Your cause is doomed if you do not win this election. Land reform, temperance reform and everything else will go to the wall.'

> There are many sides to this struggle no doubt, but at the bottom this fight is between the people and the oligarchy, between the poor man and irresponsible wealth, the landless man against the monopoly that cramp his development. England's days of aristocratic tutelage are over. No longer will we suffer aristocratic patronage. We will govern ourselves.

The Tory campaign in Elland was muted, and Trevelyan's supporters sang uninterrupted their 'Song for Tory Agents':

> God Bless the House of Lords,
> Our democratic Peers,
> Where Bishops speak for Baptists
> And Earls for engineers.
>
> God Bless the House of Lords,
> Who represent our will
> By saying 'No' when we say 'Yes',
> And 'Well' when we say 'Ill'.

And so on, for fourteen verses! When the poll was declared, though Trevelyan's vote had fallen almost a thousand from the January election, he still retained a comfortable majority.

The Liberals had counted on gaining at least thirty seats in the December election. Instead, there was now parity between Tory and Liberal. For his part, Trevelyan refused to be downcast. He fired another typical 'broadside' of a letter to his friend, Walter Runciman.[6]

> I do not know what view is generally taken of the result. To me it seems to be all that could be desired, and as decisive as an election could have been. At any rate, I hope that is the interpretation Asquith will put upon it. I suppose that we need have no anxiety but that you will now go straight ahead and pass the Parliament Bill without delay and without compromise. . . . Vigorous, confident tactics on our part are the only way of preventing a Tory attempt at real resistance.

Asquith introduced the Parliament Bill in the Commons on 21 February 1911. The Tories put up a sterner resistance than Trevelyan had expected, and it was not until 15 May that the final vote was taken. The Lords, meanwhile, introduced their own reform bill to the accompaniment of strident discord between those who would have defended the Upper House as then constituted and those who, by compromise, sought to avoid the awful wrath promised by the Commons' reforms. A temporary truce was arranged for the coronation of George V. In July, however, after an overt threat by Lansdowne that the Tory peers would not accept the Parliament Bill as sent them by the Commons, Asquith informed Arthur Balfour of the king's pledge to create Liberal peers. In the face of this information the responsible Tory leadership could only counsel their followers to accept defeat. In the Commons, the Tories gave vent to their frustration by shouting down Asquith. Trevelyan described the scene to his wife.

> Balfour hadn't the courage or decency to try and stop them. . . . I am convinced this ruffianism will alienate sympathy in the country and I should not be surprised if it leads to some Radical retaliation somewhere. We shall have crowds outside Palace Yard before long.

To his parents he wrote: 'This is a real revolution and Lord Hugh [Cecil] has at least done the service of impressing that ugly fact upon his party when they are helpless to parry it.' Trevelyan talked glibly of revolution; but the passion engendered by the fate of the Lords was scarcely noticed outside Westminster and the great houses of the land. 'Heat and the Lords are the only topics,' Trevelyan wrote to his wife on 9 August. 'The last act of the drama is come.' The next evening, by a narrow majority, the Lords accepted the Parliament Bill. Society was in a turmoil, but the nation at large was supremely indifferent.

For Trevelyan, the defeat suffered by the Lords at the hands of a Liberal Commons was the partial fulfilment of a long-held dream. Almost thirty years earlier, then a schoolboy at Harrow, he had written to his father about the crisis over the Redistribution Bill:[7]

> Let us hope there is such a row as turns out the hateful Upper House. Let us hope that within fifty years the Royal Assent may be given to the expulsion of the ancient tyrants of England who have shown themselves unworthy of the place they hold.

It would have been better had the Lords been abolished. But the Parliament Act was an important step in the right direction.

If the battle with the Lords had been the 'dominant' issue in politics – as, manifestly, Trevelyan believed it to be – why were most people so indifferent to its outcome? The answer is simple. They were much more concerned about the revolutionary ferment in British industry than about a constitutional 'revolution'. The Liberal government, fatally wedded to the virtues of compromise, was caught and being slowly crushed between the unremitting forces of Capital and Labour. For all the bold propaganda, the way to social revolution paved by the good intentions of Lloyd George and Winston Churchill had failed to capture the imagination and the sympathy of many British workers. They needed, they demanded more *immediate* improvement of their lot. Their leaders, parliamentary and trade union, appeared either not to comprehend their plight, or to ignore it. They were obliged, therefore, to make their demands in such a fashion that they could no longer be ignored. Miners, cotton spinners, railwaymen, dockers; each in turn struck for better conditions. Those who derided Parliament's patent panaceas armed themselves with a new philosophy – revolutionary syndicalism.

From the beginning of 1910 there had been violence, arson, looting, riot and death on a scale never before experienced in industrial Britain. The middle classes trembled in anxious apprehension of danger to their persons and property. The workers, enraged by righteous indignation, pressed their demands ever more violently. The owners and shareholders remained intransigent, truculent, selfishly uncomprehending. And in Parliament, the people's representatives raged over constitutional propriety and procedural niceties. Tom Mann, the old Labour leader, returned from Australia and, armed with the new syndicalist gospel, spread his good news in the monthly journal he edited, the *Industrial Syndicalist*. The tenor of these times is caught exactly by a bizarre incident in December 1910. There was a 'shoot-out' between two Russian anarchists and a detachment of the Scots Guards and police under the enthusiastic generalship of the Home Secretary, Churchill. In their barracks at St John's Wood, the Horse Artillery awaited Winston's summons to battle! Eventually, the young commander won his victory – the anarchists died in a blazing building. Tom Mann set an essay for his readers: 'If two men can keep 2,000 men employed and hold them at bay in one street, how many men would be required to defeat two or three million men, spread over the area of Great Britain?'[8]

Despite government efforts to achieve compromise, 1911 was an even more violent year than 1910. Leaders talked, working men acted, and Mr Churchill dispatched troops hither and thither. In mid-August, Trevelyan wrote to his wife:

> The labour situation may produce almost anything. The news tonight is very bad – shooting in Liverpool – and a universal railway strike within hours. . . . I fear there will be a serious situation before things get better. I think what has happened is this. A great wave of hope of a better kind of life has come over the mass of workers, of which the political success of our Government has been partly a cause and partly an evidence. On top of this feeling has come the success of several trades in London getting immense increases of wages and shorter hours after a couple of days strike. The case of the carmen and dockers was unanswerable. Everyone with a grievance everywhere says – 'I will strike to win a little success.' Hence, the heather is on fire everywhere. . . . So, we are now on the brink of a temporary overturn of society which may lead to very serious consequences.

Here, then, was the threat of violent revolution – but not the kind of revolution Trevelyan welcomed. Certainly, the instruments of revolution should be the workers, but in harmony with the bourgeoisie – even as the progressive elements in the Liberal and Labour parties were in harmony! Parliament would implement the revolution by legislation. That way alone could England become the 'green and pleasant land' they *all* desired. In 1909, after reading

Prince Kropotkin's book on the French Revolution, Trevelyan criticized the Prince's thesis. 'He wants to show that the bourgeois parties are no good and that the *sans-culottes* always do everything.... The mob are necessary to the bourgeoisie and the bourgeoisie to the mob in revolution. Some kind of collaboration alone makes for success.' But revolution in France, or Russia, was one thing. Surely, things would never come to such a pass in England?

> The Liverpool riots are very horrible, but it is a vile town with infinite poverty and unexhaustive religious bitterness hardening the feelings of the workers towards each other and to all men. I hope there are not many towns where violence would blaze up so fiercely in so short a time.

Trevelyan obviously did not comprehend the root cause of the workers' violent cry for help and understanding. Nor was he alone in his ignorance. It was impossible to know how to act because it required too great a change of philosophy, too sudden a denial of long-held opinions. It was possible to sympathize to a certain extent, to feel shock, even shame. Many found it easier to make excuses, feel alienated, or altogether ignore this unwelcome social phenomenon.

The anarchic industrial situation was a formidable embarrassment to those Liberal government supporters who, for so long and with such certainty, had proclaimed themselves the workers' accredited representatives. 1912 began with a great miners' strike. Asquith tearfully explained to the Commons the reasonableness of the compromise solution he proposed. The miners remained unaffected by the Prime Minister's lachrymose pleas. In contrast to the 1911 strike, this time there was no violence. The soldiers stood by at the ready: the workers sullenly ignored them. Tom Mann, for inciting the soldiers to make common cause with the workers, was thrust into prison. Trevelyan, incensed by the Attorney-General's explanation of this action – 'not a word to show he realized what a hole the Government is in: his whole argument left the situation as critical as ever' – circulated a lengthy and detailed memorandum to Cabinet ministers.

> I hope you will excuse me placing my view before you, which is that of a very large number of Liberals. . . . The suggestions I press upon you are –
>
> 1. This is not a matter which ought to be left any longer to the individual discretion of any Minister. . . . It is a matter of vital policy.

2. That on grounds both of Liberal policy and expediency, no more prosecutions should be undertaken from now onwards.
3. That the men already imprisoned should be amnestied as soon as the strike comes to an end.

The first point was a palpable hit at Churchill. Trevelyan then severely criticized the Attorney-General, Rufus Isaacs. He condemned the Liberal government's ineffectual conduct as most likely to raise the violent class feeling it was supposed to dampen. He ended by affirming that 'responsible Labour leaders are put in gaol . . . for expressing what at least half the Liberal party thinks they have a perfect right to say, however much they may disagree with it'. From John Morley came a swift rejoinder.

> Liberals must take care not to kick overboard the ideas, instincts and principles of *Government*. For myself, I am not prepared to allow a mob to batter the police to pieces if I have a squadron of cavalry handy. And if like [Fred] Jowett, I thought the use of the army in extreme civil disturbance wrong, I would censure the responsible Minister in Parliament. I should *not* say to soldiers they should mutiny. . . . I never have been and never will be, for dealing in milk and water with Trade Union violence.

Ministers, like Morley, might bluster, but no longer could they ignore an ugly *impasse* largely created by their own inertia and lack of sensibility. With the connivance of the Tory leaders – on this issue they did not wish to embarrass the government any more than need be – a Minimum Wages Bill for the miners was rushed through Parliament in March. It embodied Asquith's earlier proposals rejected by the men. How would they respond this time? Trevelyan wrote to the Bishop of Oxford:

> I am very much disappointed at the prospects with regards to the strike today. I feel quite certain that the men will be making a bad blunder and will alienate more public feeling from them if they do not accept what they have already won. . . . This sort of stirring up of the people is all to the good, and what I am so sorry about is that the Labour men have not proclaimed upon the house tops the immense victory in principle this short strike has won for them. It might have been a matter of twenty years without it.

The letter might have served as a primer to the miners' leaders. Asked whether they accepted the provisions of the new Act, the miners voted to continue their strike. However, on the technical point that there had not been a two-thirds majority in favour of continuing the strike, the miners' leaders accepted the Act, and announced they had won a great victory.

The workers, exhausted by their battles, took stock of their position. Perhaps this time they had been bested – more by exhaustion than by the conciliatory skills of the government. They had secured some material reward, and, more importantly, learned a great lesson. If workers were prepared to act in unison – close the mines and docks, paralyse the country's transport system – then the government would be forced to act. It certainly would not be able to ignore them. Now they needed time to plan, to co-ordinate strategy. The Liberal government might take what credit it pleased for its firm measures having resolved a difficult situation. But in their hearts, the workers knew otherwise.

NOTES

1 H. G. Wells, *The New Machiavelli*, Penguin ed., 1946, p. 150.
2 *Manchester Guardian*, 22 January 1896.
3 J. A. Spender and Cyril Asquith, *Life of Lord Oxford & Asquith*, London, 1932, vol. 1, p. 241.
4 C. P. Trevelyan to Walter Runciman, 20 November 1909, Runciman MSS. R1/12 (Newcastle University Library).
5 C. P. Trevelyan to Walter Runciman, 2 February 1910, Runciman, MSS. R1/12.
6 C. P. Trevelyan to Walter Runciman, 23 December 1910, Runciman MSS. R1/34.
7 C. P. Trevelyan to G. O. Trevelyan, 7 December 1884, G. O. Trevelyan MSS. Box 37 (Newcastle University Library).
8 Quoted Elie Halévy, *History of the English People in the Nineteenth Century*, Benn paperback ed., 1961, vol. 6, p. 454.

Note: Quotations within the text not otherwise ascribed are taken from the C. P. Trevelyan Papers. Part of this collection is lodged at Newcastle University Library, and part, by kind permission of the Trevelyan Trustees, is on loan to the author. The author wishes to thank Mrs Pauline Dower and Mr Alistair Elliot for their generous co-operation.

9
'GOD GAVE THE LAND TO THE PEOPLE'*

ROY DOUGLAS

Lloyd George's introduction of land taxes in his 1909 budget was greeted with immense enthusiasm by the Radicals. Clearly, the Chancellor had appealed to deeply-held social and political convictions. The nature of the Radicals' response may be understood only by examining what had gone before.

Proposals for land reform of one kind or another were made repeatedly during the second and third quarters of the nineteenth century; among others, by the Chartists, Cobden, Bright, Mill and Joseph Chamberlain. What most effectively focused public attention on the 'land question', however, was the violent Irish 'Land War' which sprang out of the agricultural depression of the late 1870s and eventually led to Gladstone's great Irish Land Act of 1881.

Irish agrarian disturbances continued for many years; yet after 1881 the story of the land problem in Ireland branches sharply from the main course of Radical activity in Great Britain. The Irish were more and more inclined to seek a solution on the lines of peasant proprietorship; that is, the state should buy out existing landlords with the aid of public funds – the money, or part of it, to be repaid by the peasants over a long period. Eventually, the Unionists came to recognize that a country of small proprietors would be likely to resist major social and political change. Unionist governments, therefore, greatly encouraged the process by a series of measures, culminating in Wyndham's Land Purchase Act of 1903. Peasant proprietorship attracted a good deal of interest in Scotland, while some people hoped that the English smallholdings movement would develop in a similar direction.

In 1880, while the Irish 'Land War' was very much the focus of

*From the *Liberal Land Song*, see p. 156 below.

attention, the American economist, Henry George, published *Progress and Poverty*. He argued that no man had a better right than any other to a piece of land. A person who sought exclusive possession of land should compensate the community for his monopoly by paying a yearly Land Value Tax. This tax should discount the value of any improvements introduced by human agency, and equal the total annual value of the land itself. *Progress and Poverty* was widely read in Ireland during the 'Land War', and soon was being studied with equal interest in Great Britain. Without exaggeration, it may be described as one of the dozen most influential books written in the nineteenth century. For nearly half a century after its first appearance, *Progress and Poverty* would be on the bookshelf of practically every keen Radical in Britain. Not only Radical Liberals, but socialists as well, freely admitted their debt to George's ideas.

While Henry George's theories were beginning to germinate in the minds of Radicals, a series of violent events brought the land problem to public attention in a very practical way. The Irish 'Land War' sparked off other peasant risings. The crofters of the West of Scotland were in a state of constant turmoil from 1882 until the end of the decade. Rent strikes, deforcements, battles with police, raids on deer forests, and other similar activities became widespread. By the late 1880s, the use of gunboats and marines, to enforce order among the recalcitrant crofters, was common. In Wales, a rather different kind of peasant revolt began about 1886, but was soon deflected into a movement against the payment of tithes. By their hundreds, tenants allowed their property to be sold up rather than pay dues to an alien church, and on at least one occasion there was large-scale violence. David Lloyd George, a young lawyer and local politician, was intimately involved in this agitation. One of the most consistent attitudes in his whole extraordinary career was his loathing for 'landlordism', learnt as a boy and sharpened in young manhood.

The stirring events among the Scottish crofters were reported at length in the Glasgow and Edinburgh newspapers, making a deep and lasting impression on the minds of readers, many of whom were of recent Highland extraction. Numerous mass-meetings of sympathizers were held in the Scottish towns, and no speaker was heard with more attention than Henry George, who made several lecture tours of the British Isles.

Although ameliorative legislation eventually damped down disturbances among the various groups of Celtic peasants, the

Glasgow Liberals were soon persuaded that the land problem was not an issue confined to rural areas, but had no less important urban aspects. As early as 1884 they began to pass resolutions in which the influence of Henry George's ideas was obvious.[1]

The doctrines of Henry George also spread rapidly in England. By 1889 they had become so 'respectable' politically that a motion in favour of land value taxation was carried unanimously by the National Liberal Federation. A similar statement was included as a major item in the Federation's Newcastle Programme of 1891.

In the early 1890s, the cause of urban land reform was pressed with increasing force in Glasgow, and, to a somewhat lesser extent, in London.[2] In fact, two separate, but not incompatible, demands were being made. The 'extremists' calculated that an annual tax on land values, eventually to be raised to 100 per cent, would be enough to meet all demands of state expenditure. All other taxes, both direct and indirect, could then abate in favour of a 'Single Tax' on land values. The 'moderates' confined their attention to local rating, claiming that the basis of assessment should not be the total value of the hereditament – land and improvement together – but exclusively the value of the site. Site Value Rating, therefore, was simply land value taxation applied for local purposes. Reformers argued that this policy would force idle land into use, destroy speculation, and remove the disincentives to land improvements which the current rating system produced. In 1894 the London County Council set up a body to negotiate with the government to try to secure legislation on these lines. By the autumn of 1897, about 200 assessing bodies in Great Britain were demanding the power to levy rates on the basis of site values.[3]

In 1901 the Final Report of the Royal Commission on Local Taxation appeared. The majority rejected site value rating, but a substantial minority, including the Unionist Lord Balfour of Burleigh, chairman of the commission, supported the proposal, at least within a limited context. In such circumstances, neither side could argue that the consensus of informed opinion was with it, and the whole question remained wide open for political discussion.

In the first few years of the new century, the agitation spread. By 1906 more than 500 local authorities supported site value rating. In Parliament, too, the campaign made great headway. It was not necessary to await the return of the Liberals to office for clear proof of this advance. In the Commons, despite an overwhelming Unionist majority, proposals for site value rating won increasing support. In 1904 and 1905 bills on the subject passed their second readings with substantial majorities, though the government did not allow parliamentary time for these bills to proceed to their later stages. Yet, with strongly Conservative local authorities like Liverpool supporting the movement, there could be no doubt in what direction public opinion was running.

Other kinds of land reform also attracted attention. The smallholdings movement led to a limited amount of legislation, in which the hand of the Liberal Unionist, Jesse Collings, is evident. There was also a campaign in favour of land nationalization, led by the distinguished biologist Alfred Russel Wallace. The land nationalizers proposed that, where appropriate, the state should take over land for public or social purposes, with compensation for the landowner. They sometimes contended that land should be acquired by public authorities, even when it was not immediately required, as part of a general policy to obtain ownership and control of land. The land nationalization movement was quite separate from the demand for land value taxation, and must have seemed a good deal more welcome to the landowner because of the compensation promised; but land reformers whose long-term objectives were quite disparate often co-operated with one onother. It is evident that Radicals were readily stirred by reference to any aspect of the land question, and were likely to support practically any policy which seemed inimical to the interests of the landlords.

There were, however, certain directions in which the land reformers had experienced only a very qualified measure of success. In the 1890s there had been campaigns both by land taxers and by land nationalizers in rural areas. Village meetings were widely attended and enthusiastically supported by farm labourers, but little or no permanent organization resulted.[4] After the initial excitement had died down, the essential conservatism of most agricultural workers remained unshaken.

Yet there could be no doubt about the inherent vitality of the demand for some kind of land reform. Almost without exception, the leading Liberal politicians had criticized the current land system. Campbell-Bannerman was one of the most vigorous of the critics. When the Liberals assumed office in December 1905, Campbell-Bannerman, as Prime Minister, told his fellow-Liberals in a pre-election speech at the Albert Hall:

> We desire to develop our own undeveloped estate in this country. . . . We wish to make the land less of a pleasure-ground for the rich and more of a treasure-house for the

nation. . . . We can strengthen the hands of the municipalities by reforming the land system and the rating system, in which I include the imposition of a rate on ground values.

With the Liberal party's landslide victory in the 1906 election, and a Radical Prime Minister at the helm of government, the land taxers had every reason for believing the political breakthrough for their schemes to be complete. At least site value rating would very soon be set on the statute book. The sort of time-scale on which they were thinking is well illustrated by a letter written in January 1906 by C. Llewellyn Davies, an official of the land-taxing movement, to J. C. Wedgwood, one of Henry George's keenest disciples, who had just been elected Liberal MP for Newcastle-under-Lyme. Wedgwood's correspondent expected a valuation bill 'this session', although he was prepared to concede that 'the actual taxing could then wait till next session, which would give time for the whole thing to be thought out'.[5]

Nowhere was the land reform movement stronger than in Scotland. Of the seventy-two constituencies, sixty returned Liberals and two returned Labour members. All the Liberal and Labour candidates seem to have supported land value taxation; most had made it one of their major issues at the election. Several leading members of the government, including Sir Henry Campbell-Bannerman and H. H. Asquith, Chancellor of the Exchequer, sat for Scottish constituencies, and so they were very familiar with the strength of the land taxing agitation.

Before land could be taxed it had to be valued. In 1906 most constitutional authorities agreed that the House of Lords would not interfere with a taxation Bill. A valuation Bill, however, was different. In the first parliamentary session, the Liberal government proposed a Bill to value Scottish land. This Bill, passed with an enormous majority by the Commons, was rejected out of hand by the Lords. A second government Bill to similar effect, introduced in 1908, sailed triumphantly through the Commons. This time the Lords preferred to adopt wrecking amendments rather than reject it outright, but the effect was the same.

Radicals had hoped that land in England and Wales as well as Scotland would be valued, but here they faced a quite different obstacle; not the Tory House of Lords, but John Burns, President of the Local Government Board. At first, Burns's appointment was greeted with considerable enthusiasm by the Radicals. By the turn of 1906-7, they were very unsure about him, and they eventually became convinced that he was perhaps the most determined obstructionist in the Cabinet.[6] It was evident that an English Land Values Bill would not even pass the Titan of Battersea, let alone the House of Lords.

Campbell-Bannerman retired in the spring of 1908, Asquith succeeding him as Prime Minister. Lloyd George moved from the Board of Trade, and became Chancellor of the Exchequer. These changes took place at a dismal time in the fortunes of the government. A developing depression brought in its train high unemployment, and the Liberal party suffered a run of severe defeats in by-elections. The Lords' intransigent opposition to contentious Liberal legislation bred a sense of frustration in the Radical ranks.

Some Radicals looked for developments in the direction of more intervention by public authorities in economic activities. This approach was brought to the land problem by the Land Nationalization Society, to which at one time nearly 130 MPs belonged. Yet in practice the initiative lay at least as strongly with those to whom massive state intervention seemed at best useless, and at worst profoundly harmful. Thus in 1909 Wedgwood argued that the remedy for unemployment was not state intervention, but land taxing:[7]

> Once they abolished the unemployment margin by giving the out-of-works the opportunity of working on the land or its idle raw materials the balance of the scales would be altered and capital would become the servant, not the exploiter, of labour.

Three years later, Wedgwood argued the application of the same principle to a different problem:[8]

> If you really want to see cheap and good houses you must do as you did in 1846. When you wanted cheap and good bread, you took off the Bread Tax. Will you now take off the House Tax? . . . Remove the rate from the house, and see whether you do not get cheap and good houses.

Alexander Ure, the Lord Advocate and probably the most thorough-going land taxer in the government, saw the current land system as the source of multitudinous evils:[9]

> We say to men, 'Make no use of your land; and we will invite you to pay no taxes; make good use of your land . . . and we will take good care that the more generously you spend the

> more heavily we will souse you in rates and taxes.' To the business man, the manufacturer, we say 'Lay down better machinery . . . and we will take care that for every foot of building you add and every bit of machinery you lay down we will tax you.' It is as if we had expressly designed the present standard to encourage men to make the worst possible use, or no use, of the land which the Creator has given us.

These speeches were typical of many. A growing number of Radicals – especially, but by no means exclusively, among the younger men – came to see land reform as part, if not all, of the solution to almost every imaginable social evil. Unlike a few of the more old-fashioned libertarians, however, the land taxers supported old-age pensions and other 'welfare state' proposals as keenly as did any believers in Fabian socialism. At the same time, most of the people who believed in state intervention as an inherently desirable principle were muted in their criticism of land taxation. The fundamental difference of approach between the two schools of thought still had not led to an open breach.

Lloyd George's celebrated budget of 1909 was the first government measure designed to deal with the land problem on a nation-wide scale. It is essential to appreciate that the Chancellor's detestation of 'landlordism' committed him neither emotionally nor intellectually to any particular kind of solution. His unrivalled skill as a political tactician allowed him to veer first to one course and then another, avoiding obstacles and seizing any possible advantage. Thus, the most direct approach to land taxation was to value first and afterwards tax on the basis of that valuation. Lloyd George considered this course, but then rejected it. Past experience with the Scottish Bills had shown him that the Lords would not hesitate to block a valuation Bill. Therefore he employed a stratagem which allowed him to establish the principle of land taxation, and at the same time slip in land valuation. The need to increase revenue substantially in order to meet great bills for rearmament and social welfare – a situation which most Chancellors would have viewed with grave alarm – Lloyd George manipulated to his own advantage.

The initial hurdle Lloyd George had to negotiate was the Cabinet. The first reaction of 'Loulou' Harcourt to the Chancellor's proposals in Cabinet was to slip a card to Runciman, with the comment: 'This Budget will ensure the triumph of Tariff Reform.'[10] In order to forestall some at least of the opposition, Lloyd George proposed only very light land taxes, designed to meet but a small proportion of the new revenue demands. In view of the storm that followed, it is well to remember that land taxes were intended to produce only half or two-thirds of a million pounds altogether in the current financial year. Far greater burdens were to be borne by the usual targets of a needy Chancellor: incomes, liquor and tobacco.

The proposed new land taxes were to be of three main kinds. The first would be a tax of less than a quarter per cent on the capital value of land. For two or three years at least, this would be levied only on mining royalties, ground rents and vacant land. As in these initial stages land would be valued by the owner himself, no more than a negligible amount of revenue could be expected from that source. The second proposal was a transfer tax of 20 per cent, payable when land, which had previously been valued, was later sold at an enhanced figure. The third, a Lease Reversion Duty of 10 per cent, would be payable by the lessor who benefited when a lease fell in. In spite of Lloyd George's initial doubts on the subject, a general valuation of land was also to be commenced.[11] Some concessions were made by the Chancellor during the Finance Bill's progress through the Commons. These annoyed the land taxers, and Lloyd George himself seems later to have regretted them. But what really concerned the Radicals was not so much the form of the current taxes as the institution of a system of valuation of land.

The Unionists recognized that the proposed great increases of taxation on liquor and tobacco afforded a possible lever to dislodge the government, or at least rouse public opinion against it. Accordingly they formed a Budget Protest League, to which the Liberals replied with their Budget League. At one of the early Budget League meetings, Lloyd George made his famous Limehouse speech – baiting landlords in general and ducal landlords in particular, to such an extent that they were driven in their fury to cast to the winds all ordinary considerations of political prudence. Unionists began to consider using their vast majority in the Lords in order to defeat the budget, even though this was quite contrary to the constitutional practice which had grown up over a couple of centuries and more.

Even before the Limehouse speech was delivered, there were some indications that the budget, and particularly its land clauses, might prove a useful electoral weapon for the Liberals. Oswald Partington, Liberal M.P. for High Peak, accepted junior ministerial office, and was obliged to defend his seat at a by-election. Partington's 1906 majority had been slight, and there was good reason for the Liberals to fear that he would be defeated. Fighting exclusively on the Budget proposals, however, he was successfully returned.

The enthusiasm which the land question aroused has few parallels in the political history of Britain. Great crowds roared the Liberal Land Song – and meant every word of it:

Sound the blast for freedom, boys, and spread it far and wide,
March along to victory, for God is on our side –
While the voice of Nature thunders o'er the rising tide,
  'God gave the land to the people!'
The land! The land! 'Twas God who gave the land!
The land! The land! The ground on which we stand!
Why should we be beggars with the ballot in our hand?
  God gave the land to the people!

Perhaps the most remarkable feature of the Budget dispute was the way in which the minuscule land taxes attracted far more attention than other, much larger, items of increased taxation. Lloyd George, with his infinite capacity for political manoeuvre, began to see the Budget's possibilities – not simply as a device for the introduction of land taxation, but as a means for forcing an issue between the Liberals and the Lords in which the electorate would overwhelmingly support the Government.

When the Lords were driven to the ultimate lunacy of rejecting the Budget, the main issue, at least in Great Britain, was not the beer and tobacco taxes, or the income tax, but land. A general election followed immediately, which left rather more than eighty Irish, and forty Labour members, holding the balance of power. With considerable skill, and luck, Asquith won the Irish to his side and maintained the support of Labour. The budget again passed the Commons, and this time the Lords let it through without a whimper.

With Radical encouragement, the Liberal government now sought to drive home its victory over the Lords. This took another general election, in December 1910, and a good deal of political arm-twisting. In August 1911, the Parliament Act became law, and the Lords' power to block Bills from the Commons was greatly reduced. Again, the land reformers seemed to see the road wide open to the legislation which they sought.

We have noted the exceptional interest which the land question aroused in Scotland. While the main concern was with land taxation, the idea of smallholdings was also much favoured. Attempts to introduce legislation in the first years of the Liberal government had been frustrated. In 1911, however, when the Parliament Bill was moving towards acceptance, Lord Pentland introduced a government Bill designed to encourage Scottish smallholdings. This Bill eventually became law, and was familiarly known as the Pentland Act.[12] After the initial excitement, its effects were somewhat disappointing. By the end of 1914, fewer than 500 applications for new holdings had been granted, and less than 300 existing ones enlarged.[13] Other clauses of the Pentland Act made provisions for rent reduction and the cancellation of rent arrears, but these were even less effective.

Legislation dealing with smallholdings in England and Wales was carried at about the same time as the Pentland Act, but aroused less general interest. There was also an Act carried in 1909, designed to encourage the sale of Irish land to the peasants in the 'Congested Districts' of the west. Not long before the outbreak of war, the government was planning a further Irish measure which would complete the process of land purchase throughout the country.[14] None of these measures, however, struck at the problem which mainly agitated the land reformers. In the spring of 1911, a delegation of MPs elicited from the government the depressing information that the land valuation, inaugurated by the 1909 budget, would not be completed until 1915. To the land taxers, it appeared that the government was purposely dragging its feet.

What could the reformers do? The Liberal government, after all, provided the only hope of securing the legislation they sought. It would be most unwise to declare war on that government – although they were sorely tempted to do so. Instead, they sought to convince the government that land taxing enjoyed widespread public support.

As in 1909, by-elections came to the land taxers' aid. By 1912, the general current of by-elections was again running adversely for the government. In this unfriendly climate, E. G. Hemmerde stood in the Liberal interest defending the marginal seat of North West Norfolk. Making land taxation the principal plank of his electoral platform, Hemmerde was triumphantly returned. North West Norfolk was a rural area; but a few weeks later the land reformers were able to show that land taxing could be an equally valuable vote-winner in an urban constituency. The MP for Hanley – nominally Labour, but in practice more of a Liberal – died. Hitherto, the Liberal and Labour parties had not opposed each other at Hanley. On this occasion, however, they both disputed the seat, and encountered a strong challenge from a Unionist who reasonably anticipated becoming the *tertius gaudens*. The Liberal, R. L. Outhwaite, an extreme land taxer, was palpably more radical than the Labour candidate. His campaign was fought in an atmosphere of tremendous enthusiasm. Outhwaite was returned with a comfortable majority over his Unionist opponent; the Labour candidate's vote was absurdly low. As if to make the land taxers' point in a different way, a Liberal candidate defending Crewe a few days later, but fighting on a much more conventional platform, lost the constituency to the Unionist.

The message of these by-elections was speedily appreciated by the government. Less than three months after the Crewe contest, a Land Enquiry Committee was set up, composed of government supporters. The first part of the committee's report, relating to rural land, was produced in the autumn of 1913. It proposed the establishment of a Ministry of Lands, with considerable powers to control agricultural wages, conditions of employment, smallholdings and allotments. There were also proposals to increase the tenant-farmer's security of tenure.[15]

Although not all of these recommendations were acceptable to some land reformers, they won widespread public support. From all parts of the country there came abundant evidence to suggest that the rural labourers were responding with great enthusiasm, especially to the idea of a minimum wage and perhaps a weekly half-holiday. Even tenant-farmers seemed to be showing a lively, and by no means hostile, interest in the Land Enquiry recommendations.[16]

In the spring of 1914, the committee's rural report was followed by an urban report, recommending new powers for public authorities to deal with poor housing and to acquire land and fix compensation. A measure of site value rating was also proposed. All local authorities would be compelled to levy some of their rates on that basis. A local authority which desired to collect a larger proportion in that manner would be enabled to do so. A very few weeks before the outbreak of war, the Land Enquiry's third report – concerning land in Scotland – also appeared.

The government evidently intended to act on both the rural and urban proposals. In the first half of 1914, the Cabinet was giving active consideration to the establishment of a Ministry of Lands, with powers to implement the rural recommendations.[17] The urban proposals required the separate assessment of unimproved land values for local rating purposes. This would pose rather serious procedural difficulties in Parliament; but just before the outbreak of war the government's intention was to introduce a valuation Bill in the late autumn of 1914, forcing it through Parliament in time for the 1915 budget.

The Land Enquiry's recommendations were expounded to the public through a great Land Campaign. Beginning in the autumn of 1913, this campaign was still in full flood at the outbreak of war. Large numbers of lecturers were enrolled, meetings were held at the rate of something like a hundred a day, and close on ten million items of literature were issued.[18] Though in rural areas the campaign was proving immensely effective, it was generally much less successful in the towns. At least part of the reason for this seems to have been the almost complete absence of serious opposition.[19]

The Land Campaign was also impeded to some extent by the immense public concern over the Irish issue. Almost at the beginning of the campaign, Lloyd George saw the underlying question of party strategy, and wrote to the Chief Whip, Percy Illingworth:[20]

> We must not let [the Land Campaign] flag. The Tory press has evidently received instructions to talk Ulster to the exclusion of land. If they succeed we are 'beat', and beat by superior generalship.

It is not difficult to appreciate the strategy which the government intended to follow. They would grant Home Rule in the autumn of 1914, but – thanks to an ingenious device suggested by Birrell[21] – the full complement of Irish members would still be in the Commons to give them support. If the land proposals passed the Lords, the government could point to constructive achievement. Should the Lords block the proposed legislation, then their obstruction could be used as a war-cry to rally all Radicals to the Liberal standard.

With the outbreak of war in 1914, the land reformers were scattered in every direction. What logic was there in a situation which gave Wedgwood the laurels of a war hero, yet visited upon Outhwaite, his close comrade in the cause of land reform and MP for an adjacent constituency, all the obloquy which became the lot of a pacifist? Outhwaite was to find himself associated not only with other land taxers like Charles Trevelyan, but with men like Ramsay MacDonald and Francis Hirst, whose ideas were incompatible with his own and with those of each other.

In the years which followed, the chaos grew worse. Lloyd George, as Prime Minister of the coalition government, presided over the repeal of his own land taxes. Wedgwood, like Trevelyan, eventually joined the Labour party, but for most of the time was out on a limb for his land taxing views. Outhwaite had an unhappy period in the Labour party, and then drifted into obscurity. Most of the land taxers remained in the Asquithian section of the Liberal party, but could have felt little enthusiasm for the leadership they received on the land question. All the land reformers found themselves associated with allies who did not share their particular enthusiasm, and sundered from erstwhile colleagues with whom they were in complete agreement on the land question. Lloyd George in the middle and late 1920s, and Philip Snowden as chancellor in the first two Labour governments, tried again to raise the banner of land reform; but the breach in the movement's continuity, the political dispersal of the land taxers and preoccupation with the looming hulk of unemployment caused all their efforts to run into the sands.

Obstinately, the land problem remains with us. If the analysis of Henry George was correct, and the ultimate source of human poverty and injustice is to be sought in the system of land ownership, then eventually the time must come when men will again pick up the threads which were dropped in 1914. Radicals will again become preoccupied with the land problem. Clio, after all, is a patient muse.

NOTES

1 *Glasgow Herald*, 20 November 1884.
2 See, *inter alia*, *Single Tax*, June 1894 *et seq.*: *Star*, 8 January 1889.
3 *Single Tax*, October 1897.
4 See reports of English Land Restoration League, and Land Nationalization Society, 1891-1902 *passim*.
5 C. Ll. Davies to J. C. Wedgwood, 29 January 1906. Wedgwood Papers.
6 For various views on Burns, see W. Runciman to J. C. Wedgwood, 25 December 1905; Wedgwood to wife, 27 November 1906; Wedgwood to Randolf Wedgwood, 14 February 1907 (all Wedgwood Papers); C. P. Trevelyan to C. T. Trevelyan, 29 November 1905 (G. O. Trevelyan Papers); C. P. Trevelyan to M. K. Trevelyan, 18 December 1906; J. C. Wedgwood to C. P. Trevelyan, 8 February 1907 (C. P. Trevelyan Papers).
7 *Manchester Guardian*, 14 January 1909.
8 House of Commons, 15 March 1912.
9 *Land Values*, June 1909, pp. 11-12.
10 L. Harcourt to W. Runciman, 24 March 1909 (Runciman Papers).
11 Lloyd George, Memorandum, 13 March 1909, Public Record Office, CAB 37/98/44.
12 See John Brown, 'Scottish and English land legislation', *Scottish Historical Review*, 1968, vol. 46, pp. 72-85.
13 *Land Values*, April 1915, p. 258.

14 Cabinet letter, 17 July 1913. Asquith Papers, vol. 7, f. 57.
15 Summary of Land Enquiry Committee Report, vol. 1 (Rural), *Liberal Magazine*, 1913, pp. 625-38.
16 See various reports to Lloyd George from 28 May 1914, Lloyd George Papers C/2/4/22 *et seq.*
17 See CAB 37/118, 120 *et seq.*
18 G. Wallace Carter to Lloyd George, 28 May 1914.
19 Ibid.
20 Lloyd George to Percy Illingworth (copy), 24 October 1913. Lloyd George Papers, C/5/4/7.
21 Memorandum by Birrell to Cabinet, 9 August 1913.

Note: The author wishes to thank his wife for helpful advice and criticism; the University of Surrey for a grant from the Faculty IV Research Fund; and for access to private papers, Mr Mark Bonham-Carter, the Trustees of the Beaverbrook Library, the Bodleian Library, Sir Steven Runciman, Mrs Pauline Dower and Mrs Helen Bowen Pease.

10

PENSIONS NOT DREADNOUGHTS: THE RADICALS AND NAVAL RETRENCHMENT

GERALD H. S. JORDAN

The new, all-big-gun battleship *Dreadnought* was launched on 10 February 1906. Three days later Parliament met for the first time since the Liberals had been swept into power by the electorate. Sir Henry Campbell-Bannerman's Cabinet, despite the presence of four Liberal Imperialists, had a strong Radical element. The Prime Minister had himself led the anti-war wing of his party during the South African war; Lloyd George, Robert Reid and John Burns had been fiercely pro-Boer. More temperate men, like John Morley, James Bryce, Herbert Gladstone and Lord Elgin were adamant Gladstonian anti-Imperialists and exponents of the party's traditional policy of peace, moderation and non-aggression. They could not be expected to forget that Gladstone had resigned over the 1894 naval estimates rather than participate 'in a policy that will be taken as plunging England into a whirlpool of militarism'.[1]

It was ironic, therefore, that the accession of a government so heavily weighted with Radicals should be marked by a revolution in warship construction which threatened the immediate scuttling of their programme of peace and retrenchment. The *Dreadnought* was a fact that could not be ignored. *The Times* warned on 16 February 1906 that the sudden obsolescence of every existing battleship could be expected to bring about a major reconsideration by other powers of their respective naval preparations. Former Conservative Prime Minister Arthur Balfour, a leading navalist, spelled out the implications to the House of Commons on 27 July:[2]

> While at first sight you might be inclined to say that the fact that we were the first to design and build vessels [i.e. dreadnoughts] gives us an advantage in one sense, I am afraid it

may entail upon us an expenditure which otherwise you might have avoided. And for this reason. If the new type carries out the full expectations of its designers, a squadron of four of these battleships is almost invulnerable to any existing naval combination. Therefore, if we are really to keep pace as regards battleships we shall have to build this new type at a rate equal to any two Powers.

The Liberal dilemma was obvious. Each dreadnought cost approximately £2,000,000. If the Cawdor programme of November 1905, which called for four large armoured ships (dreadnoughts and battle-cruisers) annually, accepted 'without prejudice' by Campbell-Bannerman, was put into effect, it would mean about £8,000,000 a year less for domestic social reforms. On the other hand, if the ships were not built the Royal Navy might lose control of the seas. The latter alternative was unthinkable to all but the most eccentric Radicals.

Ultimately the deciding factor lay outside Britain. By 1906 the German naval build-up had become a fact. In the context of the period, a large German navy was probably inevitable. All the other powers, France, the USA and Japan in particular, were building furiously, and every keel laid threatened the Royal Navy's two-power standard. But the German programme alone seemed to challenge Britain directly. The Navy Laws of 1898 and 1900, with their distinctly anti-British bias, called for nineteen battleships to be stationed in the North Sea by 1905. As early as October 1902, the First Lord of the Admiralty, Selborne, was 'convinced that the great new German navy is being carefully built up from the point of view of a war with us'.[3] In the winter of 1904-5 a minor war scare developed in which a new British Channel Fleet of twelve battleships – the same number as the Germans had in commission – was hurriedly established. A popular journal, like the usually moderate *Vanity Fair*, could declare in November: 'If the German fleet were destroyed the peace of Europe would last for two generations'. In February 1905, the First Sea Lord, Admiral Fisher, proposed, probably only half in jest, that an ultimatum be sent to Germany demanding that she cease naval construction or be 'Copenhagened'; that is, the German navy would be sunk inside Kiel.[4]

In the long run, Radical responses to calls for increased appropriations for the Royal Navy have to be understood in relation to the expansion of the German Navy. For a brief period, while Britain alone possessed the new super-battleship, the Radicals were able to achieve a degree of success in their efforts to limit naval expansion. By March 1908, however, five dreadnoughts were under construction in German navy yards, although the first was not commissioned for another twelve months. The amendment to the 1900 Navy Law passed by the Reichstag in February 1908 authorized a building programme of three dreadnoughts and one battle-cruiser annually from 1908-9 to 1911-12 and two capital ships a year until 1917-18. If the German fleet were allowed to become more powerful than the British, the massive German army could invade England. In order to maintain British supremacy, an expensive investment in new battleships for the Royal Navy was necessary. Although it would be wrong to blame the collapse of Radical opposition to naval expansion entirely on the German menace, it was one factor upon which their efforts consistently foundered between 1908 and the outbreak of the war. As G. Shaw Lefevre said in November 1906, 'no one in his senses . . . would dream of proposing that this country should stand still while France and Germany are carrying out their protracted programmes'.[5] To a majority of the Radicals the threat was plain, as their voting on the navy estimates demonstrated.

The character of the naval arms race helps to account for the ambivalence of Radical and socialist responses to increased appropriations for the Royal Navy. It was part of the Radical tradition that, in itself, the fleet was not to be regarded as an instrument of aggression but as a major guarantor of international peace. As the *Westminster Gazette* in 1893 had proclaimed, 'From Cromwell to Cobden good Radicals have ever insisted on an all-powerful Navy'.[6] Practically all Radicals recognized that sea power was essential to the preservation of the nation's maritime life-lines. The navy was the traditional guardian of free trade and the policeman of the world's oceanic trade routes. 'It is mainly our system of Free Trade', wrote H. Stanley Jevons, 'which gives our country the greatest foreign commerce per head of population of any country in the world, and this enables and requires us to maintain the largest merchant fleet and navy.'[7] As their writings and speeches show, the dissidents were not untouched by the Englishman's age-old pride in his navy. Almost all of them believed in it, many indeed loved it. Lady Loreburn, wife of the pacifist Lord Chancellor, in October 1909 christened the 'super-Invincible' *Indefatigable*. Walton Newbold, later the first Communist MP, wrote of 'the thrill of admiration and something akin to pride' that stirred him on viewing the Grand Fleet at Spithead in July 1914.[8] Even Stephen Reynolds, the syndicalist, declared: 'Of all our great public institutions I confess to being proudest of the Navy'.[9] Such feelings were common and not incompatible with an anti-armaments stance. Retrenchment had been a Radical rallying-cry since the days of Gladstone. The term symbolized the belief that the primary aim of social reform could not be achieved while huge sums were being expended on armaments. Every penny spent on guns was a penny that could be better spent in alleviating the miserable conditions of the lower orders of English society. Shaw Lefevre was certain that Campbell-Bannerman's government[10]

> is not behindhand in patriotic desire to maintain the British Empire, to protect its commerce, and to maintain a naval superiority over any combination which can be reasonably expected, but it also feels the pinch of the present lavish expenditure and high taxation. It has many other wants which will involve large expenditure of public money.

As a corollary of this the Radicals felt that, far from averting war, large-scale armaments were the cause of it. This meant that many of them developed contradictory love-hate feelings towards the navy. Emotionally torn between their belief in British maritime supremacy and their desire to restrict armaments expenditure, their arguments against naval appropriations were often half-hearted. Particularly after 1908, it was not unusual for Radicals to speak against navy estimates and then vote for them. They made their protest on principle but succumbed to pride and reason.

Part of the problem was how to judge what constituted a sufficient preponderance of naval power. On this question there was always disagreement. Although many Radicals felt that Britain was 'entitled to maintain a navy at least equal to those of the other two powers combined', they did not, in 1906-7, agree with the big-navy men that the new battleships altered the character of the two-power standard.[11] They were convinced that 'obsolete' vessels had still to be taken into account. Britain, they argued, not only had a head-start in dreadnoughts but also had such a massive superiority of pre-dreadnoughts that the country was not threatened by any likely combination of foreign navies. Other Radicals, however, insisted that the two-power standard itself was dangerous. Not only did it alarm other nations, it threatened 'progress in domestic reform – better housing, the improvement of roads, the care of the aged and infirm'. The government could, they asserted, 'with perfect confidence and safety abandon the maintenance of an overwhelmingly predominant navy, and adopt the more modest standard of being by a little the strongest naval power'.[12] But Henry Labouchere, the intense and cynical long-time leading light of the Liberal left wing, spoke for almost all Radicals when he declared: 'what I fear is that, if we have a navy so strong that we can crush all creation, we shall be inclined to try the experiment of crushing it'.[13]

The Radicals believed that Britain, as the world's greatest sea power, had a moral obligation to set an example and take the lead in reducing naval spending. They did not, however, wish to cut back the Royal Navy while the other powers continued their high rates of warship construction. If reductions were to be made, other nations would have to be induced to do the same. The Radical position was, therefore, that naval disarmament should be established by international arbitration and 'the illustrious example of a simple reliance on the practice of universal justice and obedience to the Christian law of universal love'.[14]

The potential strength of this position was revealed during the debates on the 1904 navy estimates. Even some Conservatives, like Gibson Bowles and Hicks Beach, had expressed their dismay at the proposed £36,899,500 appropriation, a staggering increase of about one-third since 1900. On 29 February, a Radical amendment moved by Herbert Roberts had called upon the government to approach the other great powers with a view to a general reduction of naval forces and the establishment of a permanent basis for the relative size of their fleets. The amendment was defeated by only fifty-two votes. Roberts had argued, in a line followed by Campbell-Bannerman in 1906 and 1907, that since the Royal Navy was supreme Britain could lose nothing by taking the initiative. Some dissidents went further and argued that Britain could with perfect safety set an example by adopting a measure of unilateral disarmament.

Radical views on naval disarmament were clearly explained in the Cobden Club's publication, *The Burden of Armaments: A Plea for Retrenchment*. The book, prepared by a committee chaired by Shaw Lefevre, pointed out that since 1889 warship construction had proceeded on the fear that two great European navies might combine against Great Britain. There was no longer any need for such anxiety. Admiral Togo's victory in the Tsushima Straits had exploded the myth of Russian sea-power; France was now an ally and in any case the French fleet had sunk to less than half the strength of the Royal Navy. Alarmists who were 'crying wolf' about the German navy should reflect upon the fact that British estimates were far greater than those of Russia, France and Germany combined. Additionally, recent arbitration treaties and the establishment of the International Tribunal at the Hague indicated that the time was right for conciliation between the great powers. It was, the Cobden Club concluded, 'absolutely safe to return to the peace establishment' of immediately before the Boer War.[15]

As it turned out, the Radicals were able to claim that, by effecting reductions in the 1905-6 and 1906-7 navy estimates and then scrapping the Cawdor programme, Britain had indeed seized the initiative and pointed the way to general disarmament. Two disparate pressures acted on the government. The Radicals, with most of the Irish and Labour members, who hoped to reach an accommodation with Germany, were coupled in a strange, uneasy alliance with Fisher, the dynamic First Sea Lord, who was violently anti-German and regarded war between the two nations as inevitable. But the alliance was not as unnatural as it at first appears. In many ways a Radical himself, Fisher believed that fiscal retrenchment would actually increase the efficiency of the navy. The May 1904 memorandum which introduced his naval reform scheme declared vibrantly:[16]

> The country will acclaim it! the income-tax payer will worship it, the Navy will growl at first! (they always do growl at first!) BUT WE SHALL BE THIRTY PER CENT MORE FIT TO FIGHT AND WE SHALL BE READY FOR INSTANT WAR! And in time when we get rid of our redundancies in useless ships and unnecessary men it will probably be 30% cheaper!

The country could both have its cake and eat it. If Fisher's reforms – based on ruthless cut-backs in non-essential areas – succeeded, no one would be able to complain about the navy; it would be stronger, more efficient, and would cost less. The 1904-5 estimates had been £36,889,500; those of 1905-6, Fisher's first, were £33,389,500; the estimates for 1906-7, worked out by the Cawdor Board and passed by Parliament in March, showed an additional cut-back of £1,520,000. All this was achieved by Fisher without axeing the new battleship programme. And, although Radicals in Parliament and the press supported the reforms, the economies effected by the First Sea Lord were an internal naval matter and owed nothing to outside pressures. The measures were initiated under a Conservative government and the savings redounded to their credit. Nevertheless, Fisher's providence gave the dissidents added hopes of cutting into the Cawdor programme. What the Tories had begun the Radicals would certainly try to extend.

All signs in 1906 pointed to naval retrenchment. Even Admiral Alfred Mahan, the American whose persuasive writings had done so much to promote the idea of a powerful German navy, warned in Leo Maxse's ultra-Tory *National Review* that 'naval development has become a mere matter of international competition . . . to which no logical – or what is more important, no practical – end is in sight'. The only way to stop this, he said, was 'by international agreement, as for instance an accepted limitation that no naval vessel shall be built exceeding a certain displacement'.[17] Mahan, almost venerated in naval circles, would be listened to with respect by the big-navy men and his views gave encouragement to the Radicals who were pressing for more reductions before the second International Peace Conference met at the Hague the next year. It was clear that the dissidents were not satisfied to abide by the Cawdor plan. On 9 May, the Commons expressed support for a motion by Henry Vivian, Lib-Lab member for Birkenhead, demanding that the question of armaments limitation be put on the Hague agenda. On 21 June, Campbell-Bannerman received a delegation of 120 MPs of the Reduction of Armaments Committee, led by the veteran Radical H. J. Wilson, urging a cut in the programme for the current year. The Sea Lords were not opposed. The *Dreadnought* and three 'Invincible' class battle-cruisers were fitting out under the 1905-6 programme. Fisher and his colleagues agreed with the Prime Minister that there was no need for all four big ships provided for 1906-7 under the Cawdor scheme since no vessels of the new type had been laid down by any European power. Indeed, Fisher expressed to the First Lord, Tweedmouth, his conviction that the country's 'present margin of superiority over Germany (*our only possible foe for years*) is so great as to render it absurd to talk of anything endangering our naval supremacy, *even if we stopped all shipbuilding altogether*! ! !'[18] Tweedmouth did not agree, but his objections were firmly squashed by the formidable combination of Campbell-Bannerman, Asquith, the Cabinet Radicals and Fisher. On 27 July, Edmund Robertson, the Parliamentary Secretary, announced in the Commons that the Admiralty would ask for only two armoured ships in the 1907-8 estimates, with provision for a third to be laid down if the Hague Peace Conference was unsuccessful. The compromise had been arranged by Asquith, with Haldane's help, and bears the mark of the political acumen that was to stand him in such good stead during his premiership. He was in an awkward spot. An Imperialist Chancellor of the Exchequer in a government committed to the cause of military retrenchment, he was bound to support the cry for economies to finance old-age pensions, but he would not do so at the expense of a drastic curtailment of the naval building programme. He never pushed for retrenchment as strongly as the Radicals would have liked and certainly not as strongly as Lloyd George was to in the future. Lacking the unshakeable moral convictions of a Radical, Asquith was able to adopt a middle-of-the-road stance which did much to prevent the naval construction issue from becoming a seriously disruptive factor within the Cabinet. The Radicals, although far from being satisfied, jubilantly accepted the decrease as a step in the right direction. It would be a sign for the other powers and a guide to the future.

The Tories were outraged. Even the whisper of naval reduction caused them undue concern; now they were faced with a 50 per cent cut in the next year's construction. Heaping scorn on the government and on Fisher, Balfour and Arthur Lee (a former Civil Lord at the Admiralty) attacked the compromise in the House of Commons as an inconsistent and shallow attempt to convince the Opposition that the navy remained supreme, the Radicals that the government had accomplished significant retrenchment, and Germany that Britain had only pacific intentions. To Balfour, 'the idea that these innocent, naif, unsuspecting statesmen who are going to join in the Hague Conference will be taken in by this noble appeal is really absurd'.[19] Campbell-Bannerman, however, ignored the sarcasm. For him it was a question of faith and the hope that Christian morality would guide the nations at the Hague: 'We desire to stop this rivalry, and to set an example in stopping it'.[20]

Outside the House, a torrent of indignant protest gushed from the Tory press. It developed the proportions of a minor naval scare with the announcement from Berlin in August that the first German dreadnought would be larger and more powerful than the British prototype. 'The supremacy of the British navy is endangered . . . The British margin of superiority will vanish altogether when these naval programmes are completed', screamed the *National Review*. 'The Liberal Government', the *Standard* charged, 'has in ten months done more damage to the nation than we might anticipate from conflict with a first-class European Power.' 'Excubitor' in the *Fortnightly Review* dwelt on the dangers of 'the naval aggrandisement of Germany' which had 'become a menace to British supremacy'. Even St Loe Strachey's generally staid and rational *Spectator* demanded a parliamentary inquiry into the state of the navy. As for Fisher, the *Globe* asserted that 'more than any one man the responsibility and the guilt for these reductions lies at his door'. The *National Review* rebuked the Sea Lords for their 'extraordinary *volte face*' and accused Fisher of being the compliant tool of a 'cheese-paring Cobdenite Cabinet'; if economies had to be effected, the journal said, they should be made in education and not in the country's first line of defence.[21]

The government, firmly supported by the Sea Lords and the service press, refused to be budged. But Asquith's compromise was not a great victory for the Radicals. Hard-pressed to respond to the Tory stream of invective, they found themselves forced into the difficult position of trying to persuade the other powers to discuss naval limitations at the same time as they had to defend the reductions by following the Fisher line of emphasizing the strength and superiority of the Royal Navy. Their predicament was obvious and it did nothing to enhance Radical credibility. On the other hand, the cut-back did demonstrate that there were others who, for various reasons, would support demands for retrenchment as long as they believed maritime supremacy was not endangered. In this instance Fisher's backing was crucial. As the *Manchester Guardian* pointed out, it was the fact that government policy coincided with that of the Sea Lords which enabled the reductions to be made. This did not mean that Fisher saw his economies from the same viewpoint as did the Radicals. 'The Hague Conference will be futile', he told Tweedmouth on 26 September. The Admiralty, however, was 'not going to be frightened by foreign paper programmes (the bogey of agitators!). But when foreigners, especially Germans, actually build, *then* we will double! ! '[22] From this time until his retirement more than three years later, however, Fisher was closely identified in the press with the Liberal government. His quarrel with Admiral Beresford, former Conservative MP for Woolwich and now C-in-C Mediterranean Fleet, took on a party complexion in which the 'Adullamites', as Fisher termed his enemies, sought to use the Tory party in their vendetta with the First Sea Lord. Beresford became a leader of the big-navy group and Fisher was for a short while the hero of those who sought to combine a supreme navy with fiscal economy.

Without Fisher's initiative in 1906 nothing would have been achieved. Inhibited by having to work against a government they favoured, the Radicals could accomplish little by themselves. Just before the cuts were announced, Murray Macdonald, the Radical member for the Falkirk Burghs, admitted: 'It is difficult for anyone who claims to be a loyal member of the Liberal Party to take up an attitude of opposition to the present Government'.[23] As the naval rivalry intensified, so the Radical quandary became greater. A full-scale revolt over naval armaments was out of the question. Such action would almost certainly split the party and might well result in its swinging totally into the Imperialist camp, leaving the dissidents to find a new home either in the Labour party or on their own. They found neither alternative appealing. Likewise, the Liberal Imperialists had no desire to be forced into an alliance with the Conservatives on the issue or to attempt to rule with a minority government. A major division within the Liberal party could put an end to the social reform programme, the fulfilment of which was, for most Radicals, their major goal. Therefore, both the left and right wings of the Liberal party, with a few exceptions like Commander Bellairs – 'that pestilent young ass who represents King's Lynn', as Fisher called him – supported the reductions announced in July; one group because they realized they could not get more, the other because they knew they could not get away with less. The Liberals' nominal allies, the Irish nationalists, did not have such problems. Seeing the Gladstonian tradition as the best hope for Home Rule, they could normally be relied upon to support Campbell-Bannerman's government. Only ship-building Belfast stood to gain from naval appropriations and it was Protestant and Unionist; the remainder of Ireland was essentially agricultural and had no stake in a powerful navy. Most of the Labour members also supported the scrapping of the Cawdor programme, although they were more divided among themselves than their Irish colleagues. Keir Hardie claimed that the July reductions, although they did not go nearly far enough, were a beginning that 'would be welcomed by the friends of peace and arbitration all over the world'.[24] In the light of the approaching Hague Conference, the British move was seen by the Radicals and their allies as the wedge opening the door to international conciliation and disarmament.

Once again it was Germany that stood out as the major obstacle. The dreadnought announcement of August, and rumours that Germany was answering the British reduction by an accelerated building programme, added fuel to the furnace of the 'blue funk school' – another of Fisher's sobriquets for his opponents – and poured a dampener on Radical hopes. On 16 August the Kaiser informed Sir Frank Lascelles, the British Ambassador in Berlin, that Germany would boycott the Hague Conference if the question of armaments was put on the agenda. 'What does Germany want?' asked *The Economist*. 'Everything would be cleared up if we were only sure that the aims of the German Government were not those of the Pan-German expansionists.' Germany, however, had just as good reason to query British motives. German apprehensions were understandable. Tirpitz did not doubt Campbell-Bannerman's sincerity in wanting all-round arms reductions and acknowledged that 'it is a correct religious aspiration'. But he recognized that the Prime Minister and the vast majority of Radicals took for granted the continuing supremacy of the Royal Navy. The British government was asking the powers to accept a fixed ratio at a time when the British navy was overwhelmingly superior to all other navies. In other words, it was asking Germany to agree to a perpetual position of inferiority. If Germany refused she would be held up to the world as the enemy of peace. Tirpitz put it succinctly:[25]

> Here is England, already more than four times as strong as Germany, in alliance with Japan, and probably so with France, and you, the colossus, come and ask Germany, the pygmy, to disarm. From the point of view of the public it is laughable and Machiavellian, and we shall never agree to anything of the sort.

One of Radicalism's great strengths was its puritanical moral faith which would not admit defeat. Despite the German rebuff the transparently honest Prime Minister played out the hand to the bitter end. The 1907-8 navy estimates, the first submitted by the Liberal government, were issued on 28 February. They announced a decrease of £1,135,000 in new construction costs over the previous year; the net saving on the total estimates was £450,000. This provided for two improved dreadnoughts plus a third contingent upon the outcome of the Hague Conference. It was the last time until the 1920s that the navy estimates would show a reduction. Although the *Daily Mail* complained that 'the nation gave no mandate to weaken its Navy for the sole purpose of providing funds for doles to the Socialists', the estimates moved through Parliament without trouble. Robertson assured the Commons that the two-power standard would be adequately maintained. By 1909 the Royal Navy would have seven dreadnoughts and three battle-cruisers in service as against not a single one for any other power. Even Balfour was forced to admit that the navy was stronger than any two-power standard demanded, and Lee, although pessimistic about the Conference, actually agreed to a temporary slackening of the building programme. The Radicals, led by Murray Macdonald and Sir John Brunner, the chemical magnate, made half-hearted attempts to secure greater cuts, but these were not put to the vote; the dissidents were pinning their hopes on the coming Conference.

Meanwhile, in an article on 'The Hague Conference and the limitation of armaments', which appeared in the first issue of the Radical weekly, the *Nation*, Campbell-Bannerman had pledged his government to further reductions provided the other powers did the same. Although the Prime Minister had sought Grey's approval before publication, the article had results the reverse of those intended. In Germany it confirmed the feelings voiced by Tirpitz, and at home it exaggerated suspicions that the government was falling into Radical hands. The feeling that Campbell-Bannerman was isolated from most of his Cabinet was heightened when neither Asquith nor, more surprisingly, Grey rose to his support when Balfour attacked the article, and the government's naval policy in general, in the Commons on 5 March.

The funeral oration for naval arms limitation was delivered by Chancellor Bülow in the Reichstag on 30 April. 'The German Government cannot participate in a discussion which, according to their conviction, is unpractical even if it does not involve risk.' Grey was not surprised. 'If discussion is impossible or fruitless we shall go on with the Naval expenditure which we now have in suspense.'[26] Radical reactions were mixed. The *Nation* responded with an irrational and childish outburst against the German government, German bureaucracy and the German people; even the German Radicals were held to be 'as decidedly opposed to the English policy as any of the Conservative groups'. On the other hand, the more sober *Manchester Guardian* saw a great deal of justice on the German side and called on Grey to ensure that the *entente* with France did not prevent Anglo-German conciliation. A month later, recovered from its tantrum, the *Nation* attacked the *entente* 'policy of penning in' Germany. By the end of 1907 such expressions of sympathetic understanding of the German position were frequent in the Radical press and, right up to the war, dissidents continued to blame British policy for the failure of the two powers to reach a naval agreement. 'Who began the arms race?' they queried. 'It was not Germany that built the first Dreadnought.'[27]

The Radicals had good reason to change their outlook. The Hague Peace Conference, which met between 15 June and 18 October 1907, was a disaster. Arms limitation was dismissed in twenty-five minutes on 17 August when a resolution by Sir Edward Fry, the eighty-two-year-old Quaker leader of the British delegation, declaring that it was 'highly desirable that the Governments should resume the serious study of this question', was adopted without a vote. It was, W. T. Stead declared, 'a miserable and scandalous débâcle'. But that was not all. The final nail in the coffin of Radical hopes was driven home by the British representatives. A Radical campaign for the abolition of the 'monstrous and barbaric practice' of the 'right of capture' of merchant ships carrying commercial goods in wartime had been launched earlier in the year and built on exaggerated hopes for the Peace Conference. For most Radicals adherence to right of capture was a major factor in the retention of large navies. 'Abandon the doctrine of capture and half the case for great navies would be destroyed', they argued. 'With half the world's shipping under our flag, one might suppose that our clear course if we mean to thrive by commerce rather than piracy, would be to press for every reform of international law which would protect commerce.'[28] Divergence of opinion was sharp and not simply along party lines. Commercial interests tended to oppose the doctrine; the arch-Tory member for Liverpool, F. E. Smith, for instance, found himself supporting Loreburn who presented the case in terms of Liberal morality. Asquith and Robertson gave moderate support to the Radical position but, as C. P. Scott was astounded to discover, Lloyd George was 'as much opposed as any of the Jingoes to the abolition of the right of capture of private property at sea – the real key to the situation'.[29] This time the Radicals did not have Fisher behind them. Naval opinion, with very few exceptions, was that the right of capture was inseparable from the idea of blockade, an essential part of Britain's involvement in a continental war. The capture of an enemy's shipping afforded Britain, with no army capable of invading a European state, the only effective way of seriously damaging an enemy. It was this position that Grey instructed the British delegation to uphold, and the highly respected Radical, Lord Courtney, who observed the Conference, saw it as 'a potent factor in preventing a fruitful discussion'.[30] Long afterward Radicals were lamenting that 'the increase of the German navy is tolerated by the German taxpayer mainly because successive British Governments, ill-inspired by their naval experts, have clung to the so-called Right of Capture'.[31]

The failure of the Peace Conference marked the end of any real possibility of checking naval arms competition. A disillusioned British delegate, Lord Reay, sadly observed that the Conference had 'not given a greater sense of security, rather the reverse'. From then until August 1914, the Anglo-German naval race was a continuous and dominating part of the European scene. The Conference and its aftermath dramatically demonstrated that the Radicals were powerless without firm Cabinet and, most important, naval support. This they did not get. Indeed, in 1908 Fisher was demanding six dreadnoughts and the next year he raised this to eight. Radical chidings were by this time exasperating naval officers like Herbert Richmond, then Flag Captain aboard HMS *Dreadnought*, who believed the government was dominated by small-navy men. When the inevitable war with Germany came, Richmond fumed,[32]

> Radical Governments will have been in power, ship-building will have been cut down and all expenditure on the Navy reduced to the lowest amount. Then like a whirlwind will come the quarrel, ourselves all unsuspecting and peaceful, ready to do anything to avoid war, giving way to every demand until some demand too outrageous for the mob to stand will be made . . . and while the mob is howling and the Government refusing to allow mobilisation or concentration of either ships or troops, Germany will silently take the initiative and put her well prepared plans into execution. Our people are like silly sheep waiting for their throats to be cut, or ostriches with their heads in sand, refusing to see and thinking they cannot be seen.

This was hardly fair to the Radicals, as at least one high-ranking officer recognized. Admiral King-Hall was clearly sympathetic to Radical pleas for an understanding with Germany. 'I know no politics,' he wrote to Noel Buxton, 'but I thought you would like to know that I, and I am sure thousands of other Liberals . . . long to be on better terms with Germany. They have a perfect right to build a fleet. The only thing we can do is to take care ours is strong enough to protect our Empire and enormous trade.'[33] The Admiral mirrored what was, of course, the Radical position. But majority naval opinion was behind the First Sea Lord. As for Fisher himself, he was subjected in 1908-9 to castigation from all sides. Radicals and pacifists, like Norman Angell, turned on him for putting dreadnoughts before pensions, while Conservatives and Navy Leaguers, egged on by Beresford, charged him with being a Radical and neglecting the navy.

As German building accelerated and pressures from the right wing and the navy grew, it became increasingly difficult for the Radicals to do anything other than seek to check the worst excesses of the big-navy men. Even so, their efforts were impaired by their own regard for the navy and its supremacy. Josiah Wedgwood, the Radical member for Newcastle-under-Lyme, typified their dilemma. When supporting Murray Macdonald's retrenchment motion on 2 March 1908, he affirmed his support for the two-power standard but stressed that he was interested only in effecting cuts in the army estimates. Macdonald himself, introducing a similar motion on 13 March 1911, admitted that Britain must possess 'an adequate superiority of Dreadnoughts'. And so, from 1908, many Radicals became much more concerned with attempting to bring about token reductions of the estimates, perhaps as much as anything to salve their own consciences, than in bringing about any fundamental change in naval policy. Others, a few with connections in the shipbuilding and allied industries, were forced by the slump of 1908 which put thousands out of work on the Tyne and Clydeside to support the dreadnought programme. Faced with heavy financial loss and the destitution of their workers, men like Sir Charles McLaren of John Brown and Company and Lord Furness of Palmer's of Jarrow really had no other choice.[34] Many more, perhaps the majority, simply acknowledged that there were other, more pressing things needing their attention, and slipped by the wayside. It is clear that many Radicals, especially after 1909, did not bother to attend the naval estimate debates. Radical memorials and resolutions to the government could still collect anything up to 150 signatures, but when it came to a vote in the House the response was discouraging to the old regulars like Brunner and Macdonald. The reduction motion of 17 March 1909 gained just twenty-seven Radical votes, half the number of the year before. The motion for reduction became an annual charade at which the dissident vote remained fairly constant. On 2 March 1914, the motion received thirty-four votes.

After 1907, the Radicals were fighting for a lost cause against a perceptible hardening of the government's naval policy. Campbell-Bannerman, Asquith and the successive First Lords, Tweedmouth, McKenna and Churchill, re-affirmed the two-power standard, which in practice was taken to mean the German fleet plus 60 per cent. Keeping in line with announced German increases, the British naval estimates, against which the Radicals protested to no avail, rose from £32,319,500 in 1908 (up £900,000 over the previous year) to £51,550,000 in 1914 (a net increase of £2,740,700 over 1913). Despite their inclinations, the Radicals gave way rather than threaten the social reform programme which they and the government were pushing so hard. In 1908, they agreed to two dreadnoughts, then three; by the end of the year, when the Admiralty was demanding six, they were willing to settle at four. By the time the estimates were submitted to Parliament in the spring of 1909, Asquith had persuaded them to accept the idea of four plus four; that is, four dreadnoughts to be built with four more contingent upon need, leaving the decision as to contingency with the government. This was their only reply to the Conservative cry of 'We Want Eight'. C. F. G. Masterman wrote of his fellow Radicals in February 1909, 'all the life and spirit has gone out of them . . . Morley looked rather crumpled and very old'.[35]

It was a sad end to the hopes and aspirations which had stood so high in 1907. In 1909 their cause was buried. It rose again briefly in 1911 when Churchill, who had described the 1909 navy scare as 'a false, sham, lying panic', became First Lord of the Admiralty. As President of the Board of Trade he had fought hard against McKenna and the big-navy men in that last-ditch battle. But his Radicalism smacked more of political opportunism than principle and his first navy estimates, issued in March 1912, were almost £12,000,000 higher than those of 1909.

Ultimately the Radicals had been defeated in their struggle for naval retrenchment by what seemed the overwhelming menace of the growing German navy. United, as they were in no other area, by their dedication to the supremacy of the Royal Navy, they could never bow down to such a threat. In having to oppose both the navy they believed in and the government they favoured, they found themselves unable to push their cause to its utmost, even during the brief interval when the international situation seemed in their favour. Although many of them saw the death of Campbell-Bannerman in 1908 as the turning-point, and others the navy scare of 1909, it was the Kaiser's intransigence and their own government's position at the Hague that killed the case for naval limitation. In fact, when Asquith in April 1908 replaced the ailing Campbell-Bannerman as Prime Minister, and Lloyd George went to the Exchequer, with Churchill taking over the Board of Trade, the Radicals found themselves better led than ever before. But it was already too late. Most of the tremendous energies of Lloyd George and Churchill were expended on what were, to them and most Radicals, the far more pressing issues of domestic politics. Even Lloyd George's Radicalism, as regards foreign policy, became suspect after his belligerent Mansion House speech in July 1911. Without the support of powerful governmental and naval experts, the Radicals were little more than thorns in the side of a government whose domestic policies they generally supported.

NOTES

1 John Morley, *The Life of William Ewart Gladstone*, London, 1907, vol. 2, p. 748.
2 *Hansard*, iv:162:111-12.
3 CAB 37/63/142.
4 Arthur J. Marder, *The Anatomy of British Sea Power*, New York, 1940, pp. 495-9.
5 G. Shaw Lefevre (Eversley), 'Naval scares', *Contemporary Review*, vol. 90, November 1906, p. 625.
6 A. J. P. Taylor, *The Trouble Makers*, Bloomington, 1958, p. 115.
7 H. Stanley Jevons, 'The two-power standard', *Contemporary Review*, vol. 95, February 1909, p. 131.
8 J. T. Walton Newbold, *How Europe Armed for War, 1871-1914*, London, n.d., p. 76.
9 Elie Halévy, *The Rule of Democracy, 1905-1914*, London, 1961, p. 412n.
10 G. Shaw Lefevre, op. cit., p. 636.
11 G. Shaw Lefevre, 'Rival navies', *Contemporary Review*, vol. 89, February 1906, p. 165.
12 Jevons, op. cit., pp. 131 and 135.
13 Marder, op. cit., p. 484.
14 Ibid., pp. 484-5.
15 Cobden Club, *The Burden of Armaments: A Plea for Retrenchment*, London, 1905.
16 Marder, op. cit., p. 487.
17 A. T. Mahan, 'The Far Eastern war', *National Review*, May 1906.
18 26 September 1906, in Arthur J. Marder, *Fear God and Dread Nought*, London, 1952-9, vol. 2, p. 91.
19 *Hansard*, iv:162:110-11.
20 Ibid., 117-18.
21 H. W. Wilson, 'Destroying Britain's naval supremacy', *National Review*, September 1906; *Standard*, 22 October 1906; '*Excubitor*', 'The Command of the German Ocean', *Fortnightly Review*, September 1906; *Spectator*, September 1906; *Globe*, 21 September 1906.
22 Marder, *Fear God and Dread Nought*, vol. 2, p. 91.
23 J. A. Murray Macdonald, 'Our armaments: a plea for reduction', *Contemporary Review*, vol. 91, May 1907, p. 640.
24 *Hansard*, iv:162:80.
25 9 January 1907, in G.P. Gooch and Harold Temperley (eds), *British Documents on the Origins of the War, 1898-1914*, London, 1926-38, vol. vi, pp. 2-3.
26 Arthur J. Marder, *From the Dreadnought to Scapa Flow*, London, 1961-71, vol. 1, p. 133.
27 Anon., 'An open letter from the German Michel to John Bull: the German naval case', *Contemporary Review*, vol. 95, April 1909, p. 394. The change of mood is particularly noticeable in *The Economist* and the *Nation*.
28 Henry Noel Brailsford, *The War of Steel and Gold*, 3rd ed., London, 1915, pp. 262 and 304.

29 Scott to L. T. Hobhouse, 22 August 1908, cited in Stephen E. Koss, *Sir John Brunner: Radical Plutocrat*, Cambridge, 1970, p. 232.
30 G. P. Gooch, *Life of Lord Courtney*, London, 1920, p. 549.
31 *The Economist*, 7 December 1912.
32 Arthur J. Marder, *Portrait of an Admiral: The Life and Papers of Sir Herbert Richmond*, Cambridge, Mass., 1952, p. 63.
33 Mosa Anderson, *Noel Buxton*, London, 1952, p. 49.
34 See Howard Weinroth, 'Left-wing opposition to naval armaments in Britain before 1914', *Journal of Contemporary History*, vol. 6, 1971, pp. 114-16.
35 Lucy Masterman, *C. F. G. Masterman*, London, 1939, p. 125.

11

RADICALISM AND THE ARMAMENT TRUST

CLIVE TREBILCOCK

Hostility to the Armament Trust – the fraternity of great industrial concerns devoted to military contracting – was a passion shared by many Radicals in the years before 1914. They could cite a variety of powerful reasons. Pacifists of all political colours could fasten upon the Trust as an organization selfishly interested in war, and capable of serving its interests by 'fomenting' hostilities between nations. Protagonists of welfare legislation could rail against the armament interests as the greedy recipients of the much increased expenditure by governments on 'bloated armaments'. Adherents of *laissez-faire* and the open market could point to the armament cartel as the culmination of monopoly capitalism. Conspiracy theorists could marvel in horror at the armourers' tentacular overseas affiliations and alliances. The Trust was warlike, expensive, non-competitive, and globally capitalistic – everything that was calculated to outrage the Radical preferences for peace, retrenchment, open business, and international accord.

In consequence, the roll-call of Radical groups apt to express swift and often shrill dislike for the armaments manufacturer – Shaw's 'wicked rich one' – was lengthy. 'Economists' of Cabinet rank, pledged to thrift and to social programmes, reformers like David Lloyd George, and, before his conversion to 'big-navy' appetites, Winston Churchill, were naturally unfriendly to the industrial beneficiaries of the world's defence budgets. Similarly, the Radical Liberal rank-and-file in the Commons, men like Sir John Brunner, Murray Macdonald, and the stalwarts of the Reduction of Armaments Committee – advocates of the classical precepts, peace, retrenchment and reform – were always ready to divert business from the armaments trade. The great reductionist campaigns of 1908 and 1911, aimed at the curtailment of naval and military spending, gave proof of their energy, if not of their effectiveness. Nor were such activities restricted to the Liberal MPs; some of the most effective propaganda against the armourers came from the small Labour groups in the House, particularly from Philip Snowden. Outside the legislature, also, there were powerful voices and pens among the Radical journalists and propagandists: Francis Hirst, G. H. Perris, and H. W. Massingham used the pages of *The Economist*, *Concord*, and the *Labour Leader* to good effect against 'the merchants of death'. But if dislike of the armament capitalists as a *profession* covered a wide range of opinion, the frontal attack upon the Armament Trust as a non-competitive and over-influential *institution* depended upon a more select group. In this most violent of the pre-war onslaughts directed against the various forms of defence activity, the socialist orators and the yellow journalists were responsible for the bulk of the comment.

And if the Trust was laid under siege by Radical commandos, rather than by a Radical army, it was also attacked rather late in the *ante-bellum* period. Although a generalized hostility to the arms trade was noticeable from the turn of the century onwards, the Trust itself was not picked out as a special target until the final two or three years before the First World War. There had been more than usually determined mutterings against 'the fraudulent contractor, the vampirical financier . . . the astute shipbuilder'[1] in the late 1900s, and the naval scare of 1908–9 – thought by many of a Radical persuasion to have been 'fomented' by the armament interests – tended to lend force to such animosities. But it was between 1912 and 1914 that a new form of attack, more specific, more ambitious, and certainly more imaginative, began to develop. Previously, the Radicals had directed most of their invective against official defence *policy* and against government *purchasing* of armaments – against, as G. H. Perris classically put it, 'ruinous expenditure upon unnecessary armaments'.[2] This refrain ran, as their titles clearly imply, through such Radical publications as the Cobden Club's *The Burden of Armaments: A Plea for Retrenchment* (1905), or Perris's *For An Arrest of Armaments* (1906). After 1912, however, the Radical pamphleteers discovered fresh whipping boys. Rather ahead of the pack, W. M. J. Williams, writing in *Concord* in July 1912, decided that 'expenditure on armaments is driven forward and decided practically by a number of armour plate firms and their friends, backed by a Jingoistic press'.[3] A new emphasis began to emerge: it was not government policy but capitalistic intrigue which was properly to blame for the persistence of the arms race. The armourers in collusion, national and international, moved into the centre of Radical attention as a new collective villain. But the full torrent of abuse did not fall immediately. Instead it waited upon an event far removed from the British economic and political scene: the revelations by Dr Karl Liebknecht before the German Reichstag in April 1913 of the misdeeds perpetrated by *German* armament interests. Once given an example, the British Radicals set to work with a will to find their own armament 'rings'. Within weeks of Liebknecht's allegations British journalists were firing off a new model of squib from the pages of the Radical press. The public was warned against the 'hideous octopus',[4] invited to contemplate 'an unscrupulous and inscrutable power of evil, richer than fabled Croesus, panoplied in steel . . . one of the most sinister obstacles infesting the path of national peace and international prosperity'.[5] By January 1914 a new Committee for the Reduction of Armaments, under the guidance of Francis Hirst, had decided that the real enemy was not Germany but the International Armament Trust. And by March 1914 the attack was given a new dimension, as Philip Snowden repeated the charges against the armament conspirators from the floor of the Commons in the most authoritative and potentially most damaging denunciation of the pre-war period. In conformity with the late development of these tactics, however, it is significant that the most comprehensive indictments of the Trust were delivered either just before or somewhat *after* the outbreak of the First World War – in a string of pamphlets and books including *The War Traders* by G. H. Perris (1913), *Krupp and the International Armament Ring* by H. R. Murray (1915), and *The War Trust Exposed* by J. T. W. Newbold (1916).

The eagerness with which the British Radicals took up the device of the Armament Trust is in itself suspect: it suggests a vocabulary of propaganda which, depleted by hard and unrewarding campaigns, seizes upon a new and foreign rhetoric regardless of its suitability to the native context. It is suggestive too that the Radicals, after protracted and largely unsuccessful attacks upon armament *expenditure*, should turn their disillusioned attentions so brusquely to the armament *producers*. Having failed to rally sufficient support against the government, it might seem that they sought out an alternative and more vulnerable object for attack. However this may be, the exact situation may be revealed more clearly by a critical analysis of the radicals' assumptions regarding the Armament Trust. These were threefold, with the final assumption trailing a significant implication. First, that the Armament Trust existed in Britain as a compact and concrete alliance of industrial interests with a necessarily sinister purpose. Second, that the Trust was sufficiently powerful to 'exploit' the British government and to induce it to spend lavishly on weaponry. Third, that the Trust existed also in an international aspect as the armourers of foreign nations joined hands in defiance of diplomatic alignments, penetrated the economies of client states, and employed their collective influence to reduce customers to a state of submission before the massed force of international capitalism. From this the implication followed that the Armament Trust was sufficiently powerful to encourage warfare between states so as to swell its expansive order books.

The Radicals viewed the Trust as an actual physical entity, a secret but powerful conspiracy that was also a combination of industrial producers. This collectivity, they argued, was designed to apportion orders between members, to drive up prices against the government – the single customer in the domestic market – and generally to exploit the dependence of the service ministries upon a few highly specialized armament suppliers. This was precisely the interpretation adopted by Snowden in his speech of March 1914. 'How,' he asked, 'can you get a tender from Vickers? You are getting it from Armstrong Whitworth and Co. and from William Beardmore and Co. The whole thing is a farce.'[6] In similar vein, G. H. Perris concluded that 'The great body of the War Trade is . . . a vast financial network . . . linked together by an intricate system';[7] and H. R. Murray argued that the 1900s saw 'an end to all rivalry between the great armament firms'.[8] Virtually every pamphlet or speech on the subject repeated this conviction in one form or another. Many of them, for good measure, provided corroboration of the network's existence by citing the mergers, take-overs, shared directorates, and exchanged shareholdings in which the industry abounded. The Radical critics delved into the inter-relations of the British arms trade; they researched the shareholdings, found the connections, and concluded that they had discovered an Armament Trust. Sometimes they described it as a ring, a tightly-linked circle of contractors arranged around the Government. And once the collaborationist preference among British arms firms was established, they deduced to a man, and without further investigation, that it must exist for evil and anti-social purposes.

Part of this argument was correct. A tendency towards association or merger, if not towards a full-blown Trust, was a marked characteristic of the armament industry in the two or three decades before the First World War. The main nuclei for this combination process were provided by the firms of Vickers, Armstrong Whitworth, the Coventry Ordnance Works and Nobel's Explosives Co. By 1914 Vickers could list within its industrial interests the artillery works of Maxim-Nordenfeld (1897), the shipyard of the Naval Construction Co. of Barrow (1897), a controlling share in William Beardmore and Co., the Clydeside shipbuilders (1902), and part control, with Armstrong, of the Whitehead torpedo works at Weymouth (1906). On its account, Armstrong had captured the famous Manchester gunworks of Joseph Whitworth (1897). Together, the two great armament concerns exchanged weapon designs and maintained a market-sharing agreement covering most of the world's weaponry clientele (from 1906).[9] Alongside this powerful condominium there stood the Coventry Ordnance Works (1905), itself a joint project sponsored by three warship-building firms. In explosives, Nobel's Explosives Co. had introduced into the market an even more marked element of cohesion: no less than five cordite producers were added to its assets between 1897 and 1912.[10] At the outbreak of the First World War, therefore, the armaments industry was very far from being a haven of open competition.

With most of these cases known to the Radical propagandists in substance, if not in detail, it is not surprising that they saw the Armament Trust as an institution, a comprehensive, concrete and corporate entity. However, they failed to recognize a variety of other important features, most notably that in several important cases the combination process was by no means completed, and that in many trades fierce competition remained the order of the day. In some munitions markets a deep wedge was inserted to prevent the further progress of association. In this way, Armstrong and Vickers were forced to fight hard against the intrusive Coventry Ordnance Works throughout the 1900s and Nobel's was locked in violent combat with the rival explosives concern, Kynoch Ltd of Birmingham for the major part of the period.[11] Rather than arrange itself in a single monolithic Trust structure, the arms trade formed, in fact, a series of smaller combinations and groups, sporting some interlinkages but also revealing some marked gaps where no writ of association succeeded in penetrating.

Given this qualification, however, it is clear that the armourers did prefer any workable system which reduced competition and permitted combination. The issue, and one which Radical commentators mishandled, was the construction to be placed upon their choice. To the Radicals the matter was self-evident: the armourers were moved by capitalistic greed, by the naturally conspiratorial nature of the trade, above all by a desire to exploit the government – which, if freed from such attentions, might return to the paths of retrenchment and reductionism. It was the characteristic failing of the Radical interpretation that it remained at this superficial level and probed no further. No attention was given to the high cost of entry to a trade which necessitated refined and expensive plant; to the irregularity and undependability of armament orders; to the precarious nature of a home market built round a single customer; to the unwillingness of the government to support its contractors in the lean periods between orders.[12] This failure to perceive correctly the market conditions of the armament trade led directly to an interpretation of the Armament Trust which was seriously incomplete.

In reality the specialized nature of the armament market conferred upon the government, the single customer, as well as upon its few suppliers, some unusual powers. The state, seen by the Radicals as prey to the 'ring's' machinations, was in practice an extremely tough customer. It could use generous contracts to lure firms into expanding their productive capacity, but at other times, when defence needs were less pressing, might provide no contracts at all. As a client sufficiently powerful to play price-maker rather than price-taker, it could manipulate prices with some freedom. However energetically the armourers might employ 'ring' tactics to drive up prices, they still depended on the government's *acceptance* of their price – there was no alternative source of demand within the home market once the service ministries had declined to do business.[13] Faced with this brand of customer power, a small number of large producers will tend naturally to combine. It is an economic fact of survival that monopsony – a market of one – tends to produce oligopoly – supply by the few. Combination, under such circumstances, may be needed not for the exploitation of the government but for the protection of producers against harsh market conditions. The cordite firms of which the Director of Army Contracts, the services' chief procurement official, said in 1905, 'If some of the companies are forced to give up the manufacture of cordite . . . there will still be sufficient competition to ensure reasonable prices',[14] could scarcely be blamed for arranging a 'ring' in their own defence. Similarly, when firms like Armstrong complained of an official policy which 'manufactured non-employed men'[15] – by refusing to provide support when contracts were scarce – the armourers might well have perceived legitimate reasons for organizing counter-measures. Combination offered escape from price-cutting and helter-skelter pursuit of scarce orders, as well as raising a united voice of protest against the not infrequent high-handedness of the War Office and Admiralty. The mere fact of a co-operative movement among arms firms did not, therefore, necessarily imply an anti-social or exploitative purpose – and this the Radicals did not understand.

The failure to detect the internal flaws and weaknesses of the Trust, the failure to identify its very particular market context, must necessarily lessen the force of the Radicals' charges and so reduce the viability of their propaganda. Moreover, the underestimate of the state's influence in the armament market, coming so soon after the attacks on the government's 'over-developed' initiatives in defence policy, does not enhance the credibility of the Radicals' interpretation of the Trust. As one commentator, himself a critic of the arms trade, realized after the war, there were within this interpretation 'shortcomings which can only be overcome by access to the private documents of the armament manufacturers'.[16] Lacking that access, the Radical view perpetrated inaccuracies which exaggerated the scale, the coherence, and the purpose of the Trust. Combination among armourers was made to look excessively extensive, excessively compact, excessively independent of market conditions, while the influence on the procurement side was allowed too little weight. This lack of proportion gave the Radical propaganda from the beginning an element of caricature, which perhaps explains its inability to convince parties or public.

Nowhere in the Radical treatment of the armament industry was the tendency towards hyperbole more marked than in its claims for the political influence of the 'ring'. This was a necessary feature in the Radicals' definition of the Armament Trust since it was by means of their political influence that the armourers were reckoned to control the defence expenditure of the state. Here was a mechanism which would explain both the quickening pace of the arms race – ascribed now to a simple profit motive – and the Radicals' lack of success in petitioning a government which, it was now clear, could not help itself. In consequence the Radical writers reserved the full weight of their vituperation for the armourers' political nexus, vying only in the malign influence attributed to the Trust's political echelons. Thus H. R. Murray decided that the Trust was sufficiently powerful 'not only to meet national requirements but to decide what those national requirements should be';[17] Perris saw the government as 'powerless' before the machinations of the armourers;[18] *Concord* reported on the 'impotence of Governments generally' in the face of the 'armour-plated exploiters'.[19] And these were the more moderate versions. As early as 1905, Shaw pushed the case a good deal further. In *Major Barbara* he brought the Salvation Army and the Armament Trust into bizarre juxtaposition, and allowed his armament manufacturer, Andrew Undershaft, to declare: 'The Government of your country! I am the Government of your country, I and Lazarus.' Dramatic licence might be allowed to Shaw, but others, who would not have wished to claim it, advanced very similar opinions. Thus, the *Labour Leader* claimed in 1913, 'the truth is that the Government is far more under the control of the armaments ring than under the control of the National Liberal Federation'.[20] In these interpretations, the Trust came close to exerting governmental power in its own right. It was a tall tale and needed a great deal of substantiation.

But very little was ever supplied in corroboration. The evidence advanced by the Radicals was limited: a few lists featuring the names of politically prominent shareholders in armament concerns; one or two examples of senior defence officials who had left government employment for well-paid service with the private arsenals; some hints as to the influence of the armament lobby over press statements in foreign countries. This was the Trust's apparatus of 'government'. It contained considerable flaws. The ex-officers were never intended to be more than liaison executives for their new masters and they necessarily remained single cogs in a very large procurement machine, exceedingly poorly placed to affect its speed or course. And in Britain the financial connections between the arms interests and the popular newspapers – real enough in France and Germany – cannot be substantiated with actual cases. So the entire argument must turn upon the influence exerted by the Trust through the legislature.

It was to this point that the Radicals gave most of their attention – mainly by tabulating all those members of the Lords or Commons who held interests in the defence industries. The aim was to establish a relationship between the legislature and the Trust, and to imply that elements of these organizations were interchangeable. Thus H. R. Murray compiled a list of 10 peers and 9 MPs with a clerical sub-category of 5 bishops and 1 dean, all with substantial armaments holdings. This was bettered by Newbold with 11 peers, 14 MPs and the same 5 bishops trailing the same dean in attendance. Perris, in contrast, contented himself with citing the investigation of the Armstrong Whitworth shareholders by the *Investors Chronicle* in 1909; this turned up 60 assorted noblefolk, including wives and daughters, and 8 MPs.[21] An elementary cross-reference of the identifiable names, however, reveals an overlap of some 80 per cent: the same cases were being used repeatedly by various authors. A consolidated total of peers and MPs derived from these sources would produce a group of 14 individual armament shareholders in the first category and 17 in the second. Exactly what this demonstrates is uncertain. If it is that a proportion of the armament industry's £60–70 million worth of stock – profitable and attractive stock – found its way into the hands of Britain's governing – that is, wealthiest – social groups, the modest conclusion would hardly seem to justify the Radicals' suggestions of startling revelations. Yet little is provided in the way of additional guidance. The truth was, of course, that the Radicals were not intent upon demonstration but on proposing a case by insinuation: exactly as the existence of a comprehensive Arms Trust was taken to follow from a list of connections between some firms, so the existence of a 'chain of influence' between Trust and government was left to depend upon a list of well-placed shareholders. The reasoning was less than subtle: the Radicals apparently assumed that, if influential men possessed financial interests in armament companies, they must necessarily have employed their influence to further the objectives of those companies. The scope for the exercise of political influence was not tested. Examples of its method of working were not provided. No evidence that it ever did work was led. Given the shareholding relationship, all else was simply *assumed* to follow: the methodology is one of inference rather than analysis.

And the inference had little enough on which to feed. The consolidated total of legislators with armament interests is, after all, very small: in neither House would the examples cited by the Radicals provide sufficient resources for an effective 'armament lobby'. Certainly, the claim that the members of the Trust had, in the unusually explicit words of one post-war critic, 'special means of protecting their interests in Parliament [owing to] the number of MPs who hold shares in these undertakings',[22] would seem to be belied precisely by the 'number of MPs' actually identified by the Radicals. The case for an 'alternative' government clearly cannot be entertained on the basis of such figures and examples.

On the other side, it is possible to demonstrate the implausibility of effective action by the Trust within the political arena. The

Radical thesis which translates the 'armour-plated exploiters' to the centre of official decision-making is vulnerable to questions probing the exact manner in which this invasion was accomplished. Assistance from the legislature is by no means established by the Radical manipulation of the shareholding lists. Mere ownership of shares would not guarantee that an MP or a peer would vote in a way designed to bring work to the 'ring'. Constraints of party policy would certainly influence the individual legislator – some armament shareholders before 1914 were Liberal MPs, for instance. And if the legislator were to resemble the average British shareholder, rarely investing more than £1,000 in a single venture, and preferring a spread portfolio, his financial interests themselves, in their very variety, would militate against his taking any consistent political action to favour armament interests against all others. With these cross-currents, it is exceedingly unlikely that the small group of armament shareholders and directors in Parliament could ever have wielded collective weight to influence government defence policy on behalf of the Trust.

Similarly, the Radical interpretations of the Trust's 'governmental' aspirations failed to recognize the very considerable defences standing between their capitalistic villains and the policy-making procedures of the real government. By 1914 these procedures were well-established. Military and naval policy, which would fix the armament need, was beaten out in the Committee of Imperial Defence after extensive reviews by the service departments. In the Cabinet, the Chancellor would place a price upon the defence needs, and his colleagues would consider both this sum and the policy proposals in the light of the current diplomatic, financial, and domestic situation. All deliberations would be carefully scrutinized by the Treasury. At length the military and naval ministers would each be given an allocation agreed by all Cabinet members. If either minister considered the grant insufficient, he was required to justify any additional demand in full Cabinet session. If both ministers were satisfied, they would pass the estimates to their departments, and there each section head, sitting in committee, would set a figure against his share of the total allocations. Then the individual section categories, including the weaponry allotments, were submitted for Treasury sanction. Once these were agreed, any transfer of funds between categories required Treasury approval. After this meticulous preparation the completed Estimates would be presented to the Commons in the Supply Debate. Here again conventions applied which would protect the defence proposals from undue pressure. As the Chairman of the Committee on Contracts explained it in July 1900, 'the War Office do not pay too much attention to those debates in Supply, as to what promises are made on their behalf' [sic].[23] And once the service ministers had seen their Estimates safely through the House, the armament votes came under the aegis of the Directorate of Army Contracts, the central armament purchasing agency for the two services. In order to ensure that the procurement machinery did not run amok at this late stage, the contracts administration was made subject to scrutiny by the Financial and Audit Departments of the War Office and Admiralty, the two Financial Secretaries of the service ministries, each of them an MP, the Public Accounts Committee, and, with large orders, by the respective Secretaries of State. Reasonably enough, the armourers did not rate the chances of eluding this formidable pack of watchdogs particularly high. In concentrating on what they construed as the obvious interest of the Trust in the 'arranged' sale and the manipulation of influence, the Radicals neglected almost entirely the considerable sales *resistance* of the government.

This sophistication in the processes of defence procurement enabled Britain to avoid most of the scandalous successes enjoyed by armament interests in other countries. Only very rarely did the system fail to prevent the operation of 'influence'. Not only were the failures few; they were occasioned only by the most unusual combinations of forces. One such conjunction had occurred in 1900. It was alleged that the Birmingham ammunition firm of Kynoch, managed by the brother of the Colonial Secretary, had received special treatment from the War Office as a result of its connection with the Chamberlain family. In the high Radical style, Lloyd George, who led the attack on the military's action, described the affair as revealing 'the most disgraceful condition of favouritism towards one company which has been manifested in the present century by any Government department'.[24] In reality, the incident displayed so many special characteristics that it tends to undermine rather than support the Radical assessment of the Trust's governmental affiliations. To begin with, as Lloyd George's words suggest, it was a virtually unique case; nothing of comparable stature could be found in the years before 1914. Further, there were few political names to rival Chamberlain in potency, and none so closely connected with an armament interest. And, most important, the violent stir created by the episode suggests that in Britain any serious distortion of defence procurement would generate rapid and effective political counteraction. Moreover, there was never the slightest hint that the 'Kynoch Affair' might reveal the hand of the Trust in government: the exact point of the allegations was that, owing to a special family connection, a *single* armament firm had been preferred to others. If it took the charisma of the Chamberlain name to lead the officials astray, and to so little effect, and if they were led astray so rarely, it would seem that the procurement system of the 1900s was proof against most forms of infiltration.

That fact is scarcely surprising. Unless simultaneous seduction of a great chain of officials, some military officers, some parliamentarians, ranging from the Director of Contracts to the highest ministerial levels, is deemed credible, it is clear that the system of checks and balances must have withstood any *methodical* attempts at subversion by industrial lobbyists. The Radical view of a 'capitalist plot', designed to capture the initiative in the purchasing of armaments, possessed the easy appeal of all conspiracy theories, but, like so many specimens of the genre, foundered in fact upon the magnitude of the task that it set its conspirators. The premises on which the interpretation was constructed, the assumption of an 'impotent' or 'powerless' role for the state, the conviction that the government of the country *could* be composed of 'Undershaft and Lazarus', were products of fancy and a certain political naïvety.

For the Radicals, conspiracy may have begun at home, but it did not stay there. An important feature of the Trust, according to the Radical view, was its tendency to assume an internationalist aspect. At a time when European peace was clearly under threat, the armourers of the world were supposed to be collaborating to exacerbate tensions and to swell the noise of rattling sabres. They were said to employ a variety of tactics. Arrangements between firms of different nationalities were used to effect a thorough 'penetration' of the market and the economy of purchasing countries. The formation of polyglot industrial groups was employed so as to permit armourers to exert more pressure upon governments than they could wield as individual traders. These groups might be formed over any international range, even involving firms in hostile countries – that is, as the Radicals objected, they were formed entirely indiscriminately, with a crucial loss of defence secrets. And, worst of all, according to the Radical view, was the manner in which the various groups and alliances, taken together, became a single organization with a vague but awful international potency of its own – including, implicitly, a power to cause war as a means of expanding trade.

The foundation for these allegations was a sufficiently concrete set of international relationships. The British armourers were certainly not reluctant to extend into the foreign market the 'ring' techniques which they had perfected at home. The formation of British groups for operations in particular foreign markets – usually involving the construction of arsenals or dockyards – was not uncommon: Vickers, Armstrong and John Brown combined for projects in Spain (from 1909) and Turkey (from 1910) and Vickers and Armstrong for projects in Japan (from 1907) and Russia (from 1913). Frequently these schemes would involve collaboration with native concerns in the heavy industries – as was most especially the case with British dealings in the Italian market, already by 1901 'a happy hunting ground for the manufacture of armaments' according to the trade press, disgustedly quoted by H. R. Murray.[25] Less often, an English concern would strike up a partnership with a foreign armament concern for the joint exploitation, in a number of third markets, of some profitable weaponry novelty such as the machine gun or the submarine. On a much larger and more intimate scale, there were the very rare cases of permanent and deep-rooted international liaison. In this way Nobel's Explosives Co. of Ardeer was tied to the Anglo-German Explosives Group, consisting of the Nobel Dynamite Trust and the German Powder Trust, from the 1880s, and maintained close contact with the great Rottweil Powder Works at Hamburg and Cologne[26]. Between members of the Anglo-German organization, including the Ardeer factory as a full participant, markets were meticulously divided, formulae exchanged, and profits pooled. Under these arrangements the German explosives interests even maintained considerable shareholdings in British cordite factories until 1915. Thus the widespread ramifications, the questing 'tentacles' certainly existed, and to render them operational an international armament diplomacy also existed.

The Radicals knew of many of these treaties and compacts. Perris wrote knowledgeably of the 'cosmopolitanism' of the arms trade; Newbold and Murray provided plentiful examples of the international arrangements; Snowden was able to cite the Spanish, Italian, Turkish and Russian instances.[27] Only the full extent of the Nobel empire eluded the critics. The basic facts of the armourers' overseas connections are not in dispute. What is at issue is the relevance of these data. For the pre-war Radicals, the relevance was at the same time restricted – in that the existence of the international armament connections was known to them, but virtually nothing more – and highly creative – in that the small amount of knowledge they *did* have sufficed to provoke their unsparing condemnation and possibly to lead them, by deduction from inadequate material, into an entirely extravagant view of the International Trust. For they had almost no inkling of the manner in which the international agreements actually functioned. The industrial documents, however, in revealing something of the alliances in operation, suggest a rather different interpretation.

In the first place, a closer investigation of the financial arrangements underlying many of the overseas dockyard and arsenal schemes suggests that 'penetration' of a client state's economy was achieved more rarely and with more difficulty than the Radicals imagined. When British firms joined with 'native' heavy industries in the construction of such facilities, it was usually the home-grown interests, not the armourers, who retained the whip hand in the enterprise. Despite frequent Radical claims that the British groups came to 'own' these 'outstations' of the Trust, the truth was much less dramatic. Thus, the equity share of the British interests in the Spanish dockyards at Ferrol and Cartagena was under 30 per cent, and in 1914 the Vickers participation in the Russian shipyard at Nicolaiev was still limited to 10 per cent, in the Italian arsenal at Terni to 28 per cent and in the Turkish dockyard on the Golden Horn to 40 per cent, held jointly with Armstrong.[28] Holdings of this size would hardly confer upon the armourers the power and influence in the internal affairs of customer states that the Radicals sought to imply. Given that indigenous financial and industrial elements frequently retained ownership control over the armament projects, the emphasis placed upon them by the Radical critics as puppet concerns, mere creatures of the Trust, is surely misplaced.

Furthermore, the solidarity of armament groups accused of employing collaborative tactics in their 'penetration' of foreign markets was in fact notably deficient. The treaties signed between the armament concerns, though they greatly impressed the Radicals, were often unsuccessful in preventing competition between the signatories. Thus there was a fierce contest for Japanese orders between Vickers and Armstrong in 1910, and, in the same year, a Vickers executive reported from Spain that 'there is considerable rivalry *within* the group for Spanish work'.[29] Despite Vickers' extensive market-sharing arrangements with Armstrong, the Barrow firm found its Newcastle friends energetically undermining its position in China and in Chile in 1911.[30] And even where agreements did hold firm, they were often, as the Radicals invariably failed to recognize, rigidly limited in geographical application. Thus Vickers and John Brown could collaborate in Spain from 1909 yet fight one another tooth and nail in Russia between 1908 and 1914.[31] The view of a tightly knit armament combine – a calmly organized and coldly efficient 'octopus' – working in systematic collusion to appropriate the markets of intimidated governments does not represent the actual conditions. Instead there were a number of separate treaties, often administered in a spirit of rancour and rivalry, with partners frequently more interested in subduing one another than in subduing the client. It was a most curious octopus, cut up into sections, divided in intention, the tentacles apt to fight amongst themselves.

Nor were its activities particularly indiscriminate in the political sense. For the British group, at least, the major part of overseas business, involving the supply of production facilities, was conducted in friendly or neutral countries or in alliance with armament concerns from friendly powers. Their largest ventures took place in Russia, Japan and Spain, countries which in 1914 ranked among allies or neutrals. Only the Turkish imbroglio turned out to be a venture favouring a potential enemy and this could not have been guessed at its inception. Turkey's international stance before 1914 was highly ambivalent and it was precisely the policy of the British government to provide defence aid in the hope of securing some diplomatic advantage. The most dangerous relationship for the armourers, that of close alliance with a foreign producer, whether for the construction of overseas arsenals or for the supply of ready-made weaponry, was generally used with propriety by the British firms. Before 1914 they were sufficiently sensitive to contemporary international relations to prefer affiliation with French firms. Thus in 1914 Vickers proposed a joint operation with Schneider-Creusot, 'this being most acceptable to the Russian Government from the political point of view'.[32] Similarly, Vickers and Armstrong tended to avoid involvement with the German armouries, most especially with Krupp. Admittedly, where Krupp possessed a clear technical superiority, the British were forced to seek a patent agreement – as with the Vickers–Krupp agreement on fuse manufacture in 1902. These, however, were minor matters. More usually, far from welcoming Krupp as 'the business ally of British armament firms', as H. R. Murray believed,[33] the British makers treated the Germans with great suspicion. Vickers, for instance, took action in 1901 to keep Krupp out of the European submarine trade – one of their agents referring to the Essen firm bluntly as 'the enemy' – and in 1909 again refused to make submarine patents available to the Germans.[34] Fierce British competition against Krupp in Russia – where the German methods were described in 1910 as 'too disgusting for words' – in Japan, in Greece, and in Turkey, acted to emphasize a genuine antipathy. And for the Austrian firm of Skoda, armourer to another hostile regime, the British manufacturers had no more affection. In 1911–12, while planning a rare excursion into the Balkan market, Vickers spoke firmly of keeping the project secret from Skoda and mentioned the intense competition expected from that quarter.[35]

Among the gunmakers the one major exception to the avoidance of 'counter-diplomatic' entanglements was the compact between Vickers and the German small-arms manufactory, Deutsche Waffen und Munitionsfabriken. But even here the details of the agreement tend to undermine rather than shore up any sinister implication. The understanding was a patent agreement, limited to exploitation of the Maxim machine-gun system, and it was first formed in 1891, before Germany was clearly recognized as an enemy to British interests. It could scarcely support single-handed the Radical suggestions of collusion between British and 'enemy' arms interests within a Trust which both crossed and exacerbated political demarcations. The bulk of the evidence points the other way – towards competition rather than collusion.

But not all of it: much more difficult to explain away are the immense ramifications of the European explosives trade, and particularly the many connections between Nobel's Explosives Co. and its German counterparts. These connections also were formed early on, in the 1880s, but they attained between 1900 and 1914 a completeness that no other international armament alliance could rival. However, it is exactly this feature which provides a case in mitigation. The interchange of funds and ideas between the Nobel concerns and the German Powder Group was a thing apart. It is probably safe to say that it was unique in the British industry of its day.[36] If indeed ties like those between the British and German explosives factories had existed on a wider scale, the Radical fears of an International Arms Trust might have assumed substance. But in the absence of similar arrangements maintained by Vickers, or Armstrong, or Coventry Ordnance Works, or Kynoch, or BSA, the Nobel empire remains merely a pointer to what that consortium might have been.

As it was, the amount of 'counter-diplomatic' activity by British armourers was surprisingly small; usually their alliances followed the outline of the great power alliance system. Moreover, the amount of competition between the world's armourers, an element of the international weaponry trade unrecognized in most accounts, suggests that the Radical view of the Trust as a single many-tentacled organization was a serious exaggeration. However well organized the explosives market may have been, the heavy armament and warship markets possessed quite separate characteristics. Here, many concerns from nations both hostile and friendly, British firms like the Palmer Shipbuilding Co. or the Coventry Ordnance Works, German firms like Krupp, Austrian firms like Skoda, or American firms like Bethlehem Steel, were seen by the greatest British manufacturers, Vickers and Armstrong, not as colleagues of the Trust, but as dangerous competitors. Such firms would not have agreed with Ramsay MacDonald's view of the arms race as 'a carefully studied financial plan devised by firms that are no longer competitors'.[37] In contrast, after encountering most of their foreign opponents in a contest to supply the Imperial Ottoman Navy in 1910 Vickers noted, 'with regard to Turkey the fight has been terrific'.[38] And in 1912 firms complained generally of 'the serious competition which now exists in war material'.[39] The international market in arms was not as comprehensively arranged as the pre-war Radicals believed, and consequently the lines of international political alignment were crossed less frequently than would have been the case with a true 'Trust'.

If the Trust's market penetration, organizational cohesion, and indiscriminate alliances are qualified in this way, it is clear that its status as a distinct institution is badly damaged. The tight combination of the world's gunmaking, shipbuilding and explosives concerns, a system designed to eradicate competition and wield collective influence in European affairs, seems to have been something of a *rara avis* before 1914. What then *was* 'The International Armament Consortium', 'The War Trust', 'The Secret International' so insistently sighted by the Radical ornithologists? The critics thought that they had supplied the answer and discovered the reality in their exposure of an organization known as the Harvey United Steel Co. For Newbold this was 'the War Trust in excelsis', while for Snowden, 'its internationalism was complete . . . [it was] the most up-to-date and complete form of capitalistic organization the world has ever seen'.[40]

The Harvey company was formed in 1893, refined in 1899–1900, and disbanded just before the First World War when its membership included four British, two German, two American, one Italian and three French armament concerns. The list of participants was impressive, and from the list – virtually the only evidence available to them – the Radicals deduced that the Harvey organization housed the nerve-centre of the Trust. It was a characteristic error, mistaking the venture's purpose and greatly over-rating its importance. In fact it was a patent arrangement making certain processes for armour-plate manufacture available to the world's producers. Prices were fixed by agreement, orders distributed between members, and a proportion of profits paid into a central pool. Although the Harvey enterprise initially planned to become a single polyglot *manufacturer* of armour plate, it never did so; it remained passive rather than punitive, a technical agreement before anything else. So much was admitted by Newbold when in 1936 he retracted, with some grace, his earlier allegations against the Trust.[41] And, in fact, the attempt to attach the characteristics of the Trust to any particular industrial organization never succeeded.

There is some indication that in their more pessimistic moments the armourers did dream of an international arms trust, but in a very particular style: they regarded it as a remote possibility. In May 1912 a proposal was made by a French armament industrialist, M. Léon Lévy, for the formation of a massive international pool including all the world's armourers.[42] This suggestion has a twin significance. First, it demonstrates beyond doubt that nothing similar had existed *before* May 1912. Secondly, it is interesting because of the reaction it provoked among British arms firms. Vickers certainly considered the idea as a means of counteracting the sharp international competition of the time but approached it with some suspicion. Their comments imply doubt as to whether all producers, notably Krupp and Coventry, would agree to be bound by the proposed rules.[43] It would appear that the doubts proved decisive since no further mention of the scheme occurs in the industrial archives after the summer of 1912. It is probable that the armourers found the Trust less easy to build than the Radicals found it to imagine.

Attached to the Trust, in the Radical view, was a final and especially unattractive potency: the ability to 'foment' war as a means of expanding sales. Shaw emphasized this attribute: 'You will make war', said Undershaft, 'when it suits us and keep peace when it doesn't.' Such convictions once more took as basic premise an assessment of governments as 'powerless' agencies but expanded the belief to a European or global scale. The prerogative to take the war-creating decisions was removed from the state executives – where it clearly belonged – and ascribed to private capitalistic interests – which could not have employed it. And this was done despite the self-evident historical truth that governments have rarely required assistance in the generation of disputatious issues. In this context the Radicals perpetrated a simple confusion between the provision of the means with which to fight wars – which the armourers supplied – and the provision of the pretexts upon which wars were fought – which governments supplied. Such considerations are, however, secondary: the central point must surely be that the capabilities of the armourers to 'foment' war were posited by the Radicals on a view of the Trust as an international institution which was itself inaccurate. If the Trust was not the single, tightly organized, comprehensive conspiracy it was made out to be, clearly its capacity to overturn international peace was much reduced.[44]

The pre-war Radical attack upon the Armament Trust was, in general, a sorry affair. It was the product of imitation, inadequate information, and a deficiency in economic and political sophistication – also perhaps of a certain tactical desperation. Given this combination, it tended, not unnaturally, to be associated with the more extreme Radical elements. From the beginning it suffered in being a poor cousin of the campaigns waged in Germany by Liebknecht and his colleagues. Without doubt, and as some critics of the arms trade admitted after 1918, the German armament concerns, given their influence with the Imperial government, their many connections with the press, and their notorious venality in foreign selling, offered a good deal more flank for attack than their British counterparts. The prime mistake of the British Radicals was to borrow a German technique of vilification and to apply it, almost unchanged, to firms which operated within a radically different home market – involving a specialized but ambiguous relationship with the government and a more competitive relationship with industrial rivals – and which confronted a diplomatic alignment offering differently disposed export possibilities. An element of imitation entered also, as Newbold explained some decades later, in the adoption by the Radicals of the interpretation of monopoly capitalism provided by J. A. Hobson and the early writings of Lenin[45] – an interpretation which fitted British realities only very partially. Once pointed in these directions, it is not surprising that Radical writers and propagandists could find few facts that could apply to the British armaments industry. They translated what little information they could gather about armament 'connexions' into swingeing condemnations of 'collusion', 'combination', and 'cartels'. In their hands, shadows were presented as very solid substances. From this eagerness to fit flimsy evidence into a pre-wrought framework there followed also the naïvety which ascribed far too little influence to governments and far too much to industrial organizations.

But it would be a mistake to believe that the Radicals necessarily aimed at an *accurate* portrayal of the British armaments industry. It is perfectly possible, indeed quite common, for propaganda, however crudely it may be conceived, to be politically effective. In this sense, the attack upon the Trust may be seen as the swan-song of the Radical campaign for the reduction of armaments, becoming more shrill – and more attached to the extreme Radical cadres – as the cause became more hopeless. It marks the final attempt to find a vulnerable target for Radical pacificism, the last phase of an extended process – and to this degree its tactical relevance was perhaps more important to its protagonists than its internal consistency or its descriptive accuracy. The fact remains, however, that it was ineffective on this level also. Even the parliamentary activities of Philip Snowden – marking the pre-war zenith of the campaign – achieved few political results and offered little to compare with the wasps' nest stirred up by Liebknecht's revelations. Here perhaps the inappropriateness of the Radical charges in a British context reasserted itself; the extravagance of the deductions may have produced an effect of counter-suggestion even at this early stage in their career. The employment against the Trust of inflated rhetoric and conspiratorial suggestion could make little ground within a constituency pledged to defend its mastery of the seas and encouraged in this aspiration by such Admiralty experts as Lord Fisher, his 'Fishpool' of strategically placed officers and officials, and his 'journalistic janissaries' of the press. Indeed, if the Radicals had been interested in applying their propaganda more accurately, they could have done worse than examine the Admiralty for lessons – and perhaps for targets.

NOTES

1 *New Age*, 25 March 1909.
2 *Concord*, January 1910.
3 *Concord*, July 1912.
4 *Labour Leader*, 24 April 1913.

5 *Concord*, June 1913.
6 *Hansard*, vi:95:2143.
7 G. H. Perris, *The War Traders*, London, 1913, p. 9.
8 H. R. Murray, *Krupp and the International Armaments Ring*, London, 1915, p. 135.
9 Armstrong Whitworth File, Vickers Archive (hereafter VA).
10 Nobel's Explosives Co. papers and Nobel Dynamite Trust, *Trade Agreements*, Imperial Chemical Industries Archive (hereafter ICIA). See also W. J. Reader, *I.C.I., A History*, London, 1970, vol. 1, chapter 9.
11 See Public Record Office WO/32/1248 and 9 and W. J. Reader, op. cit., pp. 145-8.
12 On these points see C. Trebilcock, 'A "special relationship" – government, rearmament, and the cordite firms', *Economic History Review*, 2nd ser. XIX (1966).
13 Ibid.
14 Director of Army Contracts Reports, 1906.
15 Evidence of Armstrong Whitworth to Government Factories and Workshops Committee (Cd 3626) 1907, Q 2291.
16 W. H. Williams, *Who's Who in Arms*, London, 1935, p. 44.
17 H. R. Murray, op. cit., p. 173.
18 G. H. Perris, op. cit., p. 24.
19 *Concord*, June 1913.
20 *Labour Leader*, 4 December 1913.
21 See Murray, op. cit., pp. 172-4; J. T. W. Newbold, *The War Trust Exposed* (1916), pp. 13-15; G. H. Perris, op. cit., pp. 21-3. Compare Snowden, *Hansard*, iv:59:2140.
22 W. H. Williams, op. cit., p. 12.
23 Committee on Contracts (Cd 313), 1900. Chairman's Speech, 24 July 1900.
24 Hansard, iii:88:414.
25 H. R. Murray, op. cit., p. 124.
26 Nobel Dynamite Trust, *Trade Agreements*, ICIA; see also W. J. Reader, op. cit., chapters 7 and 9.
27 G. H. Perris, op cit., pp. 9-16; J. T. W. Newbold, op. cit., pp. 6-9; H. R. Murray, op. cit., pp. 124-6; *Hansard*, iv:59:2138.
28 Calculated from shareholding details provided by Vickers Archive: Nicolaiev File; *La Sociedad Española de la Construcción Naval* File and J. D. Scott, *Vickers, A History*, London, 1962, p. 84; Document 22 of Vickers Evidence for *R. C. on Private Manufacture of Arms*, 1935-6; Document 54 of ibid.
29 Dardier to Zaharoff, 26 January 1910, VA, Letter Books (hereafter LB), and *The Japanese Chronicle*, 30 April 1914.
30 Donaldson to Vickers, 27 July 1911, VA (LB); Vickers to Del Val, 15 July 1911, VA (LB).
31 Vickers to Zaharoff, 5 November 1910; Barker to Caillard, 14 February 1911, VA (LB).
32 Barker to Courville, June 1914, Microfilm 215, VA.
33 Murray, op. cit., p. 168.
34 Dally to Vickers, 16 March 1901, and undated, probably late 1909, VA (LB).
35 Vickers to Pal, 19 June 1911; Vickers to von Borada, 1 February 1912, VA (LB).
36 I am indebted to W. J. Reader for confirmation of this opinion.
37 *Hansard*, iv:59:114.

38 Barker to Caillard, 14 February 1911, VA (LB).
39 Vickers to Budeassu, 27 March 1912, VA (LB).
40 Newbold, op. cit., p. 8; *Hansard*, iv:59:2141.
41 See evidence of J. T. W. Newbold to *R. C. on Private Manufacture of Armaments*, 1935-6, QQ 731ff.
42 Reported by Dardier to Orlando 16 May 1912, VA (LB).
43 Ibid.
44 See C. Trebilcock, 'Legends of the British armaments industry, 1890-1914: a revision', *Journal of Contemporary History*, 5, 1970.
45 Newbold to *R. C. on Private Manufacture of Armaments*, Q 731.

Note: The author is most grateful to Imperial Chemical Industries Ltd and to Vickers Ltd for their considerable generosity in allowing him free access to their industrial records for the period up to 1914.

12

H. N. BRAILSFORD AND THE SEARCH FOR A NEW INTERNATIONAL ORDER

F. M. LEVENTHAL

'Of the three cardinal points of the Manchester doctrine – Free Trade, non-intervention in the affairs of Europe, and *laisser-faire* in internal politics,' H. N. Brailsford noted in 1908, 'only the first remains. It is an evolution which the modern Liberal welcomes in principle. Non-intervention was a sterile and impracticable ideal.'[1] Such a peremptory dismissal of Cobdenite doctrine was not intended to imply that the *Nation*'s chief leader writer on foreign affairs had forsaken his Radical heritage. He, no less than other Edwardian Radicals, retained Cobden's hostility to needless entanglements, his distrust of traditional diplomacy, and his advocacy of a limitation on armaments. Where they differed was in their views of England's attitude towards oppressed peoples, whether victims of imperialism or of native tyranny. To Brailsford, the insularity of 'Little England' reflected a moral indifference to exploitation, a failure to recognize that 'the sympathies of our common humanity went beyond the Channel'.[2] It was the duty of Englishmen to enlist in the cause of freedom by lending their support to national struggles for emancipation. In a 1907 article in the *Daily News* which foreshadowed much of his later writing, he warned that to adopt a posture of non-intervention in places like Macedonia, Egypt, or Persia would be to leave the world to the avarice of the financiers. As an alternative to both isolationism and imperial rivalries, he proposed a restoration of a European Concert led by the Liberal powers, a partnership capable of restraining the appetite of aggressive capitalism and of upholding the ideal of 'worldwide brotherhood'.[3]

This invocation of European solidarity and sympathy for oppressed races was, in some ways, reminiscent of Gladstonian Liberalism, a tradition which Brailsford, the son of a Methodist preacher, had imbibed in his youth. Like Gladstone, he had a conception of a European cultural community whose authority transcended the parochial ambitions of an individual power. Yet Gladstone's European consciousness derived from his Christian morality and his sense of public law, both of which might be construed to sanction an occupation of Egypt in the interest of foreign bondholders. For Brailsford national honour and the sanctity of contracts, those shibboleths of Victorian politicians, had too often been utilized to vindicate aggression. While Gladstone professed his allegiance to the Concert of Europe, he had in practice sacrificed it to the more urgent claims of national interest. It was the unrealized ideal of Gladstonian foreign policy which Brailsford upheld as a standard by which to judge and criticize the conduct of a later Liberal government. If England could no longer detach herself from European affairs, neither could she evade her responsibility for the progress of freedom. Whether by example or by exertion of influence, she must challenge the forces of militarism and national self-aggrandizement. England should assume a position of leadership in resolving international tensions and thus help to usher in a new era of peace.

Brailsford was fond of quoting an exchange between Benjamin Franklin and Thomas Paine. Franklin is supposed to have said, 'Where liberty is, there is my country', to which Paine replied, 'Where is not liberty, there is mine.' His own sympathies clearly lay with Paine, and his writings between 1900 and 1914 bear witness to his profound concern for 'where is not liberty'. Born in Yorkshire in 1873, Henry Noel Brailsford grew up in Scotland and attended Glasgow University, where he came under the influence of Professor Gilbert Murray. Murray's example instilled a love of Greek civilization that inspired him to enlist in the Philhellenic Legion in the spring of 1897 during the abortive Greek uprising against the Turks. Appalled by the excesses to which patriotic exuberance could lead, he was none the less impressed by the stirrings of national consciousness that he observed in the Balkans. He visited the region twice during the following year, on assignment from the *Manchester Guardian*, and quickly developed a reputation as an authority on its politics. The Balkans – and more particularly Macedonia – were to become the touchstone of his interpretation of foreign affairs, the source of his commitment to national liberation. Upon returning from his investigation of conditions in Crete and Macedonia, Brailsford launched his career in journalism, serving during the next fifteen years as a leader writer and occasional foreign correspondent for a succession of Liberal newspapers, the *Morning Leader*, the *Echo*, the *Tribune*, the *Daily News*, the *Speaker*, and the *Nation*, as well as the *Manchester Guardian*. His speciality was Russia and the Near East, although his articles ranged broadly over the whole spectrum of international and imperial affairs. In addition, he played an active role in Radical pressure groups, like the Friends of Russian Freedom and the Balkan Committee, and it was under the auspices of the latter organization that he led a British relief mission to Macedonia during the winter of 1903-4. In 1913 he made his sixth journey to Macedonia on behalf of the Carnegie Commission of Inquiry into the causes of the Balkan Wars.

Brailsford's earliest articles reveal a sensitivity to nationalist awakenings, a shrewd appraisal of diplomatic manoeuvres, and an anti-Imperialist bias that characterized his later works as well. When the Cretans rebelled against Turkish control in 1897, the European powers vetoed union with Greece and occupied the island. Although they promised autonomy, little was done to implement the pledge, and another revolt broke out the next year. Brailsford, who spent three months in Crete at the time, blamed the British for their inactivity and complicity in continued Turkish oppression. Despite the loss of British lives during the uprising, he found it difficult to repress his sympathy for 'the ignorant and suffering mob which at last rebelled against the regime of idleness and starvation enforced by Europe'.[4] More effective European administration might at least preserve order, but it would not provide the definitive solution for this 'gallant and obstinate peasant race, in whose minds this fixed idea of union with Greece has become an ineradicable passion'.[5] In Crete, as elsewhere in the Balkans, Brailsford came to appreciate the futility of diplomatic contrivances that thwarted native aspirations.

The assertion of British power in imperial terms he found equally objectionable. Like his intellectual mentor, J. A. Hobson, he denied that the Boers had provoked the war in South Africa by their aggression. Rather he insisted that they had armed in defence against those who conspired to undermine their independence. The culprits were not the Dutch farmers, but the ministers in the Colonial Office and the financiers around Rhodes. While condemning the Boer treatment of the natives, he doubted whether the welfare of the Africans would be any more secure under British rule, given the official toleration of slavery in East Africa, Rhodesia, and Natal.[6] His criticism of British imperial policy was even more outspoken in an analysis of the Irish problem published in 1903. In Brailsford's view the ascendancy in Ireland rested upon a regime of conquest and class oppression that violated the English sense of law. Instead of protecting the majority of the people, the Constabulary operated as the agents of repression, military in organization and political in function. 'This formidable army', he declared, 'is in effect the machine which collects the rent, the force that backs the party of ascendancy in its ceaseless war upon the people.'[7] In addition to employing a military police, the British administration tampered with justice by packing juries with Protestants and subjecting magistrates to the authority of Dublin Castle. The Protestant element preserved the *status quo* by excluding the Irish Catholic majority from every vestige of power. Such methods, he observed, were 'a negation of every principle and tradition of our Constitution'.[8] Although compulsory land purchase had begun to ameliorate the situation of the Irish peasantry, many of them subsisted under conditions of misery unparalleled outside Russia and Turkey. Furthermore, he recognized that Irish discontent stemmed not merely from rack-renting or even from coercion. Only the prompt concession of self-government could rectify historic wrongs and instil among the discontented a sense of loyalty to the Empire. Allowed to manage its own affairs, Ireland might in time come to emulate Canada in its devotion to the crown. Whatever constitutional formula was adopted, 'no future scheme', he warned, 'can hope for success which does not seek to enlist in the service of Ireland the dominant passion of Irish minds – their love of country and their consciousness of nationality'.[9]

Macedonia, to which Brailsford returned in 1903 at the time of the Bulgarian uprising, presented an altogether more complicated situation. National consciousness and humanitarian sentiment might justify the emancipation of the region from Turkish tyranny, but the rival claims of the Balkan peoples and the mixture of races and religions in Macedonia itself militated against a peaceful settlement. Brailsford's initial sympathies lay with the Bulgarian Revolutionary Committee, which had effectively established its organization throughout the province, converting the villagers to its ideal of a liberated Macedonia. While conceding that the Macedonian Slavs were racially more Serbian than Bulgarian, he affirmed that the basis of nationality was not blood, but a sense of common civilization, which the Bulgarian movement had imparted. Although its methods were terroristic, the Committee was democratically constituted and was dedicated to Western ideals of freedom.[10]

The atrocities committed by the insurgents soon persuaded Brailsford that his optimism had been misplaced. 'In the Bulgarian movement', he reported, 'I see no element of hope. It is as ruthless, as brutal, as unscrupulous as the Turkish government itself. It is working rather for the ascendancy of the Bulgarian race in Macedonia than for its liberation from Turkish rule.'[11] Unlike Ireland or even Crete, where national consciousness united the people against a common enemy, Macedonia was rapidly succumbing to fratricidal slaughter. 'The atmosphere', he later remarked, 'is so poisoned with nationalism that the most enlightened patriot becomes corrupted against his will.'[12] Moreover, the rivalry of the native races distracted attention from the overriding issue – the economic exploitation and misery of the Balkan peasant. The fault lay not with the benighted insurgents, but rather with the European powers, who found it more convenient to allow the Sultan to repress the rebellion than to resolve their own conflicts in the Near East. Brailsford attributed the major share of responsibility to England, which had preserved Turkish hegemony in the Balkans in 1878 because Macedonian liberation was inconsistent with Disraeli's view of imperial interests. It was incumbent upon the British government to make amends by assuming a greater role in guaranteeing the welfare of the region. Unlike the Cretans and the Boers, the Macedonians were seeking not independence, but an end to Ottoman misrule. 'A Macedonia freed from direct Turkish rule might not be an ideal State, but at least it would be a region where a tolerable human life would be possible to men who today are only anxious to throw their existence away.'[13]

The solution which Brailsford and his associates on the Balkan Committee advocated was effective European intervention. Only the threat of concerted force would induce the Sultan to acquiesce in reforms which would include a European governor, responsible to the powers and armed with complete financial control, and a European *gendarmerie*. The watered-down version of the scheme implemented in the 1903 Mürzsteg programme, which designated Russia and Austria as the supervisory authorities, not only failed to pacify Macedonia, but left Turkish administration essentially intact. As Brailsford realized, the insufficiency of the reforms was an incitement to further local violence, the Bulgarian Committee refusing to disband until Europe had substituted international control for Turkish occupation. 'The ability to create such an anarchy at will', he contended, 'is the only effective means which the subject-races of Turkey possess of recalling Europe to her pledges and her responsibilities. The Committee will not dissolve until we impose some solution which has an air of finality; and until the Committee dissolves, there is no hope of peace in Macedonia.'[14] It was the duty of England and other Liberal powers to assert their collective authority and to divide Macedonia into administrative districts reflecting the lines of racial cleavage. He was encouraged by Lord Lansdowne's suggestion in the last months of the Balfour ministry of a reduction of the Turkish garrison and a European commission to regulate Macedonian finances.

The advent of the Liberal government seemed to offer the chance for innovations in foreign policy that would rejuvenate the Gladstonian legacy. Without weakening the posture of firmness, the Liberals might exploit new opportunities to reduce armaments, to check the growing estrangement with Germany, and to end the feud with Russia. Such initiatives represented, for Brailsford, only the beginning of a new diplomacy based, not on a rearrangement of powers, or even on common interests, but rather on the consciousness of Europe as 'a moral entity'. The formation of a Liberal bloc, devoted to the principle of peace and to the liberation of European Turkey and of Leopold's Congo, would represent 'the rallying of all that is best and most generous in Europe itself'.[15] It was Sir Edward Grey's disregard of these high expectations that outraged Brailsford and prompted his relentless criticism of British foreign policy during the next decade. Ignoring Belgian complacence in the face of Leopold's depredation of the Congo, Grey seemed content to pursue a policy of inaction instead of following the advice of E. D. Morel's Congo Reform Association. 'My own impression', Brailsford lamented in a letter to Morel, 'is that Grey is by temperament quite indifferent to all humanitarian issues and that when he talks of waiting for Belgian opinion to move, he means only that he is glad of any excuse for doing nothing himself.'[16] Rather than imperil his accord with Russia, the Foreign Secretary dissociated himself from his predecessor's sweeping proposals in regard to Macedonia and pledged himself only to judicial reform, oblivious of the fact that 'there can be no substantial advance until the agents of Europe are invested with executive authority'.[17]

Until 1905, despite a characteristically Radical antipathy to Tsarist tyranny, Brailsford regarded a *rapprochement* with Russia with a certain degree of equanimity. He envisaged Anglo-Russian understanding as the key to a resolution of the Eastern Question and advocated the recognition of Russia's paramount influence in Armenia, a concession which would not only safeguard the Armenians from the Turks, but might deflect Russia from further penetration of the Balkans.[18] It was possible to argue that the Tsarist autocracy, however repugnant to English Liberals, had proved its acceptability to its subjects and that its internal methods constituted no bar to a diplomatic understanding. But the outbreak of revolution invalidated this view, raising Radical hopes for the dawning of a new era. 'The substitution of a liberal Constitution for the present military despotism', Brailsford predicted, 'would be the most beneficial event which Europe has seen in our generation, and unquestionably it would make for the world's peace.'[19] Once it became clear that the Russian government was at war with its own citizens, it was incumbent upon the Foreign Office to proceed warily. As early as 1906 Brailsford reproached Grey for encouraging English bankers to bail out the Russian government financially in the critical months before the convening of the first Duma. When that body assembled, it encountered, not a bankrupt bureaucracy which could be compelled to submit to popular demands, but a defiant administration reinforced by an Anglo-French loan. While the progressive elements in Russia pleaded with their British sympathizers to withhold support pending the concession of reforms, the eagerness of the Foreign Office to consolidate the agreement denied to the constitutional movement its weapon of coercion. In addition, the provision of a substantial loan gave British financiers a vested interest in the *status quo,* since political instability might endanger the security of their investments.[20] In Brailsford's view the Anglo-Russian Convention made the Liberal government an accomplice to tyranny.

While it might be prudent to maintain correct relations with Russia, the desire for friendship with the Russian people precluded intimacy with their rulers. 'Liberal Governments', he insisted, 'cannot be encouraged to seek close alliance with a Power prepared . . . to dye its hands deep in the blood of its people.'[21] When Grey refuted his critics' allegation that Russia was not evolving towards constitutionalism, Brailsford seized upon reports of continued police despotism to show that 'the machine of repression was never so busy or efficient'.[22] He denounced the proposed state visit of the Tsar, whom he labelled as 'the head of a minute caste, engaged in a brutal conflict with his people'.[23] It was not merely the implications of the Convention for the cause of popular freedom in Russia that troubled Brailsford. England had allowed Russia to extend her influence at the price of Persian independence and had sanctioned the construction of a trans-Persian railway which menaced the security of India. Mutual guarantees to Persia were repeatedly violated by Russian encroachments, and in its complicity the British government was 'guilty of a treason against freedom'.[24]

In return for these concessions Grey's policy had gained for England an unreliable ally who shared neither British scruples nor Liberal ideals. The motive for such a dishonourable arrangement was immediately apparent. England was willing to sacrifice Persia in order to win Russian support for her campaign to isolate Germany. 'The whole scheme', Brailsford explained, 'is nothing but an attempt to conclude, if not a Triple Alliance, at least a Triple Entente against Germany.'[25] The danger that Russia might be drawn into the Kaiser's orbit if she were not ardently courted, the implicit assumption behind British strategy, was illusory. Only London and Paris bankers could furnish the capital needed to guarantee solvency in St Petersburg. In soliciting Russian favour, England had failed to perceive that the Tsar needed her financial backing far more than she needed the partnership. Yet, fearful lest undue pressure undermine British influence and jeopardize the accord, the Foreign Office remained impervious to Russian expansion in Persia, Finland, and the Balkans. A more honest policy 'which had simply declined Russian intimacy, or a stronger policy which knew how to use the financial weapon, would have lost nothing which subservience has gained'.[26]

To all Brailsford's hopes for the liberation of the Balkans the one inescapable obstacle was the persistence of Ottoman despotism. Indeed, he was inclined to argue that the possibility of reform was directly proportional to the degree of independence of a province from Constantinople. The revolt of the Young Turks in 1908 not only shattered his image of a moribund Turkey, but equally altered his perspective on the Balkans themselves. A liberalized empire might facilitate the internal development of Macedonia without unleashing centrifugal forces. As in the case of the Bulgarian movement, what attracted Brailsford to the Young Turks was their assimilation of Western political values. He wanted the Balkan Committee 'to assure them that no difference of religion will cause us to be slow in welcoming the essentially Liberal character of their movement'. His enthusiasm was so unrestrained as to make him actually 'prefer a renaissance of the Ottoman Empire on a basis of liberty and toleration to any partial solution which might have freed certain of the Christian races'.[27] This was a curious reversal of his earlier conviction that Macedonian freedom was contingent upon the removal of the Turkish yoke. He was now inclined to suggest that if tranquillity and civil liberty were consistent with Turkish domination, European intervention would no longer be warranted. As he commented to Noel Buxton:[28]

> The new situation robs us, while it continues, of this pretext for interfering. So long as Christians are not being killed or maltreated or denied elementary justice, through the fault of a feeble or culpable government, I don't think we have a moral right to interfere. I assume, in all that follows, that the Young Turks keep their word about assuring equal conditions to Moslems & Christians. If they don't, they deserve no consideration. . . . I am with [Edwin] Pears & yourself in desiring Home Rule for Macedonia. I go further & think it inevitable. But I no longer wish to see it imposed by diplomacy or by force.

Even when it became evident that the Young Turks, however idealistic their professions, were bent on a policy of centralization that made few concessions to Christians in the empire, Brailsford continued to counsel patience and repudiate any revival of pro-Sultan sentiment. Parliamentary government could not rapidly take root in an atmosphere poisoned by generations of repression and fanaticism. The Young Turks had achieved, if not racial equality, peace and security of property. 'To desert them, to oppose them', he warned, 'is to consign Turkey to ruin and to prepare for European war.'[29] By 1910 he was willing to acknowledge that in the Young Turk revolution efficiency and domination, not Liberalism, had triumphed and that it had failed to bring civilized rule to Macedonia and Albania. Had the Young Turks at least been willing to concede a measure of cultural freedom, they might have withstood a demand for territorial autonomy. It was their suppression of Albanian schools and language almost as much as their massacre of Albanian villagers that completed Brailsford's disenchantment.[30] He soon reverted not merely to the encouragement of Balkan separatism, but to support for German economic penetration of Turkey as well.

However ambivalent his attitude towards nationalism became, Brailsford justified it as an instrument for the political and cultural elevation of the masses – whether in Ireland or Macedonia or Egypt – and maintained that British foreign policy should seek to foster its development. At the same time he recognized that emerging national consciousness repeatedly threatened to disrupt the precarious peace. Given this explosive potential, European powers had a responsibility to avoid exacerbating local tensions by resolving their differences without intruding their rivalries in European or African trouble-spots. One of the complaints which he levelled against Grey was that the Foreign Secretary not only refused to protect national movements, but deliberately sacrificed them – as in Persia – to the exigencies of power diplomacy. Brailsford's affinity for the underdog, his aversion to Jingoism, led him increasingly to identify with German grievances. Although he had welcomed the *entente* with France, he valued it as the basis of a Liberal partnership, not as a defensive alliance against Germany. 'We do not make ourselves more valuable to France', he observed, 'by drifting into this chronic hostility towards her neighbour.'[31] The *entente* did not, in any case, inaugurate European reconciliation, but unrestrained Anglo-French exploitation of Egypt and Morocco. The inclusion of Russia convinced Brailsford that the purpose of the participants was to isolate Germany and to exclude her from opportunities for overseas investment. 'Had peace been our object', he concluded, 'we should have sought it rather at Berlin than at St Petersburg.'[32]

Germany's conduct during the Moroccan and Bosnian crises had endangered European peace and stimulated a competition in armaments, but the reasons for her behaviour were readily apparent. The noisy threats were merely a protest 'against the toils of a vast diplomatic intrigue which were gradually hemming her in'.[33] Although in the first instance Germany was voicing her objection to a secret partition of Morocco which would have excluded her enterprise, she was more generally challenging the right of other powers to close the door of 'a place in the sun' to German capital. Her desire for compensation was an intelligible goal that did not endanger her competitors. Brailsford believed that by offering concessions England and France could appease Germany's feelings of victimization and remove the ostensible reason for massive armaments. A *rapprochement* must aim not merely at the reconciliation of England and Germany, but rather at a restoration of harmony among all three powers.[34] He envisaged an Anglo-German consortium which would share in the development of the Baghdad railway, 'save Turkey as an Asiatic Power, and even restore her to prosperity'. Franco-German relations, on the other hand, might be improved if France were to open her money market to German enterprise, and Germany were to apply 'an ungrudging policy of conciliation to Alsace-Lorraine'.[35] As long as the British government assumed that a fundamental antagonism existed in European affairs which gave an exclusive character to its friendship with France, the arms race would continue. Such a proposal did not imply that Brailsford, a member of the ILP since 1907, endorsed the diplomatic machinations of capitalist states, but only that he saw the possibility of exploiting them in the interest of peace.

From the time of the Boer War Brailsford had become convinced that 'the potent pressure of economic expansion is the motive force in an international struggle'.[36] A reading of Marx shortly after 1900 and, even more significantly, the contribution of his friend Hobson, suggested a connection between Imperialism and the search for overseas markets for the investment of surplus capital. Whereas Hobson had sought to explain British Imperialism, Brailsford applied the thesis to European diplomacy in general, discovering in it the key to what he described as 'the war of steel and gold'.[37] These ideas were elaborated in a series of articles in the *Nation*[38] and more fully in the book which was to become not only his best-known work, but one of the most influential socialist tracts of the period.

The premise of the book could be succinctly stated:[39]

> Modern conditions have involved us in a rivalry of armaments which is now a conscious struggle to achieve by expenditure and science, by diplomacy and alliances, a balance of power which always eludes us, and because it is always variable and unstable condemns us to a bloodless battle, a dry warfare of steel and gold.

In the past, Brailsford asserted, the search for a balance of power had been a function of a nation's fear of invasion or loss of independence. England had formed alliances and provided subsidies in order to counter the actual threat which Louis XIV and Napoleon posed to her integrity. In contrast, European territorial frontiers, at least outside the Balkans, were beyond contention by the early twentieth century. Aside from the issue of Alsace – which Brailsford felt local autonomy could resolve – there was at stake 'nothing whatever in Europe, nothing at all that touches any vital interest of any European democracy'.[40] Indeed he was willing to venture a prediction that there would be no more wars among the major powers. The unlikeliness of war did not mean that genuine peace had been achieved. Despite the interval of more than forty years since the Franco-Prussian War, Europe had not only failed to check militarism, but found itself divided into hostile camps, each aiming to transform the balance of power in its own favour. These alliances were a symptom of the prevailing insecurity, of what G. Lowes Dickinson would later term the international anarchy. The fear which caused European powers to arm was no longer that of invasion, but of the risk that a stronger power might menace their overseas acquisitions. What were at stake were opportunities for economic penetration, places in the sun for the investment of surplus capital. Economic motives, not questions of nationality or domestic freedom, underlay the struggle for a balance of power.

Adopting the analytical framework of Hobson's *Imperialism*, Brailsford argued that capital, accumulating too rapidly to secure a profitable return at home, sought outlets in the under-developed regions of the world and then invoked the power of the modern state for its protection. 'We are engaged', he claimed, 'in Imperial trading, with the flag as its indispensable asset, but the profits go exclusively into private pockets.'[41] It was no longer true that trade followed the flag, but rather that the flag followed investment. If finance did not invariably determine the course of diplomacy, there existed a secret and capricious relationship between the two, stimulating armed competition between the capitalist powers, a war of steel and gold. During the era of free trade, Lancashire manufacturers had opposed the conquest of new territories and had viewed armaments as unproductive expenditure. A foreign policy based on the export of goods was consistent with the freedom and prosperity of one's customers, but the export of capital led directly to Imperialism. The fears aroused by imperial rivalry had generated a powerful munitions industry, closely linked with financial circles and eager to exploit the tensions among nations for profit. Brailsford cited England's experience in Egypt as an example of the way in which financial interests came to dominate government policy. The seizure of Egypt was 'the master-key of our foreign policy',[42] creating an initial breach with France, swollen armaments, and, ultimately, the search for allies in order to escape diplomatic isolation. The Egyptian occupation, undertaken to safeguard the interests of European bondholders, had eroded England's benevolent influence at Constantinople and saddled her with the burdens of administration in Cairo. Under Lord Cromer's rule, local initiative in politics and education was deliberately stifled, because foreign capitalists regarded a national government as harmful to their enterprises.

The doctrine of continuity of policy had been applied to serve the needs of imperialism, removing foreign affairs from the arena of party debate and subjecting it to the control of a coterie of government experts, colonial officials, and self-interested financiers. The Liberal press and the Radical pressure groups, as Brailsford's own experience indicated, lacked the capacity to influence the direction of policy.[43] With the enforcement of party discipline, ensuring that MPs voted for or against the government rather than on the merits of a particular foreign question, the Commons had virtually forfeited its right to criticize. Those who attempted to challenge Grey risked endangering progressive domestic legislation. Furthermore, even within the Cabinet members tended to defer to the Foreign Secretary, whose authority was rarely questioned. 'Nations aspire in vain to fraternity and peace, while the ambitions, the prejudices, and the interests of their governing caste dictate their movements and govern their intercourse.'[44]

Although Brailsford admitted that popular Jingoism reinforced the financial pressure towards expansion, he refuted Norman Angell's view that the problem was merely to persuade public opinion of the folly of war. Armaments had increased not so much to equip a nation for war as to enhance its prestige and to underpin its expansion overseas. To contend that the acquisition of territory in a war rarely benefited its victors was to ignore the fact that imperial gains were usually obtained without recourse to combat among the competing powers. Brailsford also maintained that although the pursuit of war may be senseless from the standpoint of national interest, it might still be a rational goal for certain powerful financial groups. Even if one were to accept the risk of war, instead of the unstable 'armed peace', as the danger confronting Europe, pacifist activity had proved less effective as a weapon than socialism, 'the most formidable factor in the preservation of the peace of Europe'.[45] Modern nations, obliged to rely on conscript armies, could no longer contemplate unleashing a war without taking into account the inflexible opposition of this well-organized body of opinion.

To his analysis of the economic basis of international conflict Brailsford added four concrete proposals, which he believed would pave the way for a new ordering of European relations. First, a fundamental change was needed in England's constitutional machinery to secure more democratic control of foreign policy. He suggested a separation of external from domestic issues by a scheme of federal devolution, leaving the Imperial Parliament at Westminster to concern itself with imperial questions. Within Parliament a Commons Committee for Foreign Affairs would be elected on a proportional basis from all parties to supervise the Foreign Office in a manner comparable to that of the American Senate Foreign Relations Committee.[46] Although the Foreign Secretary would retain executive responsibility, the Committee would have the right to appeal over his head to the House of Commons. The Foreign Office should be compelled to modify its traditional methods and recruit its officials on the basis of open competition.

Second, those who invested capital or sought concessions abroad must, if they wanted the protection of the British flag, restrict their activity to imperial territory. If they chose to venture into areas outside British control, they could do so at their own risk, aware that they had no claim on official aid. In order to protect undeveloped regions from ruthless exploitation, a credit bureau – not unlike the later World Bank – might be set up at The Hague to provide financial experts and to help in the negotiation of loans on reasonable terms. Third, England should agree to give up the obsolete right to capture an enemy's merchant fleet at sea. If this claim were surrendered, the motive for the Anglo-German naval rivalry would be eliminated, facilitating a reduction of expenditure on battleships. In addition, the manufacture of armaments should be nationalized to remove the private financial incentive for the accumulation of munitions. Finally, the powers should agree to merge their sectional alliances into a genuine Concert of Europe. Once England, France, and Germany resolved their few outstanding differences, there would be no further obstacle to the establishment of a council capable of mediating all disputes. The basis of their accord would be a resolution that nothing should happen in the world without the consent of all the civilized powers.

Brailsford did not disclaim a utopian aspect to many of his prescriptions, but he was convinced that education and rational calculation would eventually bring his hopes to fruition.[47]

> Let a people once perceive for what purposes its patriotism is prostituted, and its resources misused, and the end is already in sight. When that illumination comes to the masses of the three Western Powers, the fears which fill their barracks and stoke their furnaces will have lost the power to drive. A clear-sighted generation will scan the horizon and find no enemy. It will drop its armour, and walk the world's highways safe.

On that naïvely optimistic and intellectually irrefutable note, he concluded *The War of Steel and Gold*. The date was March 1914.

NOTES

1 *Nation*, 30 May 1908.
2 Ibid.
3 *Daily News*, 23 December 1907.
4 *Glasgow Herald*, 8 September 1898.
5 *North American Review*, August 1905, vol. 181, no. 2, p. 252.
6 *Morning Leader*, 30 December 1899; 6 January 1900.
7 Brailsford, *Some Irish Problems*, London, 1903, p. 9.
8 Ibid., p. 13.
9 Ibid., p. 43.
10 *Manchester Guardian*, 7 April and 18 May 1903.
11 Ibid., 8 June 1903.
12 Brailsford, *Macedonia: Its Races and Their Future*, London, 1906, p. 123.
13 *Manchester Guardian*, 10 August 1903.
14 Brailsford, *Macedonia*, p. 314.
15 *Independent Review*, October 1906, vol. XI, no. 37, pp, 59-60.
16 Brailsford to E. D. Morel, 6 September 1906, Morel Papers (London School of Economics), F. 9.
17 *Nation*, 20 July 1907.
18 *Independent Review*, August 1904, vol. III, no. 11, pp. 321-36.
19 *Daily News*, 5 August 1905.
20 *Independent Review*, September 1906, vol. X, no. 36, pp. 257-64; and Brailsford, *The Fruits of our Russian Alliance*, London, 1912, pp. 5-13.
21 *Nation*, 22 June 1907.
22 *Daily News*, 25 June 1908.
23 *Socialist Review*, July 1908, vol. I, no. 5, p. 337.
24 Brailsford, *The Fruits of our Russian Alliance*, p. 59.
25 *Socialist Review*, July 1908, vol. I, no. 5, p. 339.
26 *Nation*, 15 June 1912.
27 Brailsford to Noel Buxton, 11 August 1908, Buxton Papers.
28 Brailsford to Noel Buxton, 14 August 1908, Buxton Papers (McGill University, Montreal).
29 *English Review*, May 1909, vol. 2, p. 380.
30 *Nation*, 10 December 1910. See also *Contemporary Review*, September 1911, vol. C, no. 549, pp. 321-30.
31 *Manchester Guardian*, 5 July 1905.
32 Letter to the Editor of *The Times*, 10 September 1907.
33 *English Review*, July 1909, vol. 2, p. 787.
34 *Contemporary Review*, July 1912, vol. CII, no. 559, pp. 18-26. See also, *Nation*, 25 May and 1 June 1912.
35 *Nation*, 24 May 1913.
36 *Nation*, 18 May 1912.
37 Brailsford first used this term as the title of an article in the *Nation*, 5 June 1909. See also the *Nation*, 2 September 1911.
38 *Nation*, 11 May–29 June 1912.
39 Brailsford, *The War of Steel and Gold: a study of the armed peace*, London, 1914, p. 308.
40 Ibid., p. 46.
41 Ibid., p. 61.

42 Ibid., p. 105.
43 See Zara S. Steiner, *The Foreign Office and Foreign Policy, 1898-1914*, Cambridge, 1969, pp. 190-1.
44 Brailsford, *War of Steel and Gold*, p. 154.
45 Ibid., p. 195.
46 Brailsford outlined this proposal earlier in *English Review*, December 1909, vol. 4, pp. 122-31.
47 Brailsford, *War of Steel and Gold*, p. 317.

13

RADICALISM AND NATIONALISM: AN INCREASINGLY UNSTABLE EQUATION

HOWARD WEINROTH

The appearance of a strident nationalism during the First World War was an unsettling experience for British Radicals. Confused by xenophobic outbursts, the invasion of small states and the conflicting claims of political sovereignty over disputed areas, many were driven to reappraise the role and significance of nationalism in a world setting. Some saw it as the underlying cause of the 1914 explosion, specifically blaming the 'ramshackle Austro-Hungarian Empire for creating the pent-up force which became the Nemesis of European order'.[1] Others, chiefly disillusioned internationalists, feared it would always tend to overshadow fraternal relations between peoples. Those less pessimistic about the future nevertheless felt that the claims of emerging nationalities had to be met, for this was an essential condition of peace without which democracy would never flourish.[2] Radicals seemed strangely obsessed with nationalism, and not disinclined to indulge in the scholarly pastime of reconstructing the map of Europe on the basis of strict ethnological divisions. It was as though they were uncomfortably admitting that their Liberalism had failed to give due emphasis to one of Europe's major problems.

At least one Radical, Arnold Toynbee, not only expiated the sin of Liberal negligence but sought to explain it. Writing to the *Nation* in 1915, he observed that in the first half of the nineteenth century 'we discovered the strength of nationalism and took it for the supreme constructive force in humanity . . . [but] after 1871 we fell under the hypnotism of economics so completely that Mr Norman Angell came to represent this in turn as the sole creative factor'. Toynbee stressed that the 1914 disaster should have taught them that economics and nationality were both fundamental, irreducible factors, neither of which could be 'distorted in practice into conformity with the other's results'.[3] His explanation, reflecting a dichotomy in Liberal thinking hardly perceptible before the war, is imprecise because it wrongly suggests that Liberalism had long abandoned the principle of nationality. Certainly this was untrue of the Radicals. Their support of national movements, stemming from the days of the Polish struggle against Tsarism, had not been extinguished. Conveniently overlooking inconsistencies in Gladstone's policies, they still proudly proclaimed his concern for the fate of the Bulgarians and Montenegrins, his plea for Irish Home Rule and his ringing phrase, 'Egypt for the Egyptians'. They credited themselves with being the first to arouse their countrymen to the plight of the Armenians. By the twentieth century, this commitment to the defence of small nations was extended to the Boers, the Finns, the Persians and the Macedonians; indeed, to any people aspiring to achieve self-determination. It manifested itself in the founding of new foreign policy pressure groups, such as the Balkan and Persia Committees, in which Radicals – Noel Buxton, James Bryce, Sir Edwin Pears, H. F. B. Lynch, Philip Morrell, Professor E. G. Browne – were the moving spirits.[4] L. T. Hobhouse put their views succinctly in 1904, when deprecating the baneful legacies left by the Vienna and Berlin Congresses. National rights, he argued, 'have their assigned place in the democratic system', for 'the world advances by the free, vigorous growth of divergent types' which preserve their vitality in an organic order of life 'resting on the spontaneous co-operation' of its parts.[5] It was this credo of a plurality of nations freely coexisting and mutually benefiting one another that the Radicals unhesitatingly adopted.

Few Radicals had ever attempted to analyse the complexities of the national organism. They acknowledged *prima facie* that it had as distinct an existence within the human family as the individual had within a particular society. They ascribed that existence to a combination of factors – language, culture, race, sentiment – and concluded that a people's consciousness of its own being was sufficient warrant for political self-expression. They were unable, however, to fathom the inner depths of a nation's vitality, the historical reasons why it appeared when it did, or its perplexing dualist nature – what G. Lowes Dickinson termed the liberative and aggressive aspects of nationality.[6] Radicals identified with popular movements striving for political independence not because of a reasoned theory of nationalism but from a deep-seated humanitarianism. Above all, they were convinced that in championing the 'unliberated' they were vindicating their own noble view of Liberalism. This frequently impelled them to seek some special cause to which they could anchor their convictions. Yet in adopting 'one or another of the different races for a favourite pet', their Liberalism periodically became the victim of their partiality.[7] This, in turn, caused friction among the Radicals themselves whenever national movements came into conflict.

Nevertheless, before the war, Radicals were not acutely disturbed by the disorderliness of national self-determination; it was assumed to be a passing phase. They were, as Toynbee perceived, hypnotized by economics. They believed that the aggressiveness of states would be dampened by the universal integration of finance capital, already reflected in the sensitive if negative response of stock markets to international unrest. Interdependence on this level was bound to draw the great Powers together; and the young nations, most notably in the Balkans, would be absorbed into the civilizing centre of Europe as they rid themselves of barbaric conditions. Norman Angell took credit for this notion, though for decades Radicals in general had been embellishing what was a time-hallowed Cobdenite theme. James Bryce, for instance, rendered another variation of it. Discoursing on the evolution of man in the spatial sphere, he claimed that three major developments stood out: 'the contraction of the world, the overflow of the more advanced races and the consequent diffusion all over the world of what is considered civilisation'.[8] Armed with this theoretical framework, it is no wonder that, despite growing international tensions, the Radicals clung to an optimistic, if not unshakeable, faith in the proliferation of nationalities along pacific lines. Curiously enough, however, they were among the first to discard the full application of the principle of self-determination, and increasingly so as Europe rushed vertiginously towards disaster in 1914. To explain this paradox necessitates a study of Radical reactions to nationalism against the background of changing international relations.

Two national revolutionary developments fired Radical interest in 1908. One was the battle of the Persian constitutionalists to supplant the Shah and secure the independence of their country from foreign control; the other, the revolt of the Young Turks which finally brought to an end the tyranny of Abdul Hamid.

For the Radicals, the Persian movement had a special and sustained attraction. It is not surprising that they gave it high priority in their demands upon the Foreign Office. Persia had all the virtues yet none of the defects of the maturing nations. It was not a Turkey with a long tradition of cruelty towards its Christian subjects. It was not a Morocco, still politically backward, with little chance of avoiding the imposition of a foreign protectorate. Nor was it some remote African territory whose right of self-determination could safely be left to the distant future. The Persians were a cultured people attempting to construct a parliamentary regime on the Western model. Here were sufficient reasons for Radical concern. H. F. B. Lynch, founder of the Persia Committee, impressed this upon the Commons:[9]

> Whenever a people were engaged in a struggle for freedom . . . in a struggle for self-realisation, they always felt that England, and especially the [Liberal] party . . . would take their part and sympathise with them, and if the circumstances permitted, convert their sympathy into practical support.

The Radical journals detected an even brighter aspect in Persian constitutionalism. If it succeeded, it would serve as a beacon for political experiment in the East. Identical movements in India and Egypt would be encouraged to follow in its path. Thus, Liberalism would take root among non-European peoples. This could have proved embarrassing for the British Empire, but the Radicals were not alarmed by that prospect. They believed it possible for rising nationalist forces to co-exist with imperial rule. Had not British dominion prevailed so long precisely because it was flexible enough to grant reforms and self-government when conditions permitted? The extension of Home Rule to South Africa was a case in point.

This ideal projection of a Liberal British government acting as midwife to emerging nations was seriously strained by the Anglo-Russian Convention. This became the instrument for Russian aggression against Teheran, and for British intervention in southern Persia to quell the marauding tribes that spread disorder and ruined trade. Aroused by what they considered a betrayal of faith, the Radicals waged a tireless campaign to arrest the dangers threatening Persian independence. At every inauspicious turn of events they harangued Sir Edward Grey, subjecting the House to long, acrimonious debates, imploring the Liberal party 'to raise its voice against a policy that was alienating the Persian people'.[10] In 1912, they packed the London Opera House in protest against British collusion in the 'virtual dismemberment of this unhappy country'.[11] Inevitably there were differences between Radicals as to what ought to be done. Lord Loreburn, who regarded the Persians as a 'corrupt and hopeless lot', was indifferent; but he was in a minority of one. More typical were those moderates, like C. P. Scott, who wished to preserve the mutilated Convention, but urged incessant criticism of Grey to afford him greater bargaining power with the Russians – 'they must be told to fulfil their share of the agreement or it would not last'.[12] On the other hand, the impatient advocates of Persian freedom – Arthur Ponsonby, Silvester Horne, Philip Morrell, H. N. Brailsford – thought it better to cut the Gordian knot and extricate British policy from the Russian connection.[13]

Grey attacked this line of thought. He claimed that the Radicals were calling for a 'maximum of interference in the world at large with a minimum of friends', an obvious reference to their distaste for Anglo-Russian collaboration. In this he was mistaken. Similarly, A. J. P. Taylor when he implies that in 1912 they proposed bartering away the rights of Persians *inter alia* to 'satisfy the legitimate aspirations of Germany'.[14] What the Radicals wanted, as Ponsonby asserted, was to allow national movements to work out their own solutions.[15] To the extent they favoured German investment in Persia, it was meant partly to conciliate Germany's drive for markets, mainly to rescue the constitutional movement. This may seem odd, but the Radicals believed that a third power on the Persian scene would act as 'a counterpoise to the excessive influence of England and Russia', and thereby draw the teeth of balance-of-power diplomacy.[16] No doubt, it was an idyllic notion borrowed from nineteenth-century examples; also, an illusion, that small nations could realize self-determination despite great-power intervention. Once disabused of these illusions their agitation declined. In 1914, E. G. Browne, the Persia Committee's authority on oriental affairs, reviewing the latest developments – the Persian oil concession and the Trans-Persian railway – despairingly admitted that nothing could be done as long as Grey clung 'with tenacity of purpose . . . to his pro-Russian and anti-German policy'.[17] Bertrand Russell went a step further in an exceptional prediction.[18]

> The only hope for Persia, as the rest of Asia, seems to lie in such a weakening of all the Great Powers [in war] as shall enable more backward nations to throw off the yoke fastened on them by Cabinets and financiers of the 'civilized' States.

Nevertheless, the Radicals could not forget the Persian question! The war-time dissenters, to the discomfort of former political allies who would rather not have been reminded, maintained that the violation of Belgium was no worse than the rape of Persia. The latter was their yardstick for judging the plausibility of realizing self-determination in a world governed by the balance of power.[19]

Persian nationalism was a straightforward affair compared with the Balkan imbroglio. What complicated matters here were the number of national movements struggling one with another as well as against Turkey. The conflicting interests of the great powers added to the confusion. Even the Radicals had difficulty determining which national group – Greek, Serb, Bulgarian, Roumanian, Albanian – best merited their support. But, since the pro-Bulgarians enjoyed most influence in the Balkan Committee, they naturally gave the lead. For several years under Noel Buxton's guidance they had been criticizing the Foreign Office's apparent ineptitude on the crucial issue of Macedonian reform. The Young Turk revolution in 1908 came as a stunning surprise, overturning plans and calculations. It was a blow to those who had pinned hopes on an early realization of Macedonian autonomy; a moment of scepticism for a few unbending anti-Turks who failed to see Liberalism dawning in the East or doubted the ability of the new regime to overcome the obstacles that beset it.[20] Despite these misgivings, G. P. Gooch rightly recorded that nowhere outside Turkey was the revolution 'hailed with such enthusiasm as in England'.[21] The Balkan Committee shared his views, and one of its members waxed lyrical over the coming millennium.[22]

> What a short cut to the thousand years of joy! . . . The market place of Monastir breathes to unwonted airs of freedom's Marseillaise . . . for the first time since Titus there is joy upon Mt. Zion, and for the first time since the Crusades, the Holy Sepulchre is loud with thanksgiving.

More remarkable and to the point were the words of James Bryce, a fire-eating Turcophobe who had helped to father the Balkan Committee. To Buxton he stated his conviction that never before in history had there arisen such an opportunity 'for a reconcilement of Christians and Mussulmans on the basis of good feeling and equality'.[23] The general consensus of Radicals, reinforced by Grey's benign approval of the revolution, was summed up by the *Nation:* 'If there is a chance, even a remote chance, that the Turks may themselves work out their own solution, we shall do well to suspend any special thought of intervention on behalf of the Christian races.'[24]

Underlying this appeal for restraint and sympathy were three considerations. The Turks, having made immense efforts to reform their regime, should not be stifled by European prejudices. In the prevailing circumstances, foisting upon them a programme for Macedonian or Albanian autonomy would probably result in annexation by one of the great powers. But, most important, the renaissance of the Ottoman Empire on the basis of liberty and toleration was preferable to 'any partial solution which might have freed certain races'.[25] C. R. Buxton elaborated this point. The Turks had but two courses from which to choose.[26]

> Either . . . refuse to grant full autonomy and try to reform the Empire on the basis simply of personal security and equality before the law, or by granting such autonomy . . . risk a reactionary movement. . . . The former course means contentment for twenty millions of the human race whereas the violent disruption of Turkey could, at most, benefit six millions.

Had the Radicals then jettisoned their own commitment to national liberation? No – but it would have to wait! It could not displace their sense of equity towards Turkish liberalism or broader humanitarian considerations. In time, it would work itself out within the context of the Ottoman Empire. As Brailsford, in parrying Sir Edwin Pears's advocacy of immediate autonomy, told Noel Buxton, 'I am with Pears and yourself in desiring Home Rule for Macedonia. I go further and think it inevitable. But I no longer wish to see it imposed by diplomacy or *force*.'[27]

Objection to the use of force, if not its total abnegation, was one of the distinguishing features of the dissenting mind. It accounts for the contradictory position Radicals assumed during the 1908 Bosnian crisis and the subsequent tension between Austria and Serbia. Morally outraged by the Austrian *démarche* and Bulgaria's declaration of independence, the left-wing journals initially joined the chorus of voices condemning the flagrant repudiation of international law. The *Manchester Guardian* sadly noted that now the Treaty of Berlin 'had been placed on the dissecting table' other powers 'will carve where Bulgaria and Austria have hacked'. Both the *Nation* and the *Daily News* lashed out at the reckless 'manifest destiny' of the Habsburgs. Not only did it aggravate Serbo-Montenegrin irredentism, but it made the Slav states more conscious 'that they were at the mercy of Austrian politicians and capitalists who hold their only outlets to the world'.[28] Thus it was necessary that a European conference be held to compensate Turkey, conciliate the Slav states and grant autonomy to Bosnia-Herzegovina. But within weeks, the pendulum of Radical opinion was reversed. The conference idea, and Grey for having proposed it, were discredited.

Austria suddenly appeared generous; she was offering compensation to the Turks. As for the southern Slav states, they should submit to the *fait accompli*. 'A plebiscite' might have been the instrument for ascertaining Bosnian wishes, commented the *Nation*, 'but it had gone out of fashion'. Besides, 'autonomy would only create additional friction in that area yielding little liberty for its inhabitants'.[29] *The Economist*, seldom excited about national movements, agreed. It was unthinkable that Bosnia-Herzegovina be handed back to the Sultan, for 'Austria has settled and pacified this one-time wild and barbarous country' and 'her work was at least as beneficial as ours [in Ireland]'.[30] Since the act of annexation was irreversible, the Radicals proposed trialism – elevating the Slavs in the Habsburg Empire to the status of the Germans and Magyars as the best alternative to autonomy. It would free the Croats, Serbs, Slovaks and others from the heavy hand of Magyar domination, thus extending the area of pacification. Even better, it had the support of influential circles in Austria, the heir apparent to the throne, and slavophils in Britain.

Why this abrupt *volte face*? Sir Charles Dilke explained it in the Commons, Lord Courtney in a letter to *The Times*. Though neither Dilke nor Courtney was a proponent of Slav liberation, what they said was echoed in the Radical press. Courtney argued that international law tends towards ossification; it must yield to changing realities and the Austrian *démarche* had merely confirmed these realities.[31] But beneath his juristic defence of the *fait accompli* lay an anxious suspicion that antagonisms in the Balkans were sharpening the conflicting interests of the two European blocs, the Triple Alliance and the Triple Entente. This was bad enough, but coupled with the naval scare and Franco-German tensions in Morocco it gave a warlike appearance to the situation. Courtney, like other Radicals, doubted whether the agitation over the Bosnian annexation had served any beneficial purpose.[32]

> We have excited almost every section of opinion in Austria-Hungary . . . we are regarded with no gratitude in Servia . . . we seem to have developed some additional and quite unnecessary roughness of friction between ourselves and Germany. . . . Why could we not have seen this at once – that overpowering logic of events that we recognise today, and have been a pacificator working with that other pacificator, Germany, from the beginning instead of being dragged into acquiescence?

However much Radicals might differ in their approach to specific national issues, one thing united them – the preservation of European tranquillity. International developments in 1908–9 had demonstrated the precarious nature of that tranquillity. This, in turn, made the Radicals hesitate before championing self-determination.

The desire to preserve peace invariably drew Radicals together, providing a relatively cohesive response to related problems. The outbreak of war frequently drove them into a state of disorder, even despair. The Balkan struggles of 1912–13 did just this. Though disappointed by the Ottoman government's ruthless policies, the Radicals persisted in the belief that the Young Turks could still be induced to grant reforms to the disaffected Christian minorities. They feared what might result once local hostilities started. In the *Daily News*, Brailsford foretold the havoc and atrocities that would accompany war. Nothing, he warned, would excuse it 'except that an end must come out of the accumulated horrors of daily conquest and continuous devastation'. Yet, 'had a point been reached at which the Balkan peoples would incur a worse blood guilt by tolerating oppression' than by an appeal to arms?[33] Noel Buxton was also emotionally lacerated. Must he 'abandon the hope' that happiness could be achieved for the unfortunate subjects of Turkey 'by peaceful means and so become an advocate of war?' That was the dilemma of many, observed the *Arbitrator*, 'because the very members of the peace societies are also members of such bodies as the Anti-Slavery Society and the Balkan Committee'.[34] Conversely, the unbending moral pacifists, with Radical Positivists in the Society for Peace and Arbitration, refused to yield ground. For them the military contest in the Balkans was not a case apart.

But the old Gladstonian impulse quickly swept the field. Radical politicians – A. G. C. Harvey, D. M. Mason, Sir John Brunner, Lord Channing – welcomed the 'liberation' movement, and were joined by sections of Labour. Left-wing journals abandoned their caution as the Bulgarians, Greeks and Serbs registered stunning victories in the field. Nonconformists in general, lay and churchmen alike, showered the Balkan peoples with their blessings. So intoxicating was the euphoria that even ardent peace advocates were affected. Lady Courtney wrote in her diary, 'War in the Balkans . . . has come after centuries of slaughter and unrest and come in the best way, *if* war can ever be a good way, by the rising of the subject races and not from the outside.'[35] Canon J. H. B. Masterman, a member of the Church Peace League, maintained that sympathy for the Balkan states was 'not inconsistent with the belief that the military struggle ought not to have occurred'.[36] And Norman Angell, the inaugurator of the 'New Pacifism', turned the situation on its head. Peace under the Turks was equivalent to war; the liberation of the Balkans was the corridor to civilization.[37]

This impressionistic description conceals the inner tensions, conflicting loyalties and diverging evaluations which plagued the Radicals. Not all favoured Balkan nationalism with the same intensity of feeling, just as some were not outspokenly anti-Turkish. The London correspondent of the *Manchester Guardian* detected two extremes: the men who would drive the Turks 'bag and baggage' out of Europe, and those who were opting for 'Young Turkey' as against 'Old Russia'.[38] If the knights errant of Balkan liberation recounted the cruelties of the Turks, the latter pointed to the recent massacres committed by Bulgarian bands against innocent civilians, to the outrages perpetrated by Christian Russia against Finns and Jews. It was not that these Radicals denied the injustices suffered by Greeks, Bulgarians and Serbs; what they demanded was 'fair play' for all. It was hardly possible that any side among the belligerents enjoyed 'a balance of right', and they stressed the Russian danger that loomed behind the Balkan victories.[39] Between the two extremes was a wide range of views including anti-Russian as well as 'neutral' attachment to the cause of liberation. Because of these divisions, the short-lived Radical Foreign Policy group decided to issue a restrained and evasive statement about the Balkans. At the same time Philip Morrell advised Buxton that the Balkan Committee ought to avoid meetings on behalf of the rebel states.[40]

War also eroded the Radical conception of resolving national difficulties, especially in Macedonia. The ideal expressed by Pears, Buxton, Brailsford and Bourchier had been Home Rule for that strife-ridden province. Short of that, they urged security and reform for its inhabitants. Now, in October 1912, with the opening of hostilities, they altered their political vocabulary. The detachment of Macedonia from the Ottoman Empire seemed 'a reasonable compromise' since 'Bulgaria would have nothing less'.[41] But the Bulgarians, Greeks and Serbs had no intention of stopping at liberation. They pushed for partition as the swift strokes of their armies accomplished what decades of pained hopes and futile diplomacy had not realized. The Radicals kept in step. The *Nation*, reflecting the new mood of exhilaration, triumphantly proclaimed, 'the clean final solution of partition is incomparably preferable to the old expedient of autonomy'. The latter had been adopted by

Western peoples for 'opportunistic reasons' – out of fear that an attempted territorial division 'must result in fratricidal warfare among the races of the Peninsula'.[42] Had the Radicals all along been no more than opportunists? If so, it was because they had adhered to the Liberal outlook which, by its very nature, was bound to disavow such 'revolutionary acts' as the abrupt dismemberment of empires. On the other hand, autonomy was compatible with that outlook; it seemed to promise a framework in which peoples could progress pacifically towards full emancipation. Though a few left-wing supporters of Balkan nationalism occasionally saw partition as performing 'a permanent disposal of the [Macedonian] problem', J. D. Bourchier, The *Times* correspondent in Sofia, was probably voicing the Radical-Liberal assessment more accurately when he said it 'could *only* be arrived at by war . . . *provided* that it is carried out in accordance with the principle of nationalities . . . the Slav and Greek populations being absorbed by the kindred free states and the Albanians being independent'. Yet even then he opined that the division of spoils among the great powers might 'take a different form *which would prolong the evil*'.[43]

In one respect, Bourchier's gloomy prophecy was wide of the mark. As the perceptive Liberal diplomatist, George Young, wrote to Bryce, the trouble with the Balkan Committee and the anti-Foreign Office faction was that they 'kept plugging away at Grey as tho' the Balkans were only a third hand in the deal of which China and Persia were previous tricks', whereas the new complexion of things was that the *entente* was 'favourable to the principle of nationality in Macedonia, as it was unfavourable to it in Persia'.[44] Nevertheless, Bourchier had underlined the inherent obstacles to 'clean-slate' solutions which, in a moment of unguarded zeal, the Radicals forgot. They were deluded to suppose that the 'necessity of partition' could be combined with the image of 'races once riven by discord' coalescing. They conjured up a Balkan Federation on the threshold of civilization, but nothing of the kind happened. The victorious rebel states began to squabble over territorial arrangements. The Bulgarians stalled in Eastern Thrace, and with little gain to show for their efforts, were incensed with their allies. The Serbs seized most of the Macedonian areas provisionally allotted to the Bulgarians and refused to make concessions. In the west, the Greeks staked out claims in southern Epirus, while Montenegrins and Serbs embarked upon a campaign to lop off segments of Albania. Before the sordid calculations of the insurgents, the fleeting dream of Balkan unity receded. Faced by these facts, the Radicals bartered principles for pragmatism. They argued that 'in each delicate case of partition the interests of the local population' and not the juggling of boundaries, '*should be* decisive'. However, deviation from this strict rule *might be* legitimate – 'one could not [always] invoke the nationality principle once it had been violently overthrown'.[45] They spoke of the vital need for territorial adjustments. Though Turkish, Adrianople had to be given to the Bulgarians; the Aegean islands, perhaps Epirus, to the Greeks. Ports, predominantly inhabited by Albanians, might be handed over to the Serbs and Montenegrins. If not, then Austria must 'supply a trans-Bosnian outlet for their commerce', for 'the satisfaction of Bulgarian claims in Thrace, Greek claims in the Isles [and Slav needs in the west] must enormously simplify the adjustment of boundaries between the Allies' and reduce friction all round.[46] These pragmatic remedies were probably never seriously considered by statesmen – certainly not by the Balkan envoys to whom a prominent group of left-wing Liberals appealed in the winter of 1912.[47] Nor did they preclude the Radicals disagreeing among themselves over the rights of Montenegro to Scutari, or the injustice done to the Bulgarians in Macedonia. They are striking illustrations of the dilemma that confronted men who were bent upon the reconciliation of clashing nationalities in order to found a federation of states in south-east Europe. That the dilemma was never resolved, because the much-vaunted Balkan federation failed to materialize, suggests one reason why so many Radicals were disinclined to get 'mixed up in Eastern questions', or opposed the destruction of the Austro-Hungarian empire during the First World War.[48]

The breakdown of the Liberal conception of pacific, national proliferation was paralleled by an emotional reaction to the atrocities committed by each of the warring states. Atrocities among eastern peoples was a phenomenon that repelled English sobriety and reasonableness. Ever since the days of the 'Bulgarian Horrors', the Radicals had been ultra-sensitive to the plight of the oppressed. No campaign of theirs – whether for the Boers, the Irish, the Armenians, the Persians, the Bulgarians – was complete without reference to it. In 1913, it became an additional source of disenchantment with Balkan nationalism. Consider the distressed observations of a Balkan 'liberator' like Arthur Moore, who had anticipated 'a certain amount of horrors', but not the savage scenes he had witnessed nor the comparatively exemplary behaviour of the Turks who 'put us all in the wrong'. Or Henry Nevinson, who was disgusted by the ferocity of former allies heaping crime upon crime on one another. Bourchier saw a worse tyranny than under the Turks, but was compelled to keep 'the conspiracy of silence' because 'the *Times* will not hear of "atrocities" '.[49] It must have been this shock, all the worse for coming in the midst of general sympathy for the rebel peoples, that weaned the humanitarian Radicals away from supporting national movements and that, in 1914, evoked their angry response to the thought of submerging western civilization 'in a sea of blood to wash out a Serbian conspiracy'.[50]

Atrocities and Balkan disunity should not, however, be exaggerated. What overshadowed everything else was the state of European equilibrium: the impact that a local conflagration might have upon relations between the Triple Alliance and the Triple Entente. In this the Radicals shared a common concern. They always insisted that Turkish misrule could have been ended felicitously had it not been for the jealousies and self-interests of the great powers. They constantly harked back to the Congress of Berlin which had disregarded the aspirations of the Balkan communities, and to the Concert of Europe which had been negligent in fulfilling its promises to compel Ottoman reform. Time and again they hammered home the point that 'moral inertia would lead to strife', and that 'the small nations would take the law into their own hands'.[51] But, while they cautioned thus, they dreaded also that war would become a pretext for the great powers to pounce upon Turkey. Worse yet, there was the awesome prospect of Austria and Russia taking sides which, at the least, would reproduce the situation of 1908-9.

The paradox of 1913 was that Balkan strife resuscitated the Concert of Europe. Unexpected and unlooked for, it seemed to dispel the ominous signs that had been gathering in Europe ever since Agadir. Britain and Germany were actually collaborating in pacifying the small nations – 'a consolation for all the horror and suffering', as well as for the past errors of statesmen. The Radicals thus bestowed unstinted praise on Sir Edward Grey, so long the butt of their attacks on Foreign Office policy, for playing the role of peacemaker. Elated, they spoke of *rapprochement* as leading to an *entente* between Britain, France and Germany, and envisaged European unity replacing the mischievous balance of power.[52] But, though the Radicals were prone to self-deception, they could not entirely overlook the grave developments that had grown out of the Balkan crisis – the intensification of the arms race; the reappearance of militant revanchism in France; the current talk of an impending 'racial' conflict between Teuton and Slav. The *Nation*, in chorus with other left-wing journals, summed up the fighting in the

Balkan peninsula by noting that it 'had left a furious legacy of nationalism'.[53] Incidents such as the Albanian-Montenegrin squabble over Scutari, or smouldering Austro-Serbian tensions, could become the springboard for an all-embracing disaster. For these reasons, the Radicals, not excepting the ardent slavophils, set aside the rights of nationality. They had obtained, as Harold Spender described it, 'a furtive glance into the burning abysses that lay beneath our feet'.[54] The Concert of Europe, weak and ineffective though it might be, had to be maintained. This was of greater significance than any local consideration.

The Radicals' reaction towards nationalism at the outbreak of war in 1914 was inevitable. Their Liberal vision, of national entities gradually emerging in the mould of a pacific world, had not materialized. Hobhouse's assumption that such entities would spontaneously co-operate in fashioning a higher organic order – an assumption that relied on the Cobden/Angell forecast that international society was becoming more and more integrated and, therefore, capable of minimizing new political strains and stresses – had proved false. Even before the war it was apparent that an extreme implementation of the principle of self-determination tended to unsettle European stability. Less extreme implementation, as in the case of Persia, meant that there was no liberation. Europe, then, was governed by a rigid balance of power in which two opposing alliance systems were delicately poised. Every national change within Europe, or in areas of European interest, threatened to disrupt that balance. The Radicals did not want such disruption, if only because they had nothing to substitute for it. In so far as August 1914 marked the dissolution of the international edifice of balance, the Radicals once more felt compelled to cast about for a fundamental solution to the national question.

They never found it. The only alternative to what had been was national repartition – that is, putting the knife to traditional imperial structures for the sake of ethnographical symmetry. For the Radicals, this implied incalculable complications – a leap into the dark. They preferred, as A. J. P. Taylor has astutely suggested, to look back nostalgically to the *status quo* of 1914. Their Utopia was in the past, not in the future.[55] The Radicals were still imprisoned by a nexus of values, conceptions and beliefs which belonged to a world rapidly fading out of existence. At the core lay the *conviction* that conflict, national or otherwise, could be resolved by a process of conciliation on the basis of equitable compromise. It was this conviction that allowed middle-class idealists to escape the realities of a disintegrating order.

NOTES

1 See R. W. Seton-Watson, *The War and Democracy*, London, 1914, chapters 4 and 7. Also G. M. Trevelyan, 'On the war', *Working Men's College Journal*, May 1915, pp. 98-9.
2 C. R. Buxton, 'Nationality', in C. R. Buxton (ed.), *Towards a Lasting Settlement*, London, 1915, p. 40.
3 Arnold Toynbee, 'The new Europe', *Nation*, 26 June 1915.
4 Buxton, Bryce and Pears, together with J. D. Bourchier, *The Times*'s correspondent in Sofia, were the leading personalities in the Balkan Committee. Lynch, Morrell and E. G. Browne held a similar position in the Persia Committee. There were several Radicals, like Brailsford and Nevinson, who were dedicated to working in both groups.
5 L. T. Hobhouse, *Democracy and Reaction*, London, 1904, pp. 163-4.
6 G. Lowes Dickinson, *After the War*, London, 1915, p. 15.
7 H. W. Nevinson, *More Changes, More Chances*, London, 1925, p. 362.
8 H. A. L. Fisher, *James Bryce*, London, 1927, vol. 1, p. 330.
9 *Hansard*, iv:184:543-4.
10 *Nation*, 5 November 1910.
11 *Manchester Guardian*, 16 January 1912; *Nation*, 5 October 1912.
12 C. P. Scott Diaries: 1 December 1911, 22 January 1912, C. P. Scott Collection, BM, Add. MSS. 50,901.
13 See letter by G. H. Perris in *Nation*, 21 September 1912.
14 Grey's speech reported, *Manchester Guardian*, 22 February 1912; A. J. P. Taylor, *The Trouble Makers*, Panther ed., London, 1969, p. 113.
15 *Hansard*, v:34:629-30.
16 *Daily News*, 19 May 1910. Cf. *Nation*, 19 February 1910.
17 E. G. Browne, 'The Persian oil concession', *War and Peace*, July 1914.
18 Bertrand Russell, *The Foreign Policy of the Entente*, London, 1915, p. 63.
19 Barbara Hammond to Lady Murray, 19 August 1914, Gilbert Murray Papers, Bodleian Library, Oxford, GM-23b; Barbara Hammond to Arthur Ponsonby, 22 October 1914, Ponsonby Papers, in possession of Lord Ponsonby of Shulbrede (hereafter cited as PP); J. L. Hammond to Bertrand Russell, 19 October 1914, in Bertrand Russell, *Autobiography*, Bantam ed., 1969, vol. 2, p. 47.
20 Ponsonby in *Hansard*, iv:193:939-44. Also J. D. Bourchier to Noel Buxton, 12 September 1908, Noel Buxton Papers, McGill University (hereafter cited as BP). I am indebted to Prof. H. N. Fieldhouse for permission to use the Buxton Papers.
21 G. P. Gooch, *Under Six Reigns*, London, 1959, pp. 133-4.
22 H. W. Nevinson, *Essays in Freedom*, London, 1909, pp. 132-3.
23 James Bryce to Noel Buxton, 25 November 1908, BP.
24 *Nation*, 25 July 1908.
25 H. N. Brailsford to Buxton, 11 August (1908?), BP.
26 C. R. Buxton, *Turkey in Revolution*, London, 1909, pp. 222-3.
27 Brailsford to Buxton, 14 August (1908?), BP.

28 *Manchester Guardian*, 3 October 1908; *Nation*, 17 October 1908; *Daily News*, 30 November 1908.
29 *Nation*, 2 January 1909; Cf. *Daily News*, 1 January 1909.
30 *The Economist*, 16 January 1909.
31 Courtney in *The Times*, 23 January 1909. Also Sir Charles Dilke, 'Foreign affairs', *English Review*, Aug.–Nov. 1909, vol. 3, pp. 495-500.
32 Courtney to Editor of *The Times*, spring 1909 (never sent), Courtney Papers, LSE, (hereafter cited as CP) vol. X. Cf. *Daily News*, 1 January 1909.
33 Brailsford, 'The case for the Balkans', *Daily News*, 7 October 1912.
34 Noel Buxton, quoted in *Arbitrator*, August 1912.
35 Kate Courtney's Diaries, 31 November 1912, CP vol. XXXVI. See also Courtney to A. G. Gardiner, 14 October 1912 (copy), CP vol. X.
36 Reported in *Herald of Peace*, 2 June 1913.
37 Norman Angell, *Peace Theories and the Balkan Wars*, London, 1913, pp. 25 and 33-6.
38 *Manchester Guardian*, 24 October 1912.
39 *Concord*, November 1912.
40 Hobhouse to Courtney, 21 October 1912, CP vol. X; Philip Morrell to Noel Buxton, 18 October 1912, BP.
41 *Manchester Guardian*, 4 October 1912; *Daily News*, 1-3 October 1912.
42 *Nation*, 2 November 1912.
43 J. D. Bourchier to Noel Buxton, 3 April 1912 (my italics), BP.
44 George Young to James Bryce, 10 October 1912, Bryce Papers, Bodleian Library, Oxford, Miscellaneous File.
45 *Nation*, 7 December 1912 (my italics); Cf. ibid., 16 August 1913.
46 *Manchester Guardian*, 15 January 1913; Seton-Watson, 'Austria-Hungary as a Balkan Power', *Contemporary Review*, vol. 102, 1912.
47 See documents of Balkan Peace delegates in *Arbitrator*, February 1913.
48 C. P. Trevelyan to E. D. Morel, 9 October 1914, E. D. Morel Papers, LSE, UDC Files. Also, F. W. Hirst to C. P. Trevelyan, 6 April 1915, C. P. Trevelyan Papers, Newcastle University.
49 Arthur Moore to Noel Buxton, 18 April (1913?); and J. D. Bourchier to Buxton, 7 March 1914, BP.
50 *Daily News*, 30 July 1914.
51 *Arbitrator*, November and December 1913.
52 See H. S. Weinroth, 'The British Radicals and the balance of power', *Historical Journal*, vol. 13, no. 4, 1970, pp. 679-80.
53 *Nation*, 6 June 1914.
54 Harold Spender, *The Fire of Life*, London, 1927, pp. 186-7. See also *Nation*, 8 March 1913.
55 A. J. P. Taylor, *The Trouble Makers*, Panther ed., 1969, p. 136.

14

E. D. MOREL: FROM THE CONGO TO THE RHINE

CATHERINE ANN CLINE

On 4 August 1914 E. D. Morel, the prospective Liberal candidate for Birkenhead, met Charles Trevelyan, the Radical politician, at the latter's London house. That morning the German army had attacked Belgium, and the British government, acting on its earlier ultimatum to Germany, entered the war. Morel was seeking Trevelyan's advice in composing a letter to the executive of the Birkenhead Liberal Association explaining his opposition to the Liberal government's intervention in the war. Similarly, on the previous day when Trevelyan resigned as Parliamentary Secretary to the Board of Education on the same issue he had consulted Morel who proved to be 'a splendid strengthening, or rather, clarifying influence'.[1]

It is significant that the common response of Morel and Trevelyan to the outbreak of the war was reached after consultation. They had been acquaintances for many years, and in the period since 1911 they had both expressed alarm concerning the direction of British foreign policy – Morel in slashing public attacks, and Trevelyan in quiet private remarks to members of the Cabinet. Yet some distance remained between them in the pre-war years which is not explicable solely in terms of the restraints imposed on Trevelyan by his membership of the ministry. Trevelyan was typical of those Radical parliamentary critics of their government's foreign policy with whom Morel was never fully associated in the pre-war years. The conversations between Morel and Trevelyan on 3 and 4 August represent the coming together of two allied, but distinctive, strands of disaffection with British foreign policy which was to lead to their fruitful amalgamation during the war in the Union of Democratic Control.

E. D. Morel, who thus hastened to express his opposition to Britain's entrance into the war, had, during much of his career, cultivated an indifference to those central issues in European diplomacy which led finally to the outbreak of the conflict. As the leader of the Congo reform movement he had sought, through public pressure, to induce the British government to use its diplomatic influence to force the elimination of the barbarous rubber system imposed by King Leopold's regime in the Congo. Since Morel maintained that the abuses must be eradicated 'at whatever cost', he contemptuously dismissed any fears concerning the effect of a strong Congo policy on Britain's diplomatic position in Europe. In February 1909 he warned the Foreign Office that the Congo reformers 'are neither attracted nor interested by European rivalries and Continental "diplomacy", but . . . are interested in the fate of millions of helpless people in Africa'.[2]

Although Morel was unconcerned about the effect of a vigorous Congo policy on Britain's diplomatic position, he carefully weighed the possible effect of diplomatic developments among the European powers on Britain's Congo policy. Thus he welcomed the Anglo-French *entente* of 1904, reasoning that the new friendship with France would, by strengthening Britain's position, increase the likelihood that the Foreign Office protests concerning conditions in the Congo would lead to international action. During the first Moroccan crisis in 1905, he saw Britain's anticipated support of France against Germany simply as an opportunity for a *quid pro quo* which would advance the Congo cause. He observed that: 'France had never greater need of us than at this moment . . . as one good turn deserves another so as the price of our supporting France in Morocco, she ought to support us in the Congo matter'.[3]

Morel's insistence on viewing all foreign policy issues in terms of the Congo question made him supremely indifferent to the development that first aroused Radical criticism of the Liberal government's foreign policy: Britain's increasingly close ties with Russia. In his single-minded concentration on the Congo, Morel had no energy to spare for the ideological scruples concerning friendship with Tsarist autocracy which troubled Arthur Ponsonby or for the anxiety concerning the effect of the Anglo-Russian agreement on Persia that aroused Ponsonby's Radical colleagues in the House of Commons. When the Anglo-Russian agreement of 1907 was being concluded, Morel observed neutrally that 'it will be an unpopular treaty with a number of people', and he even urged his followers to exercise patience, excusing the hesitations of the Foreign

Secretary, Sir Edward Grey, on Congo policy as an unavoidable consequence of the difficulties facing him in the House of Commons on the issue of Russia. Since that power played no role in Africa, relations with her appeared to Morel merely as a tiresome distraction of official attention from the monumental cruelties occurring in the Congo.

Since Morel was disinclined to accept excuses for inaction where the Congo was concerned, his unwillingness to criticize Grey in this instance indicates the persistence until late in the Congo campaign of his faith in the good intentions of the Foreign Secretary and the Foreign Office, both of which he was later to denounce so bitterly. In the early stages of the Congo crusade some of the officials at the Foreign Office had encouraged him in his effort to arouse public opinion, and he wrote admiringly of the 'good men amongst the permanent officials . . . who remain year in and year out'. Over the years the slow pace of British diplomacy on the Congo question caused his enthusiasm for Foreign Office officialdom to cool, but he continued until the spring of 1909 to describe the agitation organized by his Congo Reform Association as designed to support Britain's official Congo policy.

The year 1909 marked the beginning of the shift in Morel's interest from African to European affairs and his transformation from a loyal, if somewhat nagging, ally of the Foreign Office and the Foreign Secretary into their most vociferous critic. In the course of that year Morel became convinced that the Anglo-French *entente*, far from strengthening Britain's diplomatic efforts to bring about reform in the Congo, was in fact an obstacle to an effective Congo policy. During a visit to Paris in February, he was shocked by the 'corruption', 'incompetence' and 'cowardice' of French officials as well as by their susceptibility to the influence of the financial interests surrounding King Leopold, and he concluded that the French government was discouraging the British Foreign Office from any effort to convene an international conference to deal with the Congo question. His suspicions concerning the effect of the *entente* appeared to be confirmed by Grey's warning to the House of Commons in May that if the Congo issue were 'rashly managed it might make a European question'. This remark was generally interpreted to mean that Britain must avoid undue pressure on Belgium, lest that strategically important nation co-operate with Germany in the event of a war between the Central Powers and Britain's *entente* partner, France.

It was Grey's May speech which, according to Morel, 'DROVE'

him into open denunciation of the British Foreign Office and its cherished policy, the Anglo-French *entente*. When even his supporters questioned the wisdom of embroiling the Congo cause in an assault on the entire direction of British foreign policy, Morel replied that he had 'no option'.[4]

> For the first time we were told that the Congo could not be judged on its merits but was part and parcel of the European situation. It was therefore no longer practicable for me . . . to ignore these wider issues.

To another critic he explained:[5]

> If there is one thing the Government does dread it is a campaign against the entente cordiale, and they have been told that such a campaign will be waged from Land's end to John O'Groats if they abandon the Congo natives to their fate.

While these remarks leave little doubt that Morel's initial attack on the *entente* was simply a tactic in the Congo campaign, his critique of British foreign policy raised issues of broader significance. His complaint that the Congo question was not being considered 'on its merits' was echoed by Radicals like Noel Buxton, disturbed because the interests of the Balkan nationalities whom they championed were subordinated by the British Foreign Office to concern for Anglo-Russian friendship. Although preoccupied with different corners of the world, Morel and the Radicals were objecting to the same development in their nation's foreign policy – the loss of freedom of action as a consequence of increasing entanglement in the alliance system.

Morel surmised that the involvement was more extensive than the British public had been led to believe. Two years before the publication of the secret clauses concerning Morocco included in the Anglo-French agreements of 1904, and almost five years before Grey's disclosure on the outbreak of the war of the military conversations between the two powers, Morel indicated his suspicions in declaring that he favoured the Anglo-French *entente*,[6]

> Provided that the *entente* is what the average citizen of this Empire believes it to be *viz.* a friendly bond which has eliminated old and deep-rooted misunderstandings; and not an arrangement with secret clauses, a sort of military convention which necessitates on our part a state of perennial antagonism and suspicion in our relations with another great Power.

Speculation at this time concerning the existence of secret understandings was not confined to Morel, but he was the first to suggest that such putative agreements were both improper and unwise.

Morel's disapproval of the substance of British foreign policy led him to an attack on the architects of that policy – the permanent staff at the Foreign Office. Convinced that Foreign Office officials had prolonged the agony of the Congo natives in the interest of the Anglo-French *entente*, he lashed out against their 'obstinacy', ridiculed their talk of a 'higher policy', and contrasted their devious manoeuvres with the wholesome straightforwardness of a 'Public Opinion', organized by him, which asked only that its government follow the 'moral' course. A diplomacy that, in his view, had dealt so ineffectively with the Congo Free State could scarcely be trusted to handle the explosive European situation without the sound restraint of 'Public Opinion'.[7]

Just as Morel's negative assessment of Britain's European policy sprang from his frustration with the Foreign Office's conduct of Congo policy, so he became convinced that his strategy for the solution of the Congo question would result in the reduction of European tensions. Arguing that Britain and Germany, as commercial and industrial powers, shared a common interest in the destruction of the state rubber monopoly in the Congo, he urged joint Anglo-German pressure on Brussels to compel reform. Co-operation in this cause, which would result in the elimination of forced labour in the Congo, could provide also a 'golden bridge' between Germany and Britain and would dissipate their mutual suspicions and hostilities. Dismissing the fact that the German government had displayed interest neither in the natives nor in the commercial prospects of the Congo,[8] Morel insisted that a firm and unambiguous approach by Britain would elicit German co-operation.

In the five years immediately preceding the outbreak of the First World War the vision of the 'golden bridge' assumed increasing importance in Morel's mind, while its form and purpose completely altered. With the death of Leopold II in December 1909, and the dismantling of the Leopoldian system by the Belgian government, the Congo question moved toward a satisfactory solution. Meanwhile, however, Morel had become immersed in the problems of European diplomacy, and his desire for an Anglo-German *rapprochement* mounted. He believed that the Congo could still serve as a 'golden bridge' if Britain encouraged Germany to round out her territories in Central Africa by the purchase of the Congo from

Belgium. What had originally been conceived as Anglo-German co-operation on behalf of the Congo natives had become a transfer of Congo territory on behalf of Anglo-German friendship. The transition in Morel's interests from African to European affairs was now complete.

During the years from 1904 to 1910, while Morel was waging his Congo campaign and developing his critique of British foreign policy, he enjoyed cordial, but hardly intimate, relations with the parliamentary Radicals who were later to be his allies. Determined to keep the Congo reform movement non-partisan, he was careful not to become closely associated with any political group. Some of the Radicals like Trevelyan had, to be sure, assisted the Congo cause in the House of Commons, but this was for them only one among many interests, domestic and foreign. Unwilling to appear as constant critics of their own government's foreign policy, many Radicals, like Philip Morrell, deliberately refrained from giving strong support to the Congo campaign, preferring to concentrate their attention and their attacks on Britain's complicity in the destruction of Persian independence.[9]

Thus, on the eve of the Agadir crisis of 1911, Morel's criticism of foreign policy remained distinct from that of the Radicals. Radical opposition to Grey's policy sprang from disapproval of the Anglo-Russian *entente*; Morel's criticism focused on the Anglo-French *entente*. The Radicals found friendship with the undemocratic regime of the Tsar ideologically embarrassing; Morel denounced Britain's ties with the 'corrupt' French Republic as dangerous. Persia and the Balkans engrossed the attention of the Radicals; the Congo had been, until recently, Morel's sole interest.

The similarities between Morel and the Radicals were, however, more fundamental than the differences. Like the Radicals, Morel was a Gladstonian, firmly believing that foreign policy should be based on moral principle and the rule of law. Like them, too, he considered the protection of weak nations and defenceless peoples as the most sacred responsibility of Britain. Since these high principles often conflicted with the demands of continental alliances and the maintenance of the balance of power, both the Radicals and Morel were prepared, if necessary, to disregard the latter.

The substance of their views on foreign policy aside, there were differences of tone between Morel and the Radicals. These stemmed, in part at least, from the fact that Morel was not, at this stage, a party man. However uneasy the Radicals might be with Grey's foreign policy, they shrank from pushing their protests to a point which would threaten the Liberal Government. A Conservative foreign policy would certainly be no more to their liking and would entail the loss of those domestic social programmes to which they were more deeply committed than any other section of the Liberal party. Thus Grey easily quelled the Radical revolt over the issue of King Edward's visit to the Tsar in 1908 simply by announcing that he would resign in the event of an unfavourable vote. Morel, on the other hand, would have joyfully overturned any government to further the Congo cause, and he might have attempted vainly to do so in 1909 had he not been convinced that the real culprit was not Grey but the permanent staff of the Foreign Office. Thus Morel's criticisms of British foreign policy lacked the hesitancy which often characterized the statements of Radical critics. His denunciation of British foreign policy was sweeping and unqualified.

In the aftermath of the Agadir crisis of 1911 it was just such a total condemnation that seemed necessary to many Radicals, and they turned to Morel as an effective spokesman for their discontent. Just as Morel had warned, Britain had been brought to the verge of war, not in defence of British interests, but because of her support of her *entente* partner, France, against a German threat in Morocco. Without dropping their earlier objections to the Anglo-Russian *entente*, the Radicals came increasingly to accept Morel's view that the most serious threat to peace lay in Britain's ties with France, and they joined him in denouncing 'secret diplomacy', attacking the *entente*, and demanding a *rapprochement* with Germany.

Morel was at the centre of the Radical assault on Grey's foreign policy which began in October 1911 and continued unabated until April 1912.[10] Ten years of humanitarian agitation had made him adept at creating a public outcry, and his performance during these months was impressive. A perusal of the Liberal newspapers and journals during October and November indicates the extent to which the campaign was traceable, directly or indirectly, to Morel. In October a series of five letters by him entitled 'How Wars Are Made' appeared in the *Daily News*, attacking the conduct of British diplomacy during the crisis. During the same month, he reiterated his views in an article in *Nineteenth Century and After*. In November he contributed two unsigned articles to the *Nation*.[11] That journal, in addition, published two editorials during November criticizing Grey's foreign policy and quoting from Morel's *Nineteenth Century* article, as did Noel Buxton writing in the same vein in the *Contemporary Review*. An open letter on foreign policy written by Morel in collaboration with Francis Hirst, the editor of

The Economist, appeared in pamphlet form at the same time. With the important exception of the *Manchester Guardian*, which appears to have criticized Grey without any prodding from Morel, the clamorous attack by the Liberal press on the foreign policy of the Liberal government was largely his work.

Throughout the winter of 1911-12 Morel continued to produce evidence of the 'dishonesty' of British diplomacy which was quickly taken up by the Radicals in the House of Commons. Since the days when he had proved the exploitation of the Congo natives by his analysis of the shipping records and the budgets of the Congo Free State, he had been convinced that governments could be convicted of their crimes by the evidence gleaned from their own publications. In *Morocco in Diplomacy*, published in March 1912, he applied the same technique to the published diplomatic documents, press accounts, and statements of the leading participants in the Agadir crisis. He concluded that British and French policy had been 'Machiavellian', while German policy was 'straightforward', and legally correct throughout. Most alarming for the future, however, was the fact that the nation had been 'led blindfold to the very brink of war, *as the outcome of liabilities secretly contracted by its diplomatists without its authority*'.[12]

In *Morocco in Diplomacy*, as in all his writings since 1909, Morel continued to insist on the right of Parliament, and ultimately the people, to control foreign affairs. He complained not only that foreign policy had been excluded from the process of democratization that had occurred in domestic affairs, but that parliamentary authority in this area had declined over the previous decade.[13] Pointing to the recently revealed secret clauses of the 1904 agreements with France and Spain, he charged that public opinion had been kept in ignorance of the facts while being cynically manipulated by the Foreign Office through the press. The attack on the Anglo-French *entente* thus became a defence of the rights of the people and of their representatives against the pretensions of an aristocratic elite. Nothing could have been better calculated to appeal to Radical instincts, and Radical MPs like Josiah Wedgwood and Joseph King were soon denouncing professional diplomacy in the House of Commons in Morelian language.[14]

Although the sales of *Morocco in Diplomacy* were disappointing,[15] its influence was crucial for those who were to lead the anti-war forces after 1914. In later years Ramsay MacDonald recalled his feelings on first reading Morel's *exposé:* 'I did not want to believe it, and yet its facts were so authoritative and its conclusions so logical that I had to believe it.'[16] Charles Trevelyan likewise testified that 'if Morel had not written I should never have known whither we were drifting and I would have accepted the commonplace of the injured innocence of Sir Edward Grey like any other ill-informed patriot'.[17]

This mounting Radical distress with Grey's foreign policy, which Morel had done so much to stimulate, was reflected in a flurry of organizational activity during 1911 and 1912. More than seventy Liberal MPs joined the Foreign Affairs Group in Parliament established by Noel Buxton and Arthur Ponsonby in an effort to achieve greater parliamentary control of foreign policy and to block any move which 'might seek to oppose the legitimate aspirations of Germany'. The group criticized current British foreign policy as 'based on an assumption of the desires and powers of a single continental State which cannot be substantiated; and it is felt that the policy is virtually dictated by a very small number of permanent men at the Foreign Office'.[18] The Foreign Policy Committee, founded by Philip Morrell, sought to create pressure outside Parliament in support of the goals of the Foreign Affairs Group, while the Anglo-German Friendship Society and the Albert Committee pressed with renewed vigour for an Anglo-German *rapprochement*.

Morel was sought out by the leadership of these groups both as a source of expert information and as a persuasive propagandist. He was invited, in October 1911, to become a member of the executive committee of the Anglo-German Friendship Society. The publication of *Morocco in Diplomacy* was subsidized by the Albert Committee, whose President, Theodore Rhodes of North German Lloyd, brought Morel into touch with the staff of the German embassy. The Foreign Policy Committee provided Morel with a platform to continue his *exposé* of Anglo-French diplomacy during the Moroccan crisis, and those whose chief concern was still the destruction of the Anglo-Russian *entente* attempted to enlist his support.[19]

Despite the respect with which Morel was treated in these predominantly Radical circles, his campaign against Grey remained somewhat distinct from theirs. Part of the explanation lies, no doubt, in Morel's temperament. He was an autocratic figure who did not fit easily into organizations which he did not completely dominate. A more important reason is to be found, however, in a difference of approach. The Radicals concentrated on a *rapprochement* with Germany, while arguing that such a development was compatible with the continuance of the Anglo-French *entente* as originally conceived.[20] Morel, who was thoroughly convinced that the *entente* involved secret military commitments to France, had come to believe that the exposure and rejection of these agreements must precede any significant *rapprochement* with Germany. Thus, when he found the Anglo-German Friendship Society unwilling to insist that Parliament probe into the specifics of Anglo-French understandings, he scornfully remained away from their 'banquets and amiable speeches' in order 'to avoid friction'.[21]

It was this determination to force a full revelation of the nature of the ties between Britain and France that kept Morel on the attack between April 1912 and the spring of 1913 when the Radicals' criticism of Grey's foreign policy was becoming muted. Although he, like the Radicals, welcomed the government's efforts to meet criticism by the dispatch of the Haldane mission to Berlin, he continued to pose what he regarded as the crucial questions.[22]

> What is the nature of our relations with France? To what extent are we tied by the Poincaré combination? To what degree are we involved in supporting any particular policy in the Mediterranean or elsewhere . . .?

Morel's suspicions made even those Radicals who were members of the government uneasy. When he demanded official comment on rumours that Britain was pledged to send an army to France in the event of war, Trevelyan, who was travelling in Germany, wrote commending his efforts to clarify the situation and promising 'to enter on a vigorous *private* campaign on the subject when I get home'.[23]

Such public and private pressure produced results. In the spring of 1913 the Prime Minister and the Foreign Secretary solemnly denied the existence of any military or naval commitments to France. Although it is unlikely that Morel was fully convinced, there seemed nothing further that could be said, and he turned his energies to nursing the Birkenhead constituency for which he had recently been selected as the Liberal candidate.

In the light of this background, it is hardly surprising that Morel and many of his Radical allies reacted as they did during those fateful days of August 1914. Sir Edward Grey's masterly appeal to the 'obligations' of 'friendship' left them unmoved. They had been assured by the Foreign Secretary himself that there were no 'obligations'. In later years, recalling those agonizing events, Trevelyan paid tribute to the influence of Morel's five-year-long campaign in determining the response of those Radicals who opposed the war.[24]

> Unpleasant as it was having to refuse to be a party to the most momentous action ever taken by a British Government, I shall remain to the end profoundly grateful to the man who had revealed to me enough of the truth to enable me to know how to make my decision.

NOTES

1 C. P. Trevelyan to M. K. Trevelyan, 4 August 1914, C. P. Trevelyan Papers, University of Newcastle. Trevelyan also consulted his brother George, the historian, and his friend, Geoffrey Young, the diplomatist. By letter, he communicated with Lord Bryce and Walter Runciman.

2 Morel to Walter Langley (copy), 27 February 1909, Morel Collection, British Library of Political and Economic Science. (All letters hereafter quoted are from the Morel Collection.)

3 Morel to F. W. Fox (copy), 4 April 1905.

4 Morel to Bishop of Southwark (copy), 2 July 1909.

5 Morel to T. L. Gilmour (copy), 5 October 1909.

6 Morel, *Great Britain and the Congo*, New York, 1969 (reprint of 1909 ed.), p. 262.

7 Morel's first full-scale attack on the Foreign Office is to be found in *Great Britain and the Congo*, pp. 117-234.

8 The German government did approach Britain on the Congo question shortly after the publication of Morel's *Great Britain and the Congo*, in which he first proposed such co-operation. The Foreign Office, accurately judging that the real purpose was the weakening of the Anglo-French *entente*, did not respond favourably. On Germany's Congo policy, see Jacques Willequet, *Le Congo belge et la Weltpolitik*, Brussels, 1962.

9 Philip Morrell to Morel, 4 March 1912.

10 For a discussion of this campaign, see John A. Murray, 'Foreign policy debated: Sir Edward Grey and his critics, 1911-12' in L. P. Wallace and W. C. Askew (eds), *Power, Public Opinion and Diplomacy*, North Carolina, 1959, pp. 140-71.

11 'The Anglo-German crisis of last summer', *Nation*, 18 November 1911; 'The Grey–Metternich conversations', *Nation*, 23 November 1911.

12 Morel, *Morocco in Diplomacy*, London, 1912, p. xviii.

13 Recent studies tend to support Morel's charges on these points. See Zara Steiner, *The Foreign Office and Foreign Policy: 1898-1914*, Cambridge, 1969.

14 *Hansard*, v:32:2623-4 and 2656-7.

15 Republished in 1915 under the title *Ten Years of Secret Diplomacy*, it went through six editions in the next five years.

16 J. R. MacDonald's introduction to *Ten Years of Secret Diplomacy*, p. xii.

17 *Unity*, 12 January 1924.

18 Statement of policy, as quoted, T. P. Conwell-Evans, *Foreign Policy from a Back Bench*, London, 1932, pp. 81-2.

19 Morel to John Holt, 15 January 1912.
20 For example, Noel Buxton, 'England and Germany', *Contemporary Review*, 1911, vol. 100, pp. 605-17.
21 Morel, as quoted, F. Seymour Cocks, *E. D. Morel: The Man and His Work*, London, 1920, pp. 242-3.
22 Letter to *Daily News*, 1 September 1912.
23 C. P. Trevelyan to Morel, 20 February 1913.
24 *Unity*, 12 January 1924.

15

A STUDY IN FUTILITY: THE BRITISH RADICALS AT THE OUTBREAK OF THE FIRST WORLD WAR

MARVIN SWARTZ

At the end of July and the beginning of August 1914, the British Radicals attempted, without success, to prevent the participation of Great Britain in a European war. Their activities were, in the words of a perceptive observer, 'pills to cure an earthquake'.[1] Efforts of the Radicals to maintain British neutrality in the days of crisis immediately preceding the First World War were certainly inadequate. But other and ultimately more important reasons accounted for their failure. One reason the Radicals themselves recognized, without perhaps fully understanding: the commitment of British diplomacy, and national interests, to the *entente* with France. Another was the nature of the Radical movement.

The Radicals engaged in political activity within the confines of British capitalism. They wished to improve or alter the functioning of the system of which they were a part, not to change it for another. Speaking in 1913, E. D. Morel[2] praised British colonial rule over non-European peoples as unique, because[3]

> it constitutes the first attempt at imperial government by a *democracy*, which the world has ever known. . . . The imperial rule of Britain is carried out by a popularly elected Government. The men who direct it are the men whom the British people invest with the authority to do so: men whom they appoint: men whom they can dismiss when they choose.

Morel had in mind the British parliamentary system, through which he and other Radicals hoped to achieve their aims.

They were subscribing to a myth. The House of Commons was

not elected by a majority of the British people. No woman could vote in a general election before the war, nor could four out of every ten men. Seventy per cent of the entire adult population was excluded from the polls.[4] The members returned by this restricted suffrage were a social as well as a political élite. In the House of Commons of 1906, 81 per cent of Conservatives and 73 per cent of Liberals had as their major economic interest landowning or commerce and industry. Of Liberals 33 per cent, of Conservatives 51 per cent had attended a public school; 36 per cent of both parties had been educated at Oxford or Cambridge. Two per cent of Liberals and no Conservatives were trade unionists. The socio-economic background of the Cabinet, and of under secretaries of state, was even more exclusive than that of MPs.[5]

Radicals worked for change within this framework. They wanted to broaden, not destroy it. One of their arguments for moderate reforms was that they would avoid drastic ones. When, for instance, during the budget debate of May 1914, Tories complained that the rich were overburdened with taxes, David Lloyd George, the Chancellor of the Exchequer, retorted that they might in future rue 'the days when they protested against paying 1s. 4d. extra insurance against revolution'.[6] Radicals attacked the Foreign Office and Diplomatic Service as aristocratic bastions (which they were); but they demanded that the middle classes be granted better opportunities for entry rather than that the existing institutions be levelled.[7] By encouraging Liberal co-operation with Labour, Radicals sought to pre-empt socialism.

Although the Radicals counted on achieving their aims through a Liberal government, they grew increasingly suspicious of the intentions of the leadership of the Liberal party after 1910. The parliamentary private secretary to the Liberal chief whip warned a member of the government in May 1914, 'There is no disguising the fact that just now there is a slight rot in the party, considerable distrust as to the intention of you folk who lead it.'[8] This feeling extended to the two Cabinet ministers who had for some time been considered champions of the Radical cause, Lloyd George and Winston S. Churchill.

Arthur Ponsonby, a Radical organizer of the Liberal Foreign Affairs Group in the House of Commons, drafted critiques of both men which were indicative of opinion among his colleagues. Of the Chancellor of the Exchequer Ponsonby wrote:[9]

His instincts are true but he would not be above scheming

> to keep his position. One feels about his career that there is a breathless eagerness to keep up the crescendo of fame. He must be up and doing to maintain his reputation and to keep himself looming large in the public eye . . . . He is a real democrat full of humanity with great charm and originality. He has imagination and force of character. He lacks judgment, reserve and discretion. The majority of the party are too frightened of him ever to trust him as a leader. He is not quite safe. He might let them down. He is over ambitious and there is a strange blending of commoness [sic] and refinement in his character. He is a fighter and this is always appreciated in politics and he expresses sentiments which are a true reflexion of the popular mind. He is appreciated by both sides in the House of Commons. Circumstances may make him or mar him. He has strained his powers to the limit.

Ponsonby had even harsher words for Lloyd George's associate and rival, the First Lord of the Admiralty:[10]

> Winston Churchill is still a Tory democrat. He has really been perfectly consistent and never altered. He despises liberalism and has no remote conception of what it means though he can turn liberal phrases out better than any liberal. He is brilliant in his abilities. His speeches are carefully prepared and in some ways the best that are produced today. He is never spontaneous and has shown himself to be incapable of leadership in the House. He is far better at administration because he is most painstaking & thorough. Personal ambition is the keynote of all his actions and as his instincts are quite unsound he is a great source of danger. He has an unattractive personality – conceit and inconsiderateness mixed. He is in contest with Lloyd George for the limelight but he is unpopular in both parties. At the Admiralty he is intent on some great coup – that great coup may be war which he would enjoy immensely as he fancies himself as a strategist. He is really an Imperialist of the more crude & vulgar sort. But he is intensely alive stimulating active and will as long as he lives be a strong factor to reckon with.

Churchill had four decades of political activity ahead of him, and they would testify to the accuracy of many of Arthur Ponsonby's observations.

Reinforcing their suspicions of the Liberal leadership was the

Radicals' distrust of the government's foreign policy. Many of them felt that the *ententes* of 1904 and 1907 bound England more closely than was good or necessary to the policies of France and Russia. For this tendency they blamed the secretiveness of the Foreign Office and the weakness of the Foreign Secretary, Sir Edward Grey. Ponsonby, who had served in the Diplomatic Corps and the Foreign Office from 1894 to 1902, sketched Grey's character in this way:

> a gentleman in the best sense of the word. Personal ambition & a desire to advertise himself I don't suppose he has ever felt for a single instant . . . . His House of Commons manner has been a great service to him. It is very simple very sincere dignified & direct. He is rather aloof & unapproachable which makes a certain mystery that attracts. He is a liberal & is capable of passionate devotion to a cause but he is overcautious and not really very able. He trust[s] the opinion of his permanent officials more than his own judgment and is therefore capable of making rather serious mistakes. He is out of touch with the party. I don't suppose he knows more than a score of them by name. He may be called upon one day to lead and it is very doubtful whether he would make a success of it. He has a great reputation in the country specially among Tories. His successes have been more due to chance his failures to want of perception.

To some Radicals the warts in Ponsonby's portrayal would have appeared larger than life, but they shared his anxiety over Grey's foreign policy.

The Radicals were especially concerned that England might become involved in conflict with Germany. They buttressed their arguments by citing the Franco-German confrontations over Morocco in 1905 and 1911, when British willingness to support France contrasted sharply with the refusal to make concessions to Germany. After the second Moroccan crisis, resulting from the dispatch of a German gunboat to the port of Agadir in the summer of 1911, the Radicals formed a Liberal Foreign Affairs Group of about seventy-five MPs and a Foreign Policy Committee outside parliament. These organizations advocated democratic control of foreign policy and hoped to contribute to an easing of tensions between England and Germany. Although they appeared to constitute a substantial ginger group within the Liberal party, these dissenters over foreign policy had little impact upon British diplomacy or politics. United by a common fear of war, they remained divided on other issues – even such an important one as naval estimates. The apparent improvement in Anglo-German relations dissolved whatever coherence the protesters against Grey's foreign policy might have possessed after the Agadir incident. By the spring of 1913 one Radical wanly admitted, 'Grey has done a great deal towards meeting us', and the Foreign Policy Committee considered disbanding.[11]

Neither the Foreign Office nor its critics managed to explain satisfactorily how England was able to arrive at accommodations with her traditional antagonists, France and Russia, but not with Germany. Perhaps the answer was that the French and Russian challenges were based upon specific differences on issues great and small but within definable limits; problems over which states could dicker, and sometimes even reach agreement. The German challenge appeared to be different not simply in scope but in kind. It was an almost revolutionary demand for the upsetting of an old order to make way for a new; for the resolution of difficulties not of long standing but newly created by Germany's thrust towards world power (*Weltpolitik*). This drive was relentless because it was a function not only of international relations but also of the internal political, social, and economic structure of the Wilhelmenian *Reich*.

Perhaps the English response was uncompromising, at least in part, for the same reason: that the makers of British foreign policy sensed the only way of satisfying Germany was to make concessions so far-reaching as to shake the internal order in their own country. Many members of the aristocracy and the upper middle class believed, rightly or wrongly, that their supremacy – the supremacy of the official, professional, and parliamentary élite – rested upon the strength of the Empire, navy, trade and commerce, and upon that élite's reputation as the defender of this strength. The Radicals, though ready to welcome some adjustments, accepted the domestic *status quo*. They perceived no serious challenge to it from their policy of compromise with Germany. The failure to fuse analyses of internal and external events into an intelligible synthesis was a grave weakness of the moderate left in England (and throughout Europe). It was one reason for the Radicals' being caught unawares by the crisis of July 1914.

The news of the assassination of an Austrian archduke in Sarajevo on 28 June 1914 changed few holiday plans in England. Most Englishmen, especially members of the middle and upper classes, who were not dependent upon daily wages, considered the summer a season for particular enjoyment, or at least for escaping from the city. They seemed to have no reason for making an exception of July 1914. Nor did the Foreign Office. Although Grey reminded the German ambassador that England's relations with France and Russia had 'lost none of their earlier intimacy', he apparently 'saw no reason for taking a pessimistic view of the situation' in the Balkans.[12] The Permanent Under Secretary of State, Sir Arthur Nicolson, informed the British Ambassador in Vienna that his major concern in Europe was a dispute between Serbia and Greece over Albania: 'Otherwise we have no very urgent and pressing question to preoccupy us in the rest of Europe.'[13] On the same day, 6 July, the Foreign Office received a dispatch from the Naval Attaché in Berlin reporting on the success of a recent visit by a British battle squadron to Kiel, although the sailors managed to win only one of two football matches against their German opponents and 'were entirely outclassed in all the usual sports'.[14]

After Austria-Hungary presented an ultimatum to Serbia on 23 July 1914, the Foreign Office and, more slowly, the Radicals came to recognize that an international conflict was possible. Grey personally abhorred the thought of war. He feared that it would entail 'a complete collapse of European credit and industry . . . this would mean a state of things worse than that of 1848, and, irrespective of who were victors in the war, many things might be completely swept away'.[15] Because they believed that Serbia was not worth this price, some Germans hoped that England would remain neutral while the Second *Reich* destroyed the Triple Entente, by means of diplomacy or war. A more clear-sighted official in Berlin foresaw, however, that the British government would not allow the destruction of 'the "balance of power", the maintenance of which England considers to be necessary for her own interests . . . .'[16] In fact, the Assistant Under Secretary of State in the Foreign Office, Sir Eyre Crowe, was convinced that England could not stand aloof in a war between the major European power blocs without placing herself at the mercy of the eventual victors.[17]

Grey shared this view, but, cognizant of Radical opposition, he felt that his Cabinet colleagues, parliament, and the country would not 'sanction our going to war in the Servian quarrel'. British participation, Grey correctly assumed, would depend upon the 'development of other issues'.[18] Nicolson explained the difficulties faced by the Foreign Office in a letter to the British Ambassador at St Petersburg on 28 July 1914:[19]

We, of course, living under such conditions as we do here,

> when no Government practically can take any decided line without feeling that public opinion amply supports them, are unable to give any decided engagements as to what we should or should not do in any future emergencies; but I think we have made it perfectly clear that in any case neither Germany nor Austria could possibly rely with any certainty upon our remaining neutral . . . .

As Nicolson was writing, opponents of war were beginning to voice their opinions.

The Radicals became increasingly aware of the dimensions of the diplomatic crisis during the last week of July. It reawakened suspicions of the Foreign Office and governmental leaders which in many breasts had slumbered since the repercussions of the Agadir incident had died away. C. P. Scott[20] accused the Foreign Office of inspiring a leading article in *The Times* of 27 July promising English support for France and Russia in the event of war. Although both Lloyd George and the Liberal chief whip, Percy Illingworth, doubted that *The Times* expressed the views of the Foreign Office officials on this occasion,[21] they were mistaken. In a private letter Nicolson happily pointed out, 'the tone of our press, after the first shock which was occasioned by the Austrian ultimatum, has come round to the fact that it would be difficult, if not impossible, for us to stand outside a general European conflagration'.[22] Scott exclaimed angrily: 'we should do our utmost to turn out the government, whatever the cost, if they took such a course' towards war. He warned his friend Lloyd George that if Grey 'let us into it there would be an end of the existing Liberal combination and the next advance would have to be based on Radicalism and Labour'.[23]

In parliament, Arthur Ponsonby, as chairman of the Foreign Affairs Group, tried to mobilize opposition to British participation in a continental war. He convened meetings on each of the last three days in July and again, after the weekend, on 3 August. On 29 July he informed Grey of the feelings of his associates:

> It was decided that everything possible should be done to counteract the influences which already seem to be working for our participation in what may prove to be a general European conflict. On this point very strong views were expressed and it was the feeling of the meeting that we could not support the Government in any military or naval operations which would carry this country beyond its existing treaty obligations. It was felt that if both France and

> Russia were informed that on no account would we be drawn into war even though they and other European powers were involved it would have a moderating effect on their policy.

Ponsonby enclosed with this communication a resolution expressing the view of the meeting 'that Great Britain in no conceivable circumstances should depart from a position of strict neutrality'. It was signed by ten MPs, including Philip Morrell, Noel Buxton, and Arnold Rowntree, in addition to Ponsonby himself. The Foreign Secretary replied promptly to his critics. He assured Ponsonby that England was free from obligations and asked him to keep his group 'quiet for this week'.[24]

Ponsonby also proceeded to issue protests to other leading members of the government. He warned the Prime Minister, H. H. Asquith, on 30 July 1914 that any decision for war 'would meet not only with the strongest disapproval but with the actual withdrawal of support from the Government'.[25] To Churchill on the following day he explained that 'we have held back so far in our desire not to do anything which might embarrass Grey in the slightest degree'; and he emphasized that 'we should on no account be drawn into war when our interests are not immediately affected and no treaty obligations exist to bind us'. Churchill, as Grey had done, agreed with Ponsonby: 'So long as no treaty obligation or true British interest is involved I am of your opinion that we sh[oul]d remain neutral.'[26]

The incipient Radical rebellion stiffened opposition to war within the Cabinet, though not significantly. It did simplify the task of those who, like Grey and Churchill, believed that England could not remain neutral in a great European war by clearly revealing the arguments on which opposition to British participation rested. Advocates of support for the Triple Entente knew that they would have to demonstrate that British obligations and interests were involved in defending the coast of France and the neutrality of Belgium against Germany. Churchill, who had already begun naval preparations for war, was confident that Radical fears would count for little: 'The country will be united when the issue is joined', he advised his wife on 31 July 1914: 'Be sure of it.'[27] Grey was not so sure. On the same day he nervously informed the French Ambassador:[28]

> we could not pledge Parliament in advance. Up to the present moment, we did not feel, and public opinion did not feel, that any treaties or obligations of this country

> were involved. Further developments might alter this situation and cause the Government and Parliament to take the view that intervention was justified. The preservation of the neutrality of Belgium might be, I would not say a decisive, but an important factor, in determining our attitude.

A day earlier Grey, without prior reference to the Cabinet, had rejected a German bid for British neutrality which emphasized that 'Germany aimed at no territorial acquisitions at the expense of France'.[29] Grey and Asquith, whom he had consulted, apparently misrepresented this German offer and the reply to it in more ways than one in a Cabinet meeting on 31 July. Most importantly, they made an incidental reference to Belgium into the central issue, at the same time largely (if not entirely) ignoring the question of British obligations to France.[30] In fact, the Foreign Secretary was convinced that England would have to aid France whatever happened, or did not happen, to Belgium.[31]

During the weekend of 1-2 August almost the entire Cabinet eventually agreed that British interests called for defence of the French coast and of Belgian neutrality against German aggression. The knowledge that the leaders of the Conservative party had pledged their backing for such a course undoubtedly helped Cabinet members to take this decision. As the President of the Local Government Board, Herbert Samuel, explained to his wife on 2 August, the consequence of not agreeing with Grey, Asquith, Churchill, and the other interventionists 'would have been either a Coalition Government or a Unionist Government either of which would certainly have been a war ministry'. Most ministers reckoned that they had much to lose and nothing to gain by resignation. In retrospect at least, Walter Runciman, the President of the Board of Trade, recognized the meeting of 2 August as 'The Cabinet which decided that war with Germany was inevitable'.[32]

Meanwhile, from the outspoken but inchoate opposition to war outside parliament, Radicals were forming two groups to prevent British participation. One was a British Neutrality Committee headed by the noted social scientist Graham Wallas, the other a British Neutrality League directed by Norman Angell, who for some years (with the support of the conservative Garton Foundation) had been arguing that war between industrialized nations was uneconomical. The Committee began with a telephone call from Wallas to the Radical economist J. A. Hobson on Tuesday, 28 July 1914. Wallas told Hobson that he was anxious about the situation in Europe and signs that their country might treat the Triple Entente as a binding alliance. The two men met at the National Liberal Club on Thursday afternoon, when they decided to cancel all their engagements for the next day in order to concentrate on an effort to keep Great Britain neutral. That Friday morning, 31 July, at the National Liberal Club, Wallas wrote a letter to the *Manchester Guardian* and, with Hobson and a few other sympathizers, drafted a declaration calling for British neutrality. Then he visited the House of Commons and talked to MPs, some of whom were probably already involved in the activities of the Foreign Affairs Group. On 1 August, the Saturday of that Bank Holiday weekend, Wallas and Hobson again went to the National Liberal Club, where the Parliamentary Under Secretary at the Board of Education, Charles P. Trevelyan (who as a junior member of the government 'could do nothing overt'[33]), S. K. Ratcliffe, and other Radicals joined them. They decided to obtain an office, probably enabled to do so by an offer of financial assistance from Trevelyan, and quickly established one at 19 Buckingham Street, Strand.[34]

By this time Angell had launched the Neutrality League. He first sent out telegrams to recruit supporters for a group 'to give publicity to [a] moderately worded manifesto protesting against agitation to drag this country into a European war and urging that it maintain strict neutrality'. Then, in a second telegram, he warned that 'some striking action must be taken at once' to avoid British involvement in war and solicited financial contributions to meet an 'expenditure of several thousand pounds' to pay for 'full page advertisements in all leading papers of [the] country'.[35] Despite these efforts, Angell wanted to keep his name out of any publications of the Neutrality League, probably in the hope of not alienating conservative backers of the Garton Foundation. A young associate, Dennis Robertson, was put in charge of the League's temporary offices in the Salisbury Hotel off Fleet Street, and George Benson ran a branch office in Manchester.

On Sunday, 2 August, the Neutrality Committee made overtures of co-operation to the Neutrality League. In his rooms at the Temple, Angell read to Wallas, Hobson, and Basil Williams the memorandum which the League had drafted. It was a lengthy and detailed statement to the effect that neither interests nor obligations required British participation in a European conflict. The representatives of the Committee refused to accept responsibility for it on behalf of their supporters, who had already agreed to a simpler document using quotations from past speeches by Asquith and Grey to demonstrate that England would retain complete freedom of action in case of war. Any possibility of merging the Neutrality Committee and Neutrality League thus disappeared.[36] Each organization sent its own declaration to the press. That of the Committee bore the signatures of Lord Courtney of Penwith, J. Ramsay MacDonald, Gilbert Murray, A. G. Gardiner, Graham Wallas, G. M. Trevelyan, L. T. Hobhouse, J. A. Hobson, Francis W. Hirst, J. L. Hammond, and Basil Williams. Signatories of the League's manifesto were Lord Welby, the Lord Mayor of Manchester, the Lord Provost of Glasgow, the Bishop of Lincoln, the Bishop of Hereford, Sir W. Mather, Sir A. Spicer, C. P. Scott, Sir A. Haworth, Sir W. Hartly, D. A. Thomas, J. J. Thomson, Dr Horton, Richard Whiteing, W. Stubbs, Ernest Schuster, and M. Philips Price.[37]

The feverish activities of the Radicals inside and outside parliament resulted in an exaggeration of their strength, though they had little effect upon governmental policy. 'It looks as if the Liberal rank & file will at last mobilise & put pressure on the Govt.,' Lady Courtney commented excitedly on 1 August.[38] The London correspondent of the *Manchester Guardian* reported on the same day, 'I estimate that four-fifths of the Government's supporters associate themselves informally with the position of Mr. Ponsonby and his colleagues.' Ponsonby himself had warned Asquith that the small number of MPs at the meetings of the Foreign Affairs Group was representative of Liberal sentiment in general: 'in my opinion nine tenths of the party are behind us'. The Prime Minister reduced that figure when he wrote on 2 August that 'a good ¾ of our own party in the House of Commons are for absolute non-interference at any price'.[39] This battle of fractions might have made Liberal ministers nervous; it did not deter them from taking action in regard to the greater conflict of arms in Europe. In the afternoon of 3 August, Grey, on the basis of the Cabinet decisions of the previous day, outlined to the House of Commons Great Britain's obligations to France and the defence of Belgium.

Grey's speech (followed within fifteen hours by the German invasion of Belgium) convinced many Radicals of the futility of the policy of non-intervention. Gilbert Murray, a signatory of the Neutrality Committee's declaration who was in the gallery of the House, confessed that it 'had converted him'.[40] That evening Hobson, discouraged, informed C. P. Scott: 'If there is war tomorrow, as seems pretty certain, our Neutrality Committee will drop that name, and lie low as a watching Conciliation Committee, waiting some opportunity to press for peace. Grey's speech appears to have converted some even of our friends to regard the war as justified.'[41] The shadow of impending war darkened the scenes of Radical activity during the next twenty-four hours.

The first official meeting of the British Neutrality Committee took place at noon on Tuesday, 4 August 1914. Present, in addition to Wallas and Hobson, were Arnold Rowntree, G. Lowes Dickinson, Bertrand Russell, R.C. and G. M. Trevelyan, E. R. Cross, J. L. Hammond, Basil Williams, S. K. Ratcliffe, C. R. Buxton, and John Hilton. They chose Wallas as chairman, Williams as honorary treasurer, and Ratcliffe and Buxton as joint secretaries *pro tem.* Hilton described the activities of Angell's Neutrality League, which was organizing public meetings. The Committee, in contrast, was confining its action to parliament and the press. Its members finally decided to release to the evening newspapers a declaration which Lord Courtney had dictated to Wallas earlier in the day and which Lord Bryce had amended. At another, smaller, meeting at four o'clock, Lord and Lady Courtney and Holford Knight became members of the Neutrality Committee. By this time Wallas knew that his efforts were doomed to failure. He had learned at a luncheon gathering of contributors to the Radical newspaper the *Nation* that Germany would invade Belgium.

The third and last official meeting of the Neutrality Committee convened at 11 o'clock on Wednesday morning, 5 August, twelve hours after Great Britain had declared war on Germany. The Committee decided to dissolve, appointing Holford Knight to settle its debts. Wallas returned the donations of three contributors, but inquired whether he might retain that of a fourth. 'Of course you keep what remains of the £50 as long as you can conceivably want any of it,' Charles Trevelyan replied generously. Two weeks later Wallas sent him a cheque for twenty pounds, and on 15 September remitted what was left after Knight had paid £14 5*s.* 3*d.* for such expenditures as typing, printing, postage, stationery, and clerical help. A little over four pounds went as petty cash.[42] The Neutrality Committee had spent less than £20 to stop a great war. It was not enough.

The Neutrality League expended more than sixty times that amount, with no more result. On telegrams; open air meetings; hiring of taxis, motor cars, and offices; printing; bill posting and distribution of leaflets; even sandwichmen: on each phase of his complex operation Angell, accustomed to the subsidies of private foundations, had lavished more money than Wallas had used over all. About two-thirds of the nearly £1300 spent by the Neutrality

League went towards advertising.[43] Between 3 and 5 August, 'Neutrality League Announcement No. 2' appeared eighteen times as a one-column, half-page, or, most frequently, full-page advertisement in London and provincial newspapers. It read in part:[44]

> BRITONS, DO YOUR DUTY and keep your Country out of A WICKED and STUPID WAR. Small but powerful cliques are trying to rush you into it; you must DESTROY THE PLOT TO-DAY or it will be too late.

It was already too late. Some newspapers declined to publish the League's announcement, perhaps, if polite, using an excuse similar to that offered by the London manager of the *Glasgow Herald* on behalf of his superiors: 'in view of the complex nature of the international position they were not disposed to give publicity'.[45] Angell had to confess on 5 August that 'we have not succeeded in our immediate object . . . and the League itself is now ceasing its activities, as war has been actually declared'.[46]

On 5 August 1914 Great Britain was at war. The Neutrality Committee and the Neutrality League disbanded. Charles Trevelyan, having resigned from the government, began that same day to organize a new movement in which Radicals could continue to express their dissent over foreign policy. E. D. Morel became the secretary and the directing force of this new body, the Union of Democratic Control. Many Radicals who had fought unsuccessfully against war joined it, among them Arthur Ponsonby, Norman Angell, J. A. Hobson, C. R. Buxton, and Bertrand Russell. They stressed a theme summarized by a former supporter of the Neutrality Committee: 'Secret diplomacy has again sold the European Democracy.'[47] The Radicals generally did not search for deeper explanations. Yet the words of Graham Wallas's friend, the eminent French historian Elie Halévy, must temper their criticism of Grey's foreign policy: 'There is an ignorance whose true name is connivance.'[48] Frantic Radical efforts at the end of July and the beginning of August 1914 could not deflect British foreign policy from fulfilling commitments built up over many years.

The Radicals themselves were in a large measure responsible for their own failure. They were, as A. J. P. Taylor has remarked, 'remote from "the democracy" on whom they relied'.[49] They were anxious to work within the élitist political structure of British society, not against it. Norman Angell preferred to rely on conservatives such as Sir Richard Garton, Lord Esher, and A. J. Balfour rather than on Keir Hardie and the Independent Labour party. During the first months of the war, at the same time that he was organizing the Union of Democratic Control, E. D. Morel continued to act as editor of the *African Mail*, a weekly newspaper sponsored by West African trading interests. 'We hear much of "capturing German trade" but, with a few notable exceptions, do not see much organized effort to do so', he complained in a leading article of October 1914, advising that Liverpool had a[50]

> golden opportunity . . . of capturing the palm kernel industry. . . . Let us see our great manufacturing concerns making well planned efforts to dominate the African market . . . . It is in trade our strength lies. Our arms are doing us credit in the cockpit of Europe, but the greatest victory of all will be won in the market place. We owe it to ourselves and posterity that we do win it.

Most Radicals, like Morel, identified the fortunes of their country with the success of capitalist enterprise. They remained privileged members of a society whose foreign policy they deplored.

NOTES

1 Elie Halévy, 'The World Crisis of 1914-1918: An Interpretation', in *The Era of Tyrannies: Essays on Socialism and War*, New York, Doubleday Anchor, 1965 edn, p. 210.

2 Morel had organized the Congo Reform Association and was now prospective Liberal candidate for Birkenhead.

3 'Treatment of native races', *African Mail*, 2 May 1913.

4 Neal Blewett, 'The franchise in the United Kingdom, 1885-1918', *Past & Present*, 32, December 1965, p. 31.

5 W. L. Guttsman, *The British Political Elite*, London, MacGibbon & Kee, revised edn, 1965, pp. 90, 104.

6 *Hansard*, v:62:801 (11 May 1914).

7 Zara Steiner, *The Foreign Office and Foreign Policy, 1898-1914*, Cambridge University Press, 1969, p. 20; apps 3 and 4.

8 Cecil Beck to Charles Masterman (Confidential), 26 May 1914, *D. Lloyd George MSS* C/5/15/5 (by permission of the Beaverbrook Foundation, London).

9 Arthur Ponsonby's handwritten sketches of government personalities, n.d. [? *c.* June 1914], *Ponsonby MSS* (by permission of Lord Ponsonby of Shulbrede).

10 Ibid.

11 L. T. Hobhouse to C. P. Scott, 4 June 1913, in Trevor Wilson (ed.), *The Political Diaries of C. P. Scott, 1911-1928*, London, Collins, 1970, p. 89.

12 Prince K. M. Lichnowsky to Theobald von Bethmann Hollweg (Confidential), 9 July 1914, in Imanuel Geiss, (ed.), *July 1914. The Outbreak of the First World War: Selected Documents*, London, Batsford, 1967, no. 14.

13 Sir Arthur Nicolson to Sir Maurice de Bunsen (Private), 6 July 1914, in G. P. Gooch and Harold Temperley (eds), *British Documents on the Origins of the War, 1898-1914*, XI, London, HMSO, 1926, no. 33.
14 Captain Wilfred Henderson to Sir Horace Rumbold (Confidential), 3 July 1914, ibid., enclosure in no. 7.
15 Sir Edward Grey to M. de Bunsen, 23 July 1914, ibid., no. 86.
16 Hans von Schoen to Count Georg Hertling, 18 July 1914, in Geiss (ed.), op. cit., no. 33.
17 E. A. Crowe, Minutes, 25, 27 July 1914, in Gooch and Temperley (eds), op. cit., XI, nos 101, 170.
18 E. Grey to Sir George Buchanan (Tel.), 25 July 1914, ibid., no. 112.
19 A. Nicolson to G. Buchanan (Private), 28 July 1914, ibid., no. 239.
20 The owner and editor of the *Manchester Guardian*.
21 *Diaries of C. P. Scott*, 27 July 1914, p. 92.
22 A. Nicolson to G. Buchanan (Private), 28 July 1914, in Gooch and Temperley (eds), op. cit., XI, no. 239.
23 *Diaries of C. P. Scott*, 27 July 1914, pp. 91, 93.
24 M. Swartz, *The Union of Democratic Control in British Politics during the First World War*, Oxford, Clarendon, 1971, p. 16; Cameron Hazlehurst, *Politicians at War, July 1914 to May 1915*, London, Cape, 1971, pp. 35-7; Keith Robbins, *Sir Edward Grey: A Biography of Lord Grey of Fallodon*, London, Cassell, 1971, pp. 292-3.
25 Hazlehurst, op. cit., p. 38.
26 Randolph S. Churchill, *Winston S. Churchill*, Companion Volume II, Part 3, 1911-1914, Boston, Houghton Mifflin, 1969, p. 1991.
27 Ibid., p. 1993.
28 E. Grey to Sir Francis Bertie, 31 July 1914, in Gooch and Temperley (eds), op. cit., XI, no. 367.
62 Sir Edward Goschen to E. Grey (Tel., Secret, Urgent), 29 July 1914; Grey to Goschen (Tel.), 30 July 1914, ibid., nos 293, 303.
30 Hazlehurst, op. cit., p. 82.
31 E. Grey to E. Goschen, 1 August 1914, in Gooch and Temperley (eds), op. cit., XI, no. 448.
32 Hazlehurst, op. cit., pp. 98, 93.
33 Ibid., p. 123.
34 Information on the British Neutrality Committee from Graham Wallas, 'Notes . . . on British Neutrality Committee', 6 October 1914, *Wallas MSS*, 39 (by permission of the late Miss May Wallas and the British Library of Political and Economic Science, London).
35 Copies of telegrams, undated, in *N. Angell MSS* C-42-9, A & B (by permission of the Library and Department of History of Ball State University, Muncie, Indiana). I am indebted to Dr Howard Weinroth of McGill University for these documents, as well as those cited in notes 43, 45, and 46 below.
36 'Notes on B.N.C.', *Wallas MSS*, 39.
37 *Manchester Guardian*, 3 August 1914.
38 Lady Courtney, Diary, 1 August 1914, *L. & K. Courtney MSS*, 36 (by permission of the British Library of Political and Economic Science).
39 Swartz, *U.D.C.*, p. 16; Hazlehurst, op. cit., p. 33.
40 'Notes on B.N.C.', *Wallas MSS*, 39.
41 *Diaries of C. P. Scott*, p. 95.

42 'Notes on B.N.C.'; Minutes of meetings, 4, 5 August 1914; and accounts, August, [September] 1914, *Wallas MSS*, 39.
43 Lists of receipts and payments in *Angell MSS* C-45-1.
44 *Manchester Guardian*, 4 August 1914.
45 H. Clark to N. Angell, 5 August 1914, *Angell MSS* A-10-10.
46 N. Angell to E. W. Collinson (Copy), 5 August 1914, ibid. A-33-32.
47 Roland Muirhead to G. Wallas, 7 August 1914, *Wallas MSS*, 39.
48 Elie Halévy, *A History of the English People in the Nineteenth Century – VI. The Rule of Democracy, 1905-1914*, New York, Barnes & Noble, 1961 edn, p. 438.
49 A. J. P. Taylor, *The Trouble Makers: Dissent over Foreign Policy, 1792-1939*, London, Hamish Hamilton, 1957, 1964 edn, p. 103.
50 'The War . . . and after', *African Mail*, 9 October 1914.

SUGGESTIONS FOR FURTHER READING

Lloyd George and the Boer War

A selection from an important manuscript source for this period, the Lloyd George Letters in the National Library of Wales, has appeared in K. O. Morgan (ed.), *Lloyd George Family Letters, 1885-1936* (Oxford and Cardiff, 1973).

Among general works, Elie Halévy, *Imperialism and the Rise of Labour* (London, paperback ed., 1961) and K. O. Morgan *Wales in British Politics:* 1868-1922 (Cardiff, 1963) are of prime relevance.

Of the many books on Lloyd George, the following contain most information on his activities during the Boer War: W. W. Davies, *Lloyd George 1863-1914* (London, 1939), H. Du Parcq, *Life of David Lloyd George*, 4 vols (London, 1912), J. H. Edwards, *David Lloyd George*, 4 vols (London, 1913), William George, *My Brother and I* (London, 1958), John Grigg, *The Young Lloyd George* (London, 1973), Frank Owen, *Tempestuous Journey* (London, 1954), and Harold Spender, *The Prime Minister* (London, 1920).

British Radicals and India

There is no single comprehensive study available on the Radicals and India between 1900 and 1914. The best coverage of this subject is contained in the biographies and contemporary writings of those directly involved. There are several useful chapters in Henry Cotton, *India and Home Memories* (London, 1911), D. K. Ratcliffe, *Sir William Wedderburn and the Indian Reform Movement* (London, 1923), and W. Wedderburn, *A. O. Hume* (London, 1913). *Speeches and Writings of Sir William Wedderburn* (Madras, 1918) is a valuable documentary source.

Emrys Hughes, *Keir Hardie* (London, 1956) contains only one chapter on India, but this can be supplemented by J. K. Hardie, *India: Impressions and Suggestions* (London, 1909). H. W. Nevinson,

The New Spirit of India (London, 1908) and J. R. MacDonald, *The Awakening of India* (London, 1910) provide sympathetic contemporary accounts of India's political, social and economic conditions.

Much has been written on Morley and India. Stephen E. Koss, *John Morley at the India Office*, 1905-1910 (New Haven, 1969) and S. A. Wolpert, *Morley and India*, 1906-10 (Berkeley, 1967), examine events primarily from a pro-Morley, London perspective. M. N. Das, *India under Morley and Minto* (London, 1964), provides a stronger Indian perspective, less flattering to Morley.

Much has been published on India's early nationalist leaders. Most useful for this topic are R. P. Masani, *Dadabhai Naoroji* (London 1939), V. C. Joshi (ed.), *Lala Lajpat Rai*, vol. 1 (Delhi, 1966) and D. G. Karve and D. V. Ambekar (eds), *Speeches and Writings of Gopal Krishna Gokhale*, vol. 2 (Bombay, 1966).

The Radical press

Only one major Radical paper has been the subject of detailed study, in D. Ayerst, *Guardian: Biography of a Newspaper* (London, 1971). The *Daily News* is best approached through two biographies: A. G. Gardiner, *Life of George Cadbury* (London, 1923) and S. E. Koss, *Fleet Street Radical* (London, 1973). Until A. F. Havighurst produces his biography of H. W. Massingham, H. W. Nevinson, *More Changes, More Chances* (London, 1925) provides the best picture of Massingham and the *Nation*.

Provincially, G. G. Armstrong, *Memories of George Gilbert Armstrong* (London, 1944) is a valuable though sometimes fallible source for the North-East and the *Daily News* in Manchester. P. F. Clarke, *Lancashire and the New Liberalism* (Cambridge, 1971) provides an essential orientation for the study of the North-West.

The behaviour of the press in the crucial 1906 election is analysed in A. K. Russell, *Liberal Landslide* (Newton Abbot, 1973).

Work on the Radical-Labour and Radical-Socialist press is to be found mostly in studies of particular issues. For a bibliographical project on the Labour press, see *Bulletin for the Study of Labour History*, Autumn 1972, pp. 22-39.

For the response of the Liberal and Radical press to the 'new journalism', and to political change, see A. J. Lee, *Liberalism, Democracy and the Press, 1855-1914* (London, 1974).

Laying the charges for the landslide

There is no comprehensive study of Liberal party organization in the period after that covered by H. J. Hanham, *Elections and Party Management: Politics in the time of Gladstone and Disraeli* (London, 1959).

The general bibliography in A. K. Russell, *Liberal Landslide* (Newton Abbot, 1973), contains a useful list of the more informative books and articles on the Liberal party and on Liberalism during the election period.

1906: Revival and revivalism

Memoirs by and about Nonconformist leaders are generally depressing in quality, sadly outdated and inevitably hagiographical. None the less, there is useful material quoted in T. H. Darlow, *William Robertson Nicoll* (London, 1925), J. D. Jones, *Three Score Years and Ten* (London, 1940), Sir James Marchant, *Dr. John Clifford, C.H.* (London, 1924), A. Porritt, *The Best I Remember* (London, 1922), and W. B. Selbie, *Life of C. Silvester Horne* (London, 1920). The Free Church viewpoint is given more authoritative expression in E. K. H. Jordan, *Free Church Unity: A History of the Free Church Council Movement, 1896-1941* (London, 1956), and E. A. Payne, *The Free Church Tradition in the Life of England* (London, 1944).

W. T. Stead provided a contemporary account of *The Revival of 1905* (London 1905), which is helpfully balanced by C. R. Williams, 'The Welsh religious revival, 1904-5', *British Journal of Sociology*, 3, 1952. Wales also received close scrutiny from K. O. Morgan in *Wales in British Politics, 1868-1922* (Cardiff, 1963) and in his edition of *Lloyd George: Family Letters: 1885-1936* (Oxford and Cardiff, 1973).

Electoral situations elsewhere are investigated in P. F. Clarke, *Lancashire and the New Liberalism* (Cambridge, 1971), Paul Thompson *Socialists, Liberals and Labour* (London, 1967) and Henry Pelling, *Social Geography of British Elections, 1885-1910* (London, 1967), which is sometimes exasperating but always indispensable. There are some thoughtful arguments in D. A. Hamer, *Liberal Politics in the Age of Gladstone and Rosebery* (Oxford, 1972), and a stimulating assessment in P. F. Clarke, 'Electoral sociology of modern Britain', *History*, 57, 1972.

H. G. Wells and the Fabian Society

The H. G. Wells Society published *H. G. Wells: A Comprehensive Bibliography* (latest edition, 1972). This contains nearly all that has been written in English by or about Wells up to 1967. As well as books, it lists articles, prefaces, essays from collections, correspondence printed since Wells' death, etc.

For Wells himself, it is best to go to the fountain-head, i.e. to his own *Experiment in Autobiography* (London, 1934). References to his ideas about the future are scattered through his science-fiction books and in a good many of the short stories.

The Fabian episode is briefly mentioned in the autobiography, and more fully told in the relevant chapters of Pease's *History of the Fabian Society* (London, 1916), and Margaret Cole, *Story of Fabian Socialism* (London, 1961).

Socialism and progressivism in the political thought of Ramsay MacDonald

MacDonald's more important writings before 1914 include *Socialism and Society* (1905), *Socialism* (1907), *Socialism and Government* (1909), *The Socialist Movement* (1911), *Syndicalism, A Critical Examination* (1912), and *The Social Unrest, Its Cause and Solution* (1913). A long bibliography of his writings can be found in Benjamin Sacks, *J. Ramsay MacDonald in Thought and Action* (Albuquerque, 1952).

Biographies include Lord Elton, *The Life of James Ramsay MacDonald: 1866-1919* (London, 1939), and M. A. Hamilton ('Iconoclast') *J. Ramsay MacDonald* (London, 1929).

There is a comparison of MacDonald's arguments with the writings of those who might have influenced him in the introduction to Bernard Barker (ed.) *Ramsay MacDonald's Political Writings* (London, 1972), and a discussion of Idealist elements in his thinking in A. H. Birch, *Representative and Responsible Government* (London, 1964), Chapter 7.

MacDonald's place in English socialist thought before 1900 is discussed in Chapter 9 of Stanley Pierson, *Marxism and the Origins of British Socialism* (Ithaca and London, 1973), and the importance of his arguments for the early parliamentary Labour party in Chapter 1 of Rodney Barker, *Education and Politics 1900-1951* (Oxford, 1972).

Criticisms of MacDonald appear in L. MacNeill Weir, *The*

Tragedy of Ramsay MacDonald (London, 1938), Ralph Milliband, *Parliamentary Socialism, a Study in the Politics of Labour* (London, 1961), and C. L. Mowat, 'Ramsay MacDonald and the Labour party', in Asa Briggs and John Saville (eds), *Essays in Labour History 1886-1923* (London, 1971).

Charles Trevelyan and two views of 'revolution'

There is a short article on Charles Trevelyan by his cousin Philips Price in the *Dictionary of National Biography*. Trevelyan's activities with the UDC are covered in Marvin Swartz, *The Union of Democratic Control in British Politics during the First World War* (Oxford, 1971); and several chapters in Rodney Barker, *Education and Politics 1900-1951* (Oxford, 1972) deal with Trevelyan as a minister. However, until the biography appears, the only source for Trevelyan will remain the manuscript collection of letters and papers at Newcastle University Library.

On the House of Lords crisis, Roy Jenkins, *Mr. Balfour's Poodle* (London, 1954), though frequently cited, remains rather dull, and the best general account of this episode and of syndicalism is in Elie Halévy, *The Rule of Democracy*, (London, paperback ed., 1961). George Dangerfield's always brilliant and persuasive if particular view, *The Strange Death of Liberal England* (London, 1935), is happily now available in paperback (1970).

'God gave the land to the people'

Though all the standard textbooks deal with the 1909 budget and Lloyd George's land taxes, they largely neglect the aftermath. A useful recent account that takes the story forward to 1914 is H. V. Emy, 'The land campaign: Lloyd George as a social reformer, 1909-14', in A. J. P. Taylor (ed.), *Lloyd George: Twelve Essays* (London, 1971). Surprisingly little attention has been given to E. P. Lawrence, *Henry George in the British Isles* (Michigan, 1957), which despite its title, covers the period 1880-1914.

Many books discuss special aspects of the land problem in connection with other stories, for example, Roy Douglas, *History of the Liberal Party 1895-1970* (London, 1971), F. S. L. Lyons, *Ireland since the Famine* (London, 1971), K. O. Morgan, *Wales in British Politics* (Cardiff, 1963). John Brown, 'Scottish and English land legislation, 1905-11', *Scottish Historical Review*, 46, 1968, pp. 72-85, is valuable coverage of the field indicated by its title.

The land problem and reactions to it in the early twentieth century are difficult to understand except in the context of the ideas of the previous quarter of a century. Henry George's work, especially *Progress and Poverty* (1880), is essential for this purpose. Bibliographical material plus commentary is given in John Saville, 'Henry George and the British labour movement', *Bulletin for the Study of Labour History*, 5, 1962, pp.18-26.

Pensions not dreadnoughts

No major work has been written exclusively on the Radicals and the Royal Navy. There is, however, a stimulating and provocative article by Howard Weinroth, 'Left wing opposition to naval armaments in Britain before 1914', *Journal of Contemporary History*, vol.6, 1971, pp. 93-120. Also useful are Chapter 10 in Stephen Koss, *Sir John Brunner: Radical Plutocrat* (Cambridge, 1970), and Chapters 3, 4 and 8 in A. J. A. Morris, *Radicalism Against War, 1906-14* (London, 1972).

The works of Arthur J. Marder, cited in the essay, are essential reading for an understanding of the navy during this period.

Radicalism and the Armament Trust

The propaganda directed at the Armament Trust by the pre-war Radicals was amplified and presented with increased force, and in a more accessible form, by such volumes as F. Brockway, *The Bloody Traffic* (London, 1933) and H. C. Engelbrecht and H. C. Hanighen, *The Merchants of Death* (London, 1934). A more balanced and scholarly, but still hostile, view of the arms trade and its institutions is available in P. Noel-Baker, *The Private Manufacturer of Armaments* (London, 1936).

Assessments pruned of polemical intent are of more recent origin and are gradually trickling through to publication – note, however, the perseverance, of the hardy old strain in D. McCormick, *Pedlar of Death* (London, 1965), and W. Manchester, *The Arms of Krupp* (New York, 1968). The genuine industrial inter-connections are treated in the limited number of business histories available: laconically by J. D. Scott, *Vickers: A History* (London, 1962), fully and authoritatively by W. J. Reader, *Imperial Chemical Industries, Vol. I, The Forerunners* (London, 1970).

Useful information and the beliefs and tactics of the Radical propagandists is provided by A. J. A. Morris, *Radicalism Against War, 1906-14* (London, 1972).

An attempt to describe objectively the relations between the British government and the armourers is made in C. Trebilcock, 'A special relationship: government, rearmament and the cordite firms, 1890-1914', *Economic History Review*, 1966, and a revisionist case seeking to evaluate in a dispassionate style the charges made against the British arms interests by the same author in 'Legends of the British armaments industry, 1890-1914: a revision', *Journal of Contemporary History*, 1970.

H. N. Brailsford and the search for a new international order

Brailsford's articles, most of them unsigned, are scattered through several newspapers and periodicals, most notably the *Daily News, Manchester Guardian*, and *Nation*. His most accessible works in this period are two books, *Macedonia* (1906), and *The War of Steel and Gold* (1914).

On the world of Liberal and Radical journalism, apart from those titles listed in the bibliography for Alan Lee's essay, there are Philip Gibbs, *The Pageant of the Years* (London, 1946) and H. W. Nevinson, *Fire of Life* (London, 1935).

Other works which deal with material pertinent to this essay are: Mosa Anderson, *Noel Buxton: A Life* (London, 1952), W. S. Blunt, *My Diaries*, 2 vols, (London, 1919-20), H. N. Fieldhouse, 'Noel Buxton and A. J. P. Taylor's "The Trouble Makers"', in Martin Gilbert (ed.), *A Century of Conflict, 1850-1950* (London and New York, 1967), J. L. Hammond, *C. P. Scott of the Manchester Guardian* (London, 1934), J. A. Hobson, *Confessions of an Economic Heretic* (London, 1938), J. A. Hobson, *Imperialism* (London, 1902), A. J. A. Morris, *Radicalism Against War 1906-1914* (London, 1972), Bernard Porter, *Critics of Empire* (London, 1968), and Howard Weinroth, 'The British Radicals and the balance of power, 1902-14', *Historical Journal*, vol. 13, no. 4, 1907, pp.653-82.

Biographical notes on H. N. Brailsford appear in the *Dictionary of National Biography*, 1951-60 Supplement, by Kingsley Martin, and F. M. Leventhal in vol.2, *Dictionary of Labour Biography*.

Radicalism and nationalism

Before the outbreak of war in 1914, the Radicals never formulated a comprehensive approach to nationalism. Their attitudes towards self-determination for small peoples are contained in specific studies: H. N. Brailsford, *Macedonia: Its Races and Future* (London, 1906), Noel Buxton, *Europe & the Turks* (London, 1907), R. W. Seton-Watson, *The Southern Slav Question* (London, 1911), and E. M. Durham, *The Struggle for Scutari* (London, 1913). A much better understanding of the Radical dilemma over the nationality question can be gained, therefore, by looking at war-time publications: Arnold Toynbee, *The New Europe* (London, 1915), and the same author's *Nationality and the War* (London, 1915). Both books aimed at reconstructing Europe along strictly national lines. H. N. Brailsford, *The League of Nations* (London, 1917) presents the most definitive statement of Radical reservations *vis-à-vis* self-determination. George Young, *Nationalism and War in the Near East* (London, 1915) though written in the pre-war period, serves as a sobering counter balance to Seton-Watson's somewhat biased study, *The Rise of Nationality in the Balkans* (London, 1917).

Additional works which shed light on Radicalism and nationality are: Harry Hanak, *Great Britain and Hungary during the First World War* (London, 1962), Henry Winkler, *The League of Nations Movement in Great Britain, 1914-19* (New Jersey, 1952), A. J. P. Taylor, *The Trouble Makers* (London, 1957). Unfortunately, in none of these books is there an attempt to delineate the Radical dilemma – their views on nationality are either treated unsympathetically or mentioned *en passant*.

E. D. Morel: from the Congo to the Rhine

Britain's Congo policy, which led to Morel's initial criticism of the Anglo-French *entente*, is examined in S. J. S. Cookey, *Britain and the Congo Question, 1885-1913* (London, 1968). Jacques Willequet, *Le Congo Belge et la Weltpolitik* (Brussels, 1962), suggests that Morel was far too optimistic in assessing the possibilities of Anglo-German co-operation on German policy towards the Congo.

William Roger Louis and Jean Stengers (eds), *E. D. Morel's History of the Congo Reform Association* (Oxford, 1968) is enhanced by the inclusion of valuable essays and notes by the editors.

Accounts of the Radical protest of 1911-12 are provided in T. P. Conwell-Evans, *Foreign Policy from a Back Bench* (London, 1932),

A. J. P. Taylor, *The Trouble Makers*, Chapter 4 (London, 1957). John Murray 'Foreign policy debated: Sir Edward Grey and his critics', in Wallace and Askew (eds), *Power, Public Opinion and Diplomacy* (Durham, N. Carolina, 1959) omits Morel's role but provides a helpful chronology of the Radical campaign. Later phases of Morel's career are explored in C. A. Cline, *Recruits to Labour* (Syracuse, NY, 1963) and 'E. D. Morel and the crusade against the Foreign Office', *Journal of Modern History*, 39, 1967, pp.126-37, F. Seymour Cocks, *E. D. Morel: The Man and his work* (London, 1920), and Marvin Swartz, *The Union of Democratic Control in British Politics during the First World War* (Oxford, 1971).

A study in futility

No period in history has had more written about it than the last weeks before the outbreak of the First World War. Collections of official documents, biographies, memoirs and commentaries, analytical and narrative, abound.

Part 1 of Cameron Hazlehurst, *Politicians at War, July 1914 to May 1915* (London, 1971) concentrates mainly on Cabinet activities in the crisis before Britain's declaration of war. but has some useful material on the Radical backbenchers' activities. These are more fully explored in K. G. Robbins, 'The abolition of war: a study in the organisation and ideology of the peace movement, 1914-19', an unpublished Oxford D.Phil thesis (1964).

A. J. P. Taylor, *The Trouble Makers* (London, 1957) is a splendid book, and Taylor has studied the Dissenters with insight, empathy and sparkling wit. A. J. A. Morris, *Radicalism Against War, 1906-14*, gives a narrative account of the last days of peace, concentrating on the Radicals; and the story of the key dissenters to Grey's policy is told in Marvin Swartz, *The Union of Democratic Control in British Politics during the First World War* (Oxford, 1971). The bibliographies in the last two books mentioned cover most of the primary and secondary sources for Radical attitudes to Grey's foreign policy and the subsequent organization of dissenting opinion.

INDEX